TELLING STORIES IN THE FACE OF DANGER

TELLING STORIES IN THE FACE OF DANGER

Language Renewal in Native American Communities

Edited by

Paul V. Kroskrity

UNIVERSITY OF OKLAHOMA PRESS : NORMAN

ALSO BY PAUL V. KROSKRITY

Language, History, and Identity: Ethnolinguistic Studies of the Arizona Tewa (Tucson, 1993)

(co-ed.) *Language Ideologies: Practice and Theory* (New York, 1998)

(ed.) *Regimes of Language: Ideologies, Polities, and Identities* (Santa Fe, N.Mex., 2000)

(co-author) *Taitaduhaan: Western Mono Ways of Speaking* (CD-ROM) (Norman, Okla., 2002)

(co-ed.) *Native American Language Ideologies: Beliefs, Practices, and Struggles in Indian Country* (Tucson, 2009)

Library of Congress Cataloging-in-Publication Data

Telling stories in the face of danger : language renewal in Native American communities / edited by Paul V. Kroskrity.
    p.   cm.
  Includes bibliographical references and index.
  ISBN 978-0-8061-4227-2 (pbk. : alk. paper)
1. Indians—Languages—Social aspects. 2. Language and culture—America. 3. Ideology—America. 4. Indians—Ethnic identity. 5. Anthropological linguistics—America. 6. Indians—Social life and customs. I. Kroskrity, Paul V., 1949–
  PM108.T423   2011
  306.44089'97—dc23

                    2011029294

The paper in this book meets the guidelines for permanence and durability of the Committee on Production Guidelines for Book Longevity of the Council on Library Resources, Inc. ∞

To the memory of those who filled me with their stories, especially my mother, Martha Helen Kroskrity (1914–2011); *iboso* Rosalie *Samowadi* Bethel (1916–2009); *naabi "phuuponun tádá,"* Dewey Healing (1905–1992); my academic "ceremonial father," Carl Voegelin (1906–1986); and, of course, those who still tell stories and those who continue to hear them. I also dedicate this book to my longtime friend and colleague Pamela Bunte (1948–2011), who did not live long enough to see this book, and her chapter in it, become a material reality.

CONTENTS

ILLUSTRATIONS

ACKNOWLEDGMENTS

The core of this volume began as a session, by the same title, that was first presented at the Annual Meetings of the American Anthropological Association in 2006 held in San Jose, California.

I thank the authors for their dedication to this project, but I also want gratefully to acknowledge some of the many behind-the-scenes people who helped me materialize this collection of papers and talks into the book before you. For her interest in this project and guidance through the early stages of submission and review, I thank our acquisitions editor, Alessandra Jacobi Tamulevich. For detailed copyediting and many useful suggestions on the volume, I thank John Thomas. And for other forms of helpful guidance later in the editorial process, I express my appreciation to Emily Jerman. To each of you and to others who may be unknown to me, I thank you all for your expertise, your patience, your good wishes, and your dedication to producing this volume.

TELLING STORIES IN THE FACE OF DANGER

CHAPTER 1

SUSTAINING STORIES
Narratives as Cultural Resources in Native American Projects of Cultural Sovereignty, Identity Maintenance, and Language Revitalization

Paul V. Kroskrity

I will tell you something about stories,
[he said]
They aren't just for entertainment.
Don't be fooled
They are all we have, you see,
all we have to fight off illness and death.
You don't have anything
if you don't have the stories.
Their evil is mighty
but it can't stand up to our stories.
So they try to destroy the stories
let the stories be confused or forgotten
They would like that
They would be happy
Because we would be defenseless then.

More than thirty years ago, Laguna Pueblo writer Leslie Marmon Silko attempted to reveal the power of Native American storytelling art in the powerful passage excerpted above (Silko 1977). Her words were a form of early warning not to dismiss or trivialize Native American oral traditions and a challenge to understand the more local, indigenous meanings and functions associated with these narrative traditions. Though hegemonic forms of what Dell Hymes (1996) has called "narrative inequality" have erased, reduced, or marginalized Native American oral traditions in the

3

larger society and in many Native American communities as well, in many other places those narrative traditions persist and are viewed as a culturally preferred resource to maintain, renew, and otherwise reproduce indigenous knowledge and values. In the face of dangers from the hegemonic institutions of the dominant society that include heritage language death and erasure of indigenous culture, many Native communities are turning and returning to the power of their own storytelling tradition. They are telling stories in the face of danger. This volume examines the role of stories from diverse tribal groups and from a variety of genres—including traditional, syncretic, and personal narratives—for maintaining and reproducing Native American cultural groups. In many Native groups, language ideologies valorize the importance of stories as vehicles of moral development. For the Arizona Tewa, storytelling is culturally tied not only to the growth and development of children but also to the proper development of corn and other food staples (Kroskrity 1985, 1993, 2009c). In some Apachean and Pueblo groups, members who disrupt valued cultural norms were once routinely told, "Didn't your grandmother ever teach you the stories?" as a cultural rebuke.

Beyond considering stories simply as entertainment, or art for art's sake, many, if not most, of these communities place an action-oriented emphasis on using these narratives for moral instruction, healing, and developing culturally relevant tribal and social identities (Basso 1996; Cruikshank 1998; McCarty, Romero, and Zepeda 2006; Palmer 2003; Silko 1981). Many of these narrative functions are precisely those recognized in Native accounts of the importance of language renewal (e.g., Hinton 2002a, b). Native Americans clearly see healing, teaching, and identity creation as more important than non-Indian discourses of language endangerment that emphasize "universal ownership," assess in hyperbolic and materialist imagery their "intellectual treasure," or attempt to quantify heritage language death rather than qualitatively confront it (Hill 2002a).

This collection focuses on the work that stories, storytelling tropes, and related verbal art do and have done to maintain Native cultures as vital processes of cultural and linguistic reproduction. Reproduction relates to maintaining and transforming traditions, to the ongoing traditionalization of narrative texts and verbal art performances (Bauman 1992, 2004).[1] In the context of many Native American societies, some of the most important forms of cultural reproduction occur in acts of tribal, ethnic, and clan identity making, in activities of cultural sovereignty, and in the maintenance, renewal, and revitalization of the heritage languages that are the symbolic guides to members of these distinctive cultures and their preferred medium of verbal artistic expression.

Native American writers like Silko (1981), Paula Gunn Allen (1989), and Greg Sarris (1993) have all linked storytelling to tribal, clan, gender, and personal identities. Gerald Vizenor (1999, 2008:19) has also linked the maintenance of such narratives to his notion of "survivance" as "an active sense of presence, the continuation of native stories, not a mere reaction, or a survivable name." Stories help narrators and their audiences perform this manifold identity work in a wide variety of ways that can only be briefly sampled here. Keith Basso's (1996) studies of Western Apache historical and other narratives demonstrate how these tales create discursive webs linking places, place names, words of the ancestors, and moral lessons. Andie Diane Palmer's (2005) studies of situated biographical narratives among the Secwepemc (formerly known as the Alkali Lake Sushwap, British Columbia) display an indigenous tradition of telling one's life stories episodically, in a nonlinear fashion, while being in the context of relevant places for gathering food. This practice contrasts markedly with the linear and highly formulaic life stories that many community members must tell as a responsibility of attending Alcoholics Anonymous meetings. White Mountain Apache elder Eve Tulene Watt (Basso 2004) relates family stories that provide important local knowledge and alternative histories for her younger kin. Storytellers from the Dane-zaa (Ridington and Ridington 2006) and the Tewa (Kroskrity 1993) deliberately include details about hunting and other traditional technologies as a means of transmitting and keeping this knowledge available for younger generations.[2] In some groups like the San Juan Paiute or the Arizona Tewa, certain traditional genres—like winter stories—can be performed only in the heritage language (Kroskrity 2009c; Bunte, this volume). In other communities, like the Nahuatl-speaking communities in the Malinche Volcano area of northern Mexico or a group of contemporary Navajo poets performing their works, code switching, or code alternation, and code mixing provide an appropriate resource for expressing personal stories and episodes (Hill 1995; Webster 2009a, b). These are but a few of the many ways that stories assist in identity work by discursively connecting people to places, to social groups, to ancestral ways, and to their ancestors. People's various identities are developed and shaped by the kinds of stories they can hear and those to which they are denied access to hearing (Silko 1981).

For the federally recognized tribes that enjoy the limited political sovereignty of "domestic, dependent nations," what has come to be termed "cultural sovereignty" is the development, maintenance, and renewal of distinctive cultural practices and institutions that contribute to their nation building (Goldberg and Champagne 2002; Richland 2008, 2009; Tsosie 2002). These tribes already enjoy a limited political sovereignty as different nations, but what good is this relative autonomy if all cultural differences between the dominant society and the Native nations are erased? Cultural sovereignty has important community-building functions as well as important political implications in regard to the dominant society. By promoting institutions and practices that are indexed to indigenous worldviews and value systems, Native nations foster the maintenance of difference rather than the complete assimilation of indigenous groups into the larger sociocultural regime of the more encompassing nation-state.

This is, of course, valuable for those who want to preserve, maintain, or syncretize local cultures and their associated identities, but it is also critical in a political sense. If Native groups were to lose all distinctive aspects of their societies and cultures, how would they legitimate their status as Indians and their claim to special legal treatment (Cattelino 2008)? Insofar as storytelling is concerned, many Native groups have local ideologies that view these practices as a critical part of socialization to the group. Given those cultural beliefs, it is little wonder—except to outsiders—why stories and storytelling should be taken so seriously in Native American communities. Although the marginalization and trivialization of Native American oral traditions clearly have political, economic, and racist motivations, there are also some fundamental differences in the communicative norms of Native American and dominant Euro-American societies that promote misrecognition of narrative performance practices, thus further contributing to the construction of their "narrative inequality."[3] One of these differences stems from the fact that almost all Native American groups engage in some storytelling of both personal and traditional narratives that are open to children. Even though all groups have some genres that require more segregated audiences (e.g., clan elders, religious sodality members, gender-specific groups) and story performers see themselves as speaking to adult audience members as well as to children in such "mixed audiences," this indexing of storytelling to children has been distorted and magnified by the dominant society so as to transform much of the Native American oral tradition into exclusively a child's domain.

This misinterpretation emerges from very different norms of participation in cultural events. For most Native Americans, as Susan Philips (1983) found for the Warm Springs Indian community, important cultural events and indeed most activities involve all generations within the community. But in contemporary Euro-American society, age segregation is important in event structures, and most "serious" events are viewed as "adults only." This factor is compounded by a second indexical that further prompts Euro-Americans to dismiss Native American stories as mere "child's play." Humor, from verbal slapstick to dramatic irony, is a conspicuous feature of traditional stories in all Native American groups. Though there are many stories that display little or no humor, the salience of characters like Old Man Coyote, Hare, Raven, or other tricksters (Radin 1956) provides a basis for mistakenly seeing traditional stories as merely evanescent, humorous forms of entertainment. Whereas Euro-American audiences dismiss such stories as strangely humorous, Native audiences are more attuned to their serious, and sometimes sacred, moral interpretations (Beck, Walters, and Francisco 1977:61). This tension emerges in a dialogue between the mythographer Barre Toelken and a Navajo consultant whom he identifies as "Yellowman." In his ethnographic questioning of Yellowman, Toelken assumes the role of naïve interviewer:

> Why then if Coyote is such an important character (whose name must not even be mentioned in the Summer months), does Yellowman tell such funny stories about him? Yellowman's answer: "They are not funny stories." Why does everyone laugh, then? "They are laughing at the way Ma'i does things, and at the way the story is told. Many things about the story are funny, but the story is not funny." Why tell the stories? "If my children hear the stories they will grow up to be good people; if they do not hear them, they will turn out to be bad." Why tell them to adults? "Through the stories everything is made possible." (Toelken and Scott 1997:101–102)

Toelken's questions are clearly grounded in discourse assumptions rooted in mainstream Euro-American discursive culture that tends to index humor and juvenile audiences to performances that are merely entertaining. But Yellowman's answers indicate his firm belief in an alternative stance in which stories are serious business and represent vital forms of moral instruction.

Another bias that motivates mainstream misrecognition and discursive marginalization (Kuipers 1998) of Native American storytelling springs from a discursive ethnocentrism deeply rooted in literacy and associated

Western literary conventions. This bias has two distinct strands that can be analytically untangled. One of these involves the ethnocentric valorization of Western literary conventions as a standard for the evaluation of narrativity rather than the anthropological exploration of alternative cultural models of narrative performance. Indeed there is a long-standing academic tradition that includes such foundational nineteenth-century researchers as Henry Schoolcraft and Frank Hamilton Cushing and their routine practices of erasing indigenous narrative performance conventions and ornamentalizing those same narratives with more familiar Western tropes (Bauman 1993; Bauman and Briggs 2003:226–54; Tedlock 1983:33–36).[4]

The second, and more pernicious, of these biases is the pejorative view of oral traditions as primitive and inferior to literacy. In a scholarly attempt to counter this view, Dennis Tedlock (1983:159) critiqued an older academic tradition and popular cultural perspective by contending that oral narratives are "something other than just primitive ancestors of written prose fiction." Based on firsthand research on storytelling practices of the Zuni and Quiche Maya, Tedlock and other writers of the ethnopoetics movement have rightfully maintained that stories are part of an oral tradition "more like one-person theater than like conventional, block-paragraph, written prose." Failures to recognize this critical aesthetic difference and to evaluate Native American stories according to indigenous criteria would compel typical Western academic and popular audiences to rely solely on their displaced narrative expectations in order to appreciate these narratives. But, of course, the lack of shared expectations and reduction of verbal art performance to printed text would most often lead to misunderstanding.[5]

Even sympathetic academic linguists studying the indigenous narrative traditions of Central California groups like the Yokuts and Western Mono could only "mis-read" their attributes as "deficient" when judged by Western standards of literary narratives (Kroskrity 2007). Thus, for example, a "lack" of descriptive detail was noted in Central California narratives that have an indigenous design to move the plot forward, rely on what is already known by the audience, and provide a narrative vehicle that emphasizes a theatrical appreciation of the dialogue of story characters. Rather than locating artfulness in the innovation and elaboration of narrative detail—like scene-setting description and indirect characterization of story figures—the Yokuts and Mono narratives were in fact textualizations of oral performances, performances rarely heard and appreciated by literacy-deafened linguists who seemed not to recognize their orality and performance orientation. This becomes then another instance in which professional language ideologies, at the level of "practical consciousness," about literacy were involved in the construction of difference and hierarchy rather than in the project of bridging difference and creating equality that is often associated with the positive effects of literacy (Collins and Blot 2003:74; Kroskrity 2000b).

Though movements such as the ethnography of communication (Gumperz and Hymes 1964, 1972) and the study of verbal art as performance (rather than as text) (Bauman 1977) provided important critical resources with which to study others' and one's own expressive communication, the most important critiques of earlier research on Native American narratives and storytelling and the most ambitious attempts to appreciate different patterns of organization and alternative aesthetics date back to the beginnings of the ethnopoetics movement and the works of Hymes (1981, 2003) and Tedlock (1972, 1983). Though this movement transformed earlier ethnocentric preoccupations with Native American verbal art and opened the door to a better understanding of indigenous aesthetics of narrative performance, to discoveries of Native patterns of organizing text rather than mere recasts in Western frames, and to explorations of the poetic and interactional dimensions of "the oral tradition," its main thrust was usually to promote a better understanding of indigenous artistry through the close examination of texts, translations, and contexted performances (Berman 1992; Bright 1984; Kroeber 1998; Sherzer 1990).

Though approaches in ethnopoetics, the ethnography of communication, and verbal art as performance provided a critical preparation for more contemporary work, these attempts to understand culturally distant textbuilding and performance practices differ from more recent research, including that presented here, in several respects. Perhaps most important, the studies here attempt to represent what members are doing with stories in order to advance their own projects. In addition to their performance projects as verbal artists, many Native American storytellers and poets are also attempting to advance community projects. Though it is clear that we must understand the immediate context of interaction to appreciate works of verbal art, recent work informed by emphases on poetics and politics (Bauman and Briggs 1990; Briggs and Bauman 1992) as well as language ideologies (Bauman and Briggs 2003; Kroskrity 2000a; Kroskrity and Field 2009; Schieffelin, Woolard, and Kroskrity 1998) attempts to locate relevant and more encompassing political economic contexts as an often invisible yet relevant stage upon which social actors perform their narratives, respond to and coconstruct their storytelling events, and select the language(s) for verbal art performances (Kroskrity 2009a; Webster 2009a).

In much of North America and Mesoamerica, one of the critical and encompassing contexts in which stories are told is the pervasive pattern of language shift toward state languages, heritage language death or attrition, and community efforts at language renewal (Hill 1985; Krauss 1997; Meek 2009; Messing 2007; Reynolds 2009; Zepeda and Hill 1991). As for indigenous languages throughout the world, most of the remaining indigenous North American languages—perhaps as many as 90 percent of the two hundred plus languages—are either moribund or significantly threatened. This is not a reflection on the aesthetic beauty or linguistic complexity of these languages (Mithun 1998) but primarily a consequence of linguistic oppression by the dominant society. Educational institutions were one of the key contexts in which Native American children experienced the brute force of an assimilationist, missionary model of the intolerance of Native American languages (House 2002; Zepeda and Hill 1991) and the promotion of a complete conversion to English language practices. Many of these institutions forcibly removed children from their families and communities, denigrated their languages and cultures, and physically punished them for speaking their heritage languages (Hinton 1994; Lomawaima 1994). In addition to such "force" was the omnipresent hegemonic role of English in Native American lives. Because all Indian communities were economically marginalized through underdevelopment, Native Americans needed to find a means of participating in the cash economies in which they were increasingly engulfed. As the symbolically dominant language, English was often the key to such participation even if it only provided a place on the lower rungs of the socioeconomic ladder while heritage languages were indexed to increasingly marginalized, subsistence economies. Hegemonic English also reigned supreme in terms of its deployment by the mass media in the United States. Though languages like Lakhota and Navajo might be heard on some local radio stations, English otherwise dominated television, radio, and Internet communication.

Indeed, given both the history of linguistic discrimination against Native American languages—a history finally officially repudiated, but only as late as 1990 and 1992 with the passage of the Native American Languages Act—and longstanding hegemonic relations, it is remarkable that Native American languages persist at all. Though the passage of this act is undeniably a victory for tribal communities and their linguistic activists, in so many ways it is a case of "too little, too late." It is too little because there is no significant economic compensation to repair the damage from past government policies. It is too late because 90 percent of Native American languages are either dead, moribund, or in desperately threatened conditions. Almost all Native American communities verbally support efforts at heritage language renewal, but this is not an easy task. Tribal resources are often insufficient to mount the necessary five- and ten-year plans. And community members are often in need of what scholars of language renewal as well as heritage language activists term "ideological clarification" because of the rather large gap between their stated language renewal goals and their personal beliefs and practices, as Nora Marks Dauenhauer and Richard Dauenhauer (1998) found for the Tlingit and other southeastern Native Alaskan communities (Kroskrity 2009b). But even though the prospect for success is dim and the factors that must be struggled against are daunting, most communities and many of their members have chosen to struggle to renew these heritage languages rather than to surrender the cause.[6]

It is within this context of linguistic emergency that many tribal members are turning and returning to the storytelling practices that have long been associated with their very survival as a people. But before looking at the sample of case studies contained in the following chapters, I want to address certain issues associated with the imagery of "language endangerment" and with the tone of alarm that the very title of this work suggests. "Telling Stories in the Face of Danger," some reviewers tell me, is too sensationalistic and not properly respectful of local Native sensibilities about their stewardship of their own heritage languages. It is true, some scholars have argued, that the very imagery of language endangerment creates an uncalled for sense of emergency, an emergency that some interpret as suggesting the need for intervention by "outside experts."[7] I have no interest in asserting that Native communities need the "one-size-fits-all" universal program of reversing language shift that some outside experts advocate. Indeed I feel strongly that only Native communities themselves can make the decisions about what kind of linguistic adaptations they want to make in regard to their heritage languages. For some communities, reversing language shift and restoring the heritage language, either as a dominant language or as a part of a bilingual repertoire, is especially desired and within reach. Others view English as a linguistic resource they could not do without and seek only to restore and preserve the heritage language in key domains and for certain valued cultural practices.

Though I reject any intervention that is not consistent with Native self-determination in linguistic matters, I think non-Native scholars have failed to appreciate fully the sense of loss that many, if not most, heritage language speakers feel when they ponder the current and future status of their heritage languages. Most English-speaking linguists cannot properly imagine the finality of losing an indigenous language in which much of the associated cultural knowledge is stored in an undocumented oral tradition, with which living people connect to their ancestors and to their cultural sense of spirituality. A Tlingit language activist and gifted writer and scholar, Nora Marks Dauenhauer, and her Euro-American linguist husband, Richard, express this finality especially well when they write, "In contrast to the immigrant languages in the United States, which have homelands in which the languages grow and develop, the American continent is the homeland of the Native American languages. . . . If Native languages die here, there is no homeland to which one can go and find it living" (Dauenhauer and Dauenhauer 1998:94).

It is my experience, and that of the other authors in this volume, with dozens of Native communities currently challenged by language attrition, that the majority of tribal members do see heritage language loss as a matter of grave and urgent concern and, for many, as a call to action. These communities are telling, or attempting to tell, stories in the face of danger.

CHAPTERS IN THIS VOLUME

This volume is not about stories and their artful organization but rather about the uses—the larger projects—that many tribal members and communities have found for their stories. Storytelling processes underlie maintenance, intercultural adaptation, and linguistic and cultural revitalization. The following chapters provide a sampled glimpse at what today is a large and growing movement to deploy traditional stories in the educational service of Native children and young people who are themselves struggling to learn their heritage languages and cultures. As with even a small sampling such as this, we find a range of tribes and a wide variety of storytelling adaptations. The chapters are divided into two somewhat uneven halves. In part I, most chapters suggest that tribes are successfully attempting to maintain or revitalize and renew their narrative traditions or adapt them to new institutions like schools. In part II, we look at cases of partial success or even possible failure as well as cases displaying alternative adaptations. All the researchers are familiar with the communities they write about either because they are members (Gus Palmer, Jr., and Bernard Perley) or because of their extensive and original research in those communities. Though no attempt was made to do a systematic sample of Native North American linguistic and culture areas or to constrain the types of narrative examined, I did attempt to locate studies that emphasize the ongoing use of stories as vehicles of cultural and linguistic reproduction in communities struggling to maintain their languages and cultural values while exploring narrative practices and their associated ideologies as acts of resistance and persistence.

In chapter 2, Gus Palmer, Jr., reflects on the importance of what he characterizes as "oral storytelling" from his perspective as a heritage language speaker who is also charged with helping to revitalize these languages in his position at the University of Oklahoma. His emphasis on the oral dimension invokes one of the most telling differences between traditional Native American verbal art and the more literacy-based verbal art forms of the West. Using Bauman's performance orientation (e.g., Bauman 1977, 1986, 2004), Palmer highlights the creativity of the storyteller by discussing the storytelling "frame" (Goffman 1974; Tannen 1993) and addresses the indexical connections that storytelling has for Kiowas, including the belief that storytelling provides a potent medicinal value of locating people in their lands and their culture. This appreciation extends Palmer's (2003) earlier research on Kiowa storytelling. Palmer cannot help but be somewhat ambivalent in tone, since it is clear that the conditions for full traditional performance are now eroding as people's linguistic and storytelling knowledge have diminished since the time Kiowa was the dominant language of the community. Yet he finds hope in the fact that younger Kiowas are attempting to reconnect to Kiowa storytelling through language renewal efforts that may never fully restore the former richness of the Kiowa oral tradition but will permit younger Kiowas to maintain a key aspect of their cultural heritage.

In chapter 3, Pamela Bunte describes several recent San Juan Southern Paiute storytelling sessions at which traditional winter narratives were told. This would not normally be unusual, since of all the Southern Paiute communities the San Juan have the most speakers and are the only ones whose storytelling tradition has continued into the present. However, these particular sessions, conducted in 2006, were significant because they were not normal sessions with one storyteller sometimes followed by another;

rather, they were collaborative sessions with a reproductive and instructive agenda: the tellings were a community response to the emergency need to produce a wider pool of speakers who know both the stories and recitatives (sung dialogue). Bunte discusses the aesthetics and language ideologies associated with traditional storytelling as well as the heightened awareness of the negative impact of the dominant or hegemonic Euro-American culture. She also analyzes members' metadiscursive and metanarrative talk during these sessions as they re-create what it means to be Southern Paiute. This study is thus an extraordinary example of the thoughtful and deliberate strategies that Paiutes enact in order to foster and protect their linguistic and cultural heritage.

In chapter 4, Sean O'Neill explores the language ideologies and sociopolitical realities associated with the highly localized storytelling traditions of northwestern California, where elements of a shared tale often undergo radical transformation when passing from one speech community to the next. Home to a staggering diversity of languages, this region has long been the center of a thriving multilingual culture area. As Edward Sapir once noted, the Hupa, Yurok, and Karuk languages represent three of the major linguistic stocks of the North American continent, though the speakers of these languages eventually settled on a common way of life based on salmon fishing and the acorn harvest. As frequent partners in trade and marriage, these groups have long been closely aligned in matters of myth, ritual, religion. In this setting, storytelling has been critical in transmitting the mythologies and values associated with the religious life.

Yet rather than strictly promoting convergence, contact between these groups provides a strong ideological motivation for asserting local differences at the village level, a trend that continues to be significant in maintaining the sometimes subtle linguistic and ethnic boundaries between these groups in the context of current revitalization movements. Thus, despite the partial sharing of narrative and linguistic resources as a way of providing a larger, northwestern California Native identity, speakers continue to work at maintaining distinctive aspects of their stories and storytelling traditions in order to maintain tribally specific cultures and identities.

In chapter 5, Amber A. Neely examines the "traditionalizing" relationship between the stories and discourses of the Kiowa elder Alecia Gonzales and corresponding ideologies of traditional and modern values in terms of language revitalization efforts and teaching in the community today. Using both texts created by Gonzales and her teaching practice, Neely carefully illustrates how one Kiowa language activist uses storytelling and related forms to transmit Kiowa cultural knowledge and values, which she accomplishes by stressing the importance of honoring familial responsibilities and the arts, both visual and oral. Yet it is a functional art form, relevant in entertainment, childhood development, family connections, and community participation but also an expression of one's creativity. Both the form and content of Gonzales's Kiowa language textbook and multimedia storybooks, as well as her use of these in classroom settings, illustrate a syncretism of traditional Kiowa knowledge and values as well as those institutionalized in contemporary national society. Whereas traditional tales in Gonzales's books emphasize proper cultural behavior and kinship ties, the discourses, a type of mini-stories, focus additionally on "modern" values, including the importance of reading and studying. Gonzales's storytelling usage, both written and oral, incorporates new words and concepts and therefore defies the stunting effects of what has been called "elder purism" (Loether 2009; Meek 2007). Rather than conform to such ideologies and their delegitimization of adaptive language change, Gonzales attempts to create and support a syncretic heritage language that betters serve the needs of the community and helps to erase some of the differences that currently divide community efforts to revitalize the highly endangered Kiowa language.

In chapter 6, Margaret C. Field continues the theme of stories in the classroom and previews the progress of a language revitalization program directed at the Kumiai of Baja California. Researchers on this project, like Field, have concluded that the oral traditions of preliterate communities often provide valuable resources that can be made into pedagogical texts for the purpose of introducing heritage language literacy. Her close examination of the "Rabbit and Frog" story demonstrates how such stories reveal cultural values and resonate with cultural identities. But she also points out dangers in working in communities where there is a great deal of dialect variation and an intense localist stance that promotes identification with one's own dialect but not those of others, no matter how closely related. She suggests that this local language ideology needs to be respected by linguistic researchers seeking to assist the community in its language revitalization efforts, since only pedagogical texts that conform to the community's sense of its language will be accepted and utilized. Her suggestion extends as well to learning local practices involving how storytellers both authenticate and traditionalize (Bauman 1992) their narratives.

In the second part of the book we turn to the topic of "Storytelling Troubles and Transformations." In the first two chapters we see problems that arise from both the disruption of the storytelling tradition and attempts to restart and revise those traditions. In chapter 7, M. Eleanor Nevins and Tom Nevins explore local theories of teaching and storytelling and their relation to language endangerment. Based on prior research in the White Mountain Apache community, they strongly caution academic linguists and other applied linguists against assuming an isomorphism between academic models of storytelling and endangerment and those of the local Native community. Regarding the apparent crises of cultural and linguistic production, they ask, "To what extent is our model of a crisis in cultural re-production, and the role stories might play in addressing such a crisis, mir-rored in discourses and practices within Native American communities?" This approach directs attention to the language ideologies of local com-munities wherein speakers often attribute significantly different meanings to "language loss and maintenance" (Collins 1998a, b; Hill 2002a; Nevins 2004).

There are significant differences not only between the views of insiders and outsiders but also among those of community members themselves. The Nevins explore generational differences in language ideologies, in-cluding beliefs regarding storytelling transmission and storytelling con-ventions. Elders emphasize that storytelling requires the recognition of mutual obligation between tellers and audience and criticize younger speakers for not knowing how to do their part. Younger generations do not fully appreciate this larger system of responsibilities and instead view the elders as "stingy" people who will not provide the stories.

Regarding the storytelling conventions, many misinterpretations also work to produce or deepen cultural divides within the community. One such misunderstanding concerns the heavy use of the hearsay quotative *ch'idii* in traditional narratives. Young people associate these evidentials with speech acts like gossip rather than appreciating them as a convention that acknowledges the collective wisdom and special authority of the an-cestors. Elders can only derisively view what they see as a lack of respect for the stories and the ancestors. One of the sources of younger people's lack of traditional knowledge regarding storytelling and language, accord-ing to the Nevins, is their exposure to formal language maintenance pro-grams and institutions of formal education that often produce alternative sources of authoritative language practice based more on academic than on traditional expertise. The Nevins conclude that the influence of such institutions is often resisted by members who, quite legitimately, view them as potentially dangerous because they both undermine the indigenous elders and promote an "erasure" (Irvine and Gal 2000; Kuipers 1998) of local discursive practices that amounts to a further marginalization of the indigenous community and its distinctive culture via the influence of the dominant Euro-American society.

In chapter 8, I analyze an especially valorized genre of Arizona Tewa traditional stories, *pééyu'u*, by emphasizing ideologies of storytelling, narrative practices, and the indexical orders in which they are embedded. Tewa storytelling practices are culturally indexed to plant and human growth, to the moral development of children, and to the reproduction of the Arizona Tewa community. Native performance aesthetics encourage "speaking the past," yet traditional stories should not be viewed as conforming examples of Bakhtin's "authoritative word." Intertextuality is also considered, especially "generic regimentation" (Bauman 2004), and the influence of a dominant discourse model of "kiva speech" (Kroskrity 1993, 1998) is detected. I examine conflicts that have arisen between groups who want to delegitimize stories that depart from the traditional canons of performance. Many younger people lack sufficient linguistic skills, so they require some modification of the current system in order to participate at all—thus revealing debates within the Arizona Tewa community that are contestations not of the importance of Tewa language maintenance for maintaining Arizona Tewa identity but of the norms of storytelling performances. I argue that these community-internal debates are highly consequential not only for the persistence of storytelling but also for the very heritage language that this remarkable community has proudly maintained in diaspora for more than three hundred years (Kroskrity 1993, 2009c). Very much in accord with the folk view, I follow local beliefs that the failure to revive and expand storytelling is consubstantial with the maintenance of the Arizona Tewa language and the identities that are so tightly tethered to it.

The final two chapters look at the development of related but alternative forms of verbal art that are moving into the functional domain often dominated by traditional narratives. In the first of these, Bernard Perley explores the representation of storytelling in his own heritage language, Maliseet. He examines anthologies of verbal art that included Maliseet and other Algonquian languages of the Northeast produced in the late nineteenth and early twentieth centuries during the "salvage" period of research on Native American languages and cultures. Perley notes that many of the collectors of Native American verbal art excused themselves from working directly with Native communities in part by prematurely declaring these storytelling traditions to be defunct. One such collector, Charles Leland, chose to model his translation style of Algonquian stories after Scandinavian mythology and, like Schoolcraft (Bauman and Briggs 2003) before him, imposed his own ethnocentric form of versification rather than attempt to understand the forms in terms of a more indigenous aesthetic perspective. Another strategy was to represent Maliseet storytelling as "children's literature" and to rationalize all the simplifying tropes as appropriate because of the presumed primitiveness of its speakers.

Though Perley examines the language ideologies of representation, he is also examining those beliefs and feelings that directly contributed to the endangerment of Maliseet. He concludes his chapter by innovating a new genre of revitalization texts: graphic novels written in Maliseet and designed to appeal to the young people. If earlier translations pushed Maliseet closer to the void of extinction, Perley contends that these new translations may help push the storytelling traditions away from such a fateful precipice. He concludes: "The graphic novel is not supposed to sit on a shelf and collect dust. It is designed to defy the silence before the void. It is designed to provoke Maliseet community members to *tell* the story to one another in Maliseet."

In the volume's final chapter, Anthony K. Webster analyzes the relationship between the oral tradition of storytelling among Navajos and contemporary written Navajo poetry that can be and is performed orally. When Navajos talk of contemporary poetry in Navajo, they often speak of poetry as *hane'* 'narrative, story.' In fact, many Navajo poets directly link their poetry with the oral tradition (here understood as encompassing narratives, chants, and song). Webster explores the language ideologies associated with proper speaking and with connecting to traditional Navajo poetic values that are expressed by contemporary Navajo poets like Laura Tohe, Luci Tapahanso, and Rex Lee Jim. He examines such devices as the use of place names, the deployment of the quotative *jiní* and poetic deployment of linguistic purism, and the use of Navajo in bilingual poetry to demonstrate the intertextual relations between contemporary poetry and the Navajo oral tradition.

As Webster also indicates, Navajo poetry is not unitary and Navajo poets do disagree about the uses of Navajo in their poetry and how their poetic practices relate to identity. Contradictions between an idealized view of Navajo in the world and the sociolinguistic realities of the Navajo Nation—as well as tensions concerning the role of the Navajo language and its relation to English in contemporary life—fuel a range of diverse opinions among Navajo poets regarding their poetic representation of their heritage language and culture. Although considerable variation exists, contemporary Navajo poets generally promote a connection to the traditional Navajo verbal art that makes it into a resource for fashioning their own identities as Navajo poets today.

And so the cultural struggle goes on in its many forms. Today, tribes and their members face their grandest challenges not from the physical might of the overarching nation-state but rather from the hegemonic attraction of its symbolic domination. Hegemony, as the political philosopher Antonio Gramsci (1971) has observed, is always taking on new forms to encourage compliance by its citizen-subjects. Hegemony, in Native American terms, is remarkably like the shape-shifting Trickster. I lend my voice to Stephen Greymorning's (2004:15) sage advice: May the stories (and the languages) keep this Trickster at bay!

NOTES

1. Bauman's (1992) instructive notion of "traditionalization" was important historically because it provided a successful means to view properly the activities of textual tradition as the performance work of the narrator rather than as an inherent property of certain texts that could be labeled "traditional" on the basis of "local" or "expert-comparative" criteria.

2. The Dane-zaa is a Northern Athapascan, First Nations group in Canada that has also been called Beaver. See also DeMallie (1993) regarding the importance of narratives for the transmission of history both within Native groups and as a critical vehicle of ethnohistorical analysis.

3. See Fixico (1998) and Littlefield (1991) for discussion of political economic exploitation and marginalization. See Biolsi (2001), Hinton (1994:165–79), and Meek (2006) for different points on what Balibar (1991) has termed the "spectrum of racisms."

4. My goal here is to emphasize to readers who may be unfamiliar with these earlier researchers the claim that they were "foundational" figures. Bauman and Briggs (2003) regard Henry Schoolcraft (1793–1864) as occupying a parallel pioneering role in the modern study of folklore to Boas for anthropology. Frank Hamilton Cushing (1857–1900), on the other hand, has been regarded as the first ethnographer and perhaps inadvertent inventor of what would come to be more routinely termed "participant-observation" (Eggan 1979:xii).

5. For a useful critique of ethnopoetic approaches to narrative, see Parker (2003:80–100). For important critiques of literacy-centered approaches to Native American narratives, see Farnell (1995). For performance-based CD-ROM alternatives to print-preoccupied appreciations, see Farnell's (1993) pioneering *Wiyuta: Assiniboine Storytelling with Signs*—a work that inspired *Taitaduhaan: Western Mono Ways of Speaking* (Kroskrity, Bethel, and Reynolds 2002).

6. See Hinton (1994:181–87) for a useful discussion of this legislation in which the rationale for protecting Native American languages is that "languages are the means of communication for the full range of human experiences and are critical to the survival of cultural and political integrity of any people."

7. For relevant critiques of the language endangerment literature and of regimes of revitalization that would impose expert models, see Cameron (2007), Hill (2002a), Moore (2006), Whiteley (2003).

PART I

STORYTELLING AS CULTURAL RESOURCE

CHAPTER 2

KIOWA STORIES EXPRESS TRIBAL MEMORY, IDEOLOGY, AND BEING

Gus Palmer, Jr.

Terms intended to denote, clarify, or explain oral production are many. We hear such terms as "verbal performance" (Tedlock 1983), "oral poetry" (Finnegan 1977), "ethnopoetics" (Rothenberg 1983), "oral traditions" (Momaday 1970), and "oral verse" or "versifying," among others. I prefer "oral storytelling." I choose this term because it is based on both the oral delivery and social context where oral stories and poetry take place. Because storytelling has from its inception been a *telling* rather than a *writing*, storytelling is itself a live performance (Bauman 1977, 1986; Palmer 2003). This distinguishes it from written forms of literature. Storytelling also occurs in a social setting; it requires, insists on, a listener or audience. Listeners more or less participate in the telling of a story. Kiowas do this by nodding their heads or by giving some external sign, verbal or not, that they follow what is being said and give tacit approval. Other times a listener often participates by simply replying, *hàu:* 'yes.' In any case, oral storytelling is a live performance and therefore is immediate and generally unrehearsed. In societies where there is no writing, storytelling may be one of the only means of live entertainment and teaching (Foley 1997; Ong 1982; Palmer 2003).

Because storytelling is a performative event, it relies on language features that distinguish it from ordinary speech (Finnegan 1977; Hymes 1974; Palmer 2003; Sarris 1993; Tedlock 1983). By ordinary speech I mean conversation as it might take place on a daily basis. Words and the ways they are arranged in a line or utterance in performed stories tend to be highly charged and pleasing to the imagination and mind. It is perhaps for this reason they are memorable and can be handed down through the generations. There is not much written about how stories resonate in the mind with the peculiar kind of music they bring to hearers. This tends to be a tenet of poetry. For the most part, storytellers also select and have selected their words carefully because they realize that a story could cease to exist from one telling to the next. Storytelling has always been a tenuous affair down through the years. A good question is to ask how it is that so many oral narratives have been transmitted across generations yet remained intact almost to the word?

Greek literary scholar Milman Parry puzzled over this very question early in the twentieth century. His concern was how the great epic poems the *Iliad* and *Odyssey* were created orally and seemingly survived from ancient Greek times to the present day. It raised some important questions of how storytellers and poets were able to create great epic poems and stories without the aid of writing. Unfortunately, many of the questions Parry raised were not answered satisfactorily in his time, but his son, Adam Parry, picked up the study where he left off and, as Walter Ong (1982:20) stated, "beautifully traced the fascinating development of his father's thought, from his MA thesis at the University of California at Berkeley in the early 1920s till his untimely death in 1935." This inquiry about orality was just the beginning of what scholars came to aptly dub the Homeric Question, questions of exactly how the Homeric poems came to be created by oral methods of composition. This study lead to other questions concerning how comparable verses were created among other cultural groups, without the aid of memorization or other mechanical means.[1]

Such features include rhyme, alliteration, parallelism, formulaic openings and closings, rhythm, song, story framing, intertextualization, verisimilitude, and knowing when to tell a story in the midst of ordinary conversation. Because oral storytelling is a process of language, it is found in most human societies.

To understand how different people produce or perform storytelling, one should go out into the field where storytelling takes place (Finnegan 1977; Foley 1997; Hymes 1972; Ong 1982; Sarris 1993; Tedlock 1983). It is here where one can hear storytelling firsthand and participate in it socially. The first time I went out in the field to work on storytelling, I had to take into account much of the activity and context going on in the stories and storytelling that I had imagined but taken for granted until then. While growing up I had listened to the stories and been more or less unconscious of the surrounding social conditions and events that I later learned informed the story. I knew nothing then of how stories were contextualized to fit a story setting, or how the same story could be recontexualized to fit a new setting and time, or that you could minimize or maximize the contextualization gap in a story to make the theme or other story aspects relevant (Basso 1990; Foley 1997).[2] But, as I have stated, it took doing fieldwork and reeducating myself to get a better grip on how storytelling was achieved among a storytelling people—in this case, the Kiowas.

Oral storytelling is a cultural phenomenon. It draws heavily on the customs and traditions found in speech communities. To follow a story well, the people in the setting need to be familiar with the themes and values inherent in storytelling. At best, storytelling consists of a kind of cultural give and take—that is, both storyteller and listener have an equal share in the responsibilities of making the storytelling a completed human performative event. Each brings to storytelling some widely shared beliefs that make that event meaningful and understood (Hymes 1981; Sarris 1993; Tedlock 1983). Because storytelling is a product of a close encounter between storyteller and listener, storytelling should be viewed as a significant human event, and therefore worthwhile.

Arguably, oral storytelling, or oral literature, if you will, is as vital to Kiowas as the Bible and the Homeric verses are to Western civilization (Foley 1986). The only difference is that in the case of the Kiowas many stories have come down exclusively by word of mouth. But that the Kiowas or any other indigenous peoples do not have a tradition of writing down their stories does not make them any less a society than those who invented writing. We have to understand that many cultures provided for their own entertainment, teaching, and the recording of their histories and the events affecting their lives by means of an oral tradition, and that this ability contributed to their way of life in extraordinary and unknown ways that still baffle us today. Milman Parry (1928; and see Parry 1971) helped to elucidate the Homeric verses by suggesting that the *Iliad* and *Odyssey* were created not by the mere memorization of word and phrase lines but through some form of oral-formulaic versifying (Lord 1960; Ong 1982). According to Parry, who succeeded in undercutting the Homeric scholarship to show that the *Iliad* and *Odyssey* were composed almost strictly by memory, oral-formulaic verse is achieved by means of the formulaic ordering of words and phrases in the poem. Because the oral mind is largely dependent upon a repertoire of epithets constructed of metrical word schemes to fit ideas and themes, Parry argued, it was possible to compose the epic poem within the oral tradition (Ong 1982). The argument goes that many early oral epic poems have come down to us almost entirely intact, including the books of the Bible and other sacred texts. Clearly, early civilizations possessed the ability to preserve and hand down to succeeding generations those things that required safekeeping, if anything for the perpetuation of themselves as a people. So-called primitive peoples relied on the spoken word to advance their way of life. What appears crude to us—removed as we are in terms of time, place, and distance from early societies—was effectively accomplished by word of mouth, which brings us to the topic of communities that rely on an oral tradition and its place in the scheme of things.

Ong (1982) and Havelock (1963) maintain that oral cultures are by no means "primitive" or "savage" constructs. This argument has given rise to new ways of studying oral performance. Foley suggests that scholars like the Chadwicks and Ruth Finnegan "have shown, often using evidence gathered from first-hand experience of fieldwork in oral societies, this is indisputably a general phenomenon; no matter where we look in the world, we find traces of an oral tradition that preceded (and in some cases still subsist alongside) written traditions or an ongoing oral tradition still very much alive" (1986:2). For our sake, I hope these forms of narrative performance continue to nurture and entertain us as a human species. Their still being with us is a modern-day miracle in and of itself, something worth contemplating in these times of rapid change and language loss.

In a talk at Princeton in 1970, Kiowa author N. Scott Momaday suggested that "oral storytelling involves an oral dimension which is based markedly upon such considerations as memorization, intonation, inflection, precision of statement, brevity, rhythm, pace, and dramatic effect" (1970:56). To illustrate the dynamic efficiency and efficacy of the spoken word, Momaday recounted the story of the arrowmaker and his wife. The arrowmaker and his wife are alone in their tipi. While the wife busies herself in domestic chores, the arrowmaker, who is straightening an arrow, suddenly becomes conscious of someone outside spying through a small opening above the tipi door. At first the arrowmaker tells his wife not to become alarmed that someone is watching them. Then he tells her to go on talking as if of ordinary things. By and by, he speaks directly to whoever it is watching them and tells him that if he understands what he is saying he will go away, but the stranger does not. All the while the arrowmaker talks he is setting an arrow onto a bow, pointing it here and there in the manner of shooting a moving target. Finally, when he is ready, the arrowmaker takes aim in the right direction, letting the arrow go straight into the enemy's heart.

The point Momaday made in his talk about the spoken word in 1970, which, by the way, still resonates today, is graphic and powerful.[3] It is a reminder to us that at best words can sometimes make the difference between whether a person should live or die. In just a brief moment, the stranger who was looking in on the couple had a chance to move away and live, but because he could not understand what the arrowmaker was saying he stayed and perished. Momaday was both talking about the efficacy and power of words and saying something about the oral nature of storytelling. The story of the arrowmaker is old and powerful. Whether the event actually occurred is not known and perhaps is not important in terms of the story itself. That this remarkable story should come down to us at all, and by word of mouth, is a miracle of sorts, Momaday liked to say.

For Momaday, it is not a great distance between the real world of events and the world of the imagination, the world imagined in a story. As Momaday was and is still fond of saying, each time a story is told it is a *relived event*. Perhaps that is the key to it all. A story is by its own nature an act of the imagination and imaginative, and it is relived every time the story is told. Put another way, any story created as an act of the imagination and but one generation removed from possible extinction should serve to remind us of the importance of storytelling as a relived event. And because we relive the events over and over, they resonate in our minds and memory and may be summoned up every time we need to tell the story. Indeed, we are reliant on such things as stories and memoirs, personal reminiscences and historical events, for they are constant reminders of our own human condition, as they should be. Stories, then, are the imagined and relived moments that give us our humanity.

In this chapter I generally discuss traditional Kiowa *hêjègà* 'storytelling, poetry.' In particular, I examine those linguistic features that make Kiowa stories the distinctive and distinguishing performances they are, and how through systems of a Kiowa language ideology of storytelling Kiowas are able to maintain and renew their tribal identity.

THE STATE OF KIOWA STORYTELLING

One of the biggest obstacles I encountered while doing a storytelling ethnography in Kiowa Country in 2000 was locating Kiowas who could tell stories in the old way in the native Kiowa language. In many instances contemporary Kiowa storytellers substituted English for Kiowa. Aitchison (1991:242) notes that "the first generation of bilinguals is often fluent in both languages. But the next generation down becomes less proficient in

the dying language." For the Kiowas, language change and loss have occurred and are occurring right now. We Kiowas are near the point where
the language will cease to exist very soon. During my fieldwork, for the
first time in my life, I realized to just what extent Kiowa was disappearing.
Languages are disappearing or changing at an alarming rate everywhere in
Indian country (Crystal 2000; Hinton and Hale 2001). Where once tribal
people spoke heritage languages every day, now many are speaking only
English. Where Kiowas once told stories in the language of their ancestors, stories are now produced in English or a mixture of English and Kiowa.
Gone is the language I heard as a child. Even though ours was a bilingual
speaking home when I was a boy, Kiowa was the language spoken most of
the time, particularly for telling stories.

Old Kiowa people came to our house often to visit and pay their respects. Though most of these visiting elders were relatives, many were
close friends of my grandparents. Some came in wagons drawn by teams
of horses. This was in the 1950s. Even at that late date Kiowas depended
on horse-drawn wagons to get around much of the time. This was because
there was a shortage of automobiles after World War II. Fuel was also in
short supply. To be sure, it was a slower time and most rural people took
their time getting about. This was especially true of Kiowas and other
American Indians. I remember relatives coming to our home, sometimes
staying over several nights.

One thing that struck me as curious later on was the fact that there
always seemed to be plenty of food to eat, and I have often wondered how
this came to be, because, like many Indians around home, my grandparents did not work the way non-Indians did. Social Security benefits were
nonexistent back then, as was SSI (Supplemental Security Income), forms
of financial assistance we tend to take for granted these days. There were
only small subsidies of income from Indian-owned lands leased for graz-
ing livestock and raising crops. Occasionally, Indians received windfalls
from oil and gas leases. In the 1980s, some oil leases brought in as much
as a million dollars to Indian landowners. But to get back to the subject
of food, I have to say Kiowas always had plenty of it, especially meat, or
beef, if you will. And, as I have said, I find myself at a loss to explain how
my relatives acquired all the food they did. My grandmother, for example,
seemed to make food appear magically on the table, and it was always a
source of delight for everybody to see just how much there was and how
delicious it tasted. Kiowas employ numerous words based on the root *cí:*
'meat' itself, such as *císàun* 'boiled meat' and *cí:tàp* 'dried meat, jerky.' It

was unthinkable for any respectable Kiowa family to sit down at the table without the central dish of boiled or fried meat, some cooked right over an open fire outside, weather permitting. The smell of cooking filled the homes of Kiowa families all along the three-mile dirt road that stretched between our house and the houses of our relatives. While cooking took place in the kitchen, visiting and storytelling were always going on in the background. Telling *hêjègà* in Kiowa was the favorite form of entertainment. Food, especially *cí:*, was a great catalyst for telling stories. It might be said that meat was the cultural engine that drove storytelling, because there was plenty of it. And many of the stories I remember were on issues involving the food product, meat. Consider the following story told by the late Delos K. Lonewolf, who speaks of how long ago the Kiowas split up to form two tribes.[4]

àu:zâithàu:hyòp (The Udder Dissidents)

1 *á hó:à:hèl nàu hájêl tháp ø hólhèl*
   They drove along and somebody killed a deer.

2 *á fè:nè nàu qájái:qì ø chánhèl*
   They were butchering when the chief arrived.

3 *tháp ø fêndàu:mè:dè ø bó:hêl*
   He saw the deer that was butchered
   gàu àu:zâi[gàu] é háu:hèl
   And he took the udders.

4 *nàu qí:gà câudèqàjài:qì: ø chánhèl*
   And the next time the other chief arrived
   gàu àu:zâi ø kú:thàu:dè
   and wanted a share.

5 *nàu câudèqàjàiqì "háu:nê," ø jó:nê*
   And the other chief said, "no."

6 *háun ø áu:nâuhèl*
   He did not want to share any.

7 *nàu câudè, "áudèpkò náu áu:," ø jó:nê*
   And the other one said, "give me the other one."

8 *nàu câudè, "háu:nê," ø jó:nê*
   And the other said, "no."

9 *nègáu é:dè ø sáuàudèhèl gàu hègáu*
   and so this one became angry and so
   áu:gâudè qà:hyòp gàu mà:yóp, jé:pàui:,

his own men and women, every one of them,
èm tó:dé:hèl gàu hègáu ém hó:thàlhêl
abandoned everybody and cut themselves off from everybody [the tribe].
10 *úigàu háyá ém hó:a̱u:zòn:hèl*
  These other ones vanished.
11 *nègáu háun gáu hái:gâu, háyá á bá:cádè*
  And so you do not know who they are or where they went.
12 *máun hágá á tháu:*
  They probably reside somewhere.
13 *àu:zâithà̱u:hyòp àn ém ka̱umàu*
  They generally refer to them as the Udder-Dissidents.
14 *hágá á tháu:dê cáuigú*
  It is said that somewhere there dwell some Kiowas.

A favorite Kiowa delicacy, *àu:zái:* is indeed delicious. It had such power that it broke up an Indian tribe, and the Kiowas never forgot. The story and the circumstances leading up to it are told again and again. When Kiowas sit down to eat *àu:zái:* they are reminded of that fateful day long ago when two chiefs bickered over it. They like to tell the story and remember. Somehow or another *àu:zái:* is embedded in tribal memory and carries deep meaning for Kiowas. The matters leading up to the event are fraught with Kiowa ideological and identity issues and concerns. Like many Indian tribes, Kiowas engaged in and still engage in much intratribal conflict. As in the story of how the Kiowas split in half, many stories concern events surrounding tribal life that explain the frame of mind of a people that continues today. Many stories define the people's deepest concerns about themselves. They engage the minds and memories of the people in significant ways and come down by word of mouth.

Oftentimes, past narratives are recontextualized into more recent events—that is, stories acquire a certain sheen of meaning and that in turn is reconstituted into the fabric of every day tribal life. Bakhtin suggests that much of this can be explained through the special treatment of language:

The event that is narrated in the work and the event of narration itself (we ourselves participate in the latter, as listeners or readers); these events take place in different times (which are marked by different durations as well) and in different places, but at the same time these two events are indissolubly united in a single but complex event that we might call the work in the totality of all its events, including the external material givenness of the work, and its text, and the world represented in the text, and the author-creator and the listener or reader; thus we perceive the fullness of the work in all its wholeness and indivisibility, but at the same time we understand the diversity of the elements that constitute it. (1981:255)

What I take this passage to mean is that a narrator—say, a Kiowa narrator—selects a code to conduct his or her narrative. This storytelling register is a conscious selection on the part of the storyteller. Any storyteller knows that the selection of the right register to tell the story is based on the kind of hearers present in the storytelling event, to be sure, a speech frame for storytelling. The point is that it is "the totality of all its events" that is taking place, what Bauman termed "integrative" or "indivisible work." This is not a new discovery, as Bauman (1986:112) has pointed out, but a "formulation of the crucial nexus" like the one offered earlier by Bakhtin.[5]

Not too long ago, Kiowas sat around and told stories based in the language chosen to best reach their listeners. Perhaps they wanted to entertain others, teach others, instruct some aspect of living—being a friend, protecting the tribe, being valiant in war and in life. A good many stories require a metanarrative to drive home complex ideas or concepts that are the goal of the storytelling. Tedlock (1983) tells us that Zunis told stories at night because this was the magical hour to let the mind wander at will, and they could remember and best fabricate stories hidden in the shadows after daylight hours. For many Indians this was for the most part and still is an ideal time to tell stories. By and large, most people, Indians and non-Indians alike, tell stories in the evening or at night. During daylight hours people generally work. There is little time to relax and dream when people are up and about. Still, no matter what culture, people generally enjoy the afterhours when they can sit back and recount the events of the day or remember events of the past. They invoke poetry and song sometimes. The mind wanders, memory stirs. This blending of the memory and mind resonates into the creative expressionism we call the imagination. Poetry is a process and product of the imagination, a communicative practice of societies that expresses deep human feeling in memorable and linguistic ways. Humans have a need and the capacity to express such emotions, including anger, love, wonder, awe, concern for truth and error, delight, passion, lust, desire for power, kindness, error, human warmth, hope. Much poetry was and still is created and recited when people are moved by deep feeling.[6] For Kiowas, this might happen when someone remembered the old days and perhaps was so moved by the feeling that they could not help but express how they felt with the best words they knew. If one wanted to relive memories, one need only retell old stories or make a new song or poem, recontextualizing the emotion or some aspect of his or her being, tribal tradition, or beliefs into the lyric.

In terms of telling stories, it is not a far leap from past ideological practices or tribal ways to the present time. Once a person summons up a story about bravery, stamina, foresight, wisdom, or personal and collective strength, this same person can sit down and tell certain stories or recite certain songs or poems based on these human values. Once there were genres of Kiowa storytelling—fictional *hêjègà*, personal narratives, and *tàu:hêjègà* 'nonfiction or oral traditions'—which included the origin cycle of stories and tribal history. All these stories were recounted in Kiowa. There was no need to speak anything but Kiowa, because all or most Kiowas spoke and understood the Kiowa language. Besides, what respectable Kiowa would tell stories in any language other than Kiowa? Speaking Kiowa was, in the words of Irvine and Gal (2000), the "ideologically iconized" way of being Kiowa so as to live life as a Kiowa. Nothing short of tribal identity. Language had such a huge bearing on who you were and what you were about in the world that, if you were truly a member of that human society called Kiowas, you expressed yourself in the only language that was required, and that was Kiowa. There was nothing more to be said than that your living language was everything you were.

Old Kiowas used to say that once you lay down your language, figuratively, you are not the same person you once were. You have changed. Indeed, if you were speaking any other language this suggested that you were, in terms of identity, "going down the wrong road," as some Kiowa might say. My grandfather used to like to say that, if you were so unfortunate as to lose your way, you were a lost human being, indeed, without direction, purpose, and Kiowa soul. One spoke Kiowa for the good reason that this made you a Kiowa. You did not wish to share your language with strangers because they had no logical reason to use it. Someone, perhaps a stranger, might want to possess your language. Every Kiowa knows that it is dangerous to allow any stranger to know your deepest, truest thoughts, which could only happen by way of or through spoken words.

Another typical Kiowa idea might go something like this: If, for any reason, you should put your language aside, in exchange for one, say, such as English, this might suggest that you no longer wish to be a Kiowa, that you somehow have allowed your deepest Kiowa being to be exposed to the light, and in this way you deny something essential in the ideological way that sets you apart from bad foreign influences. In the Kiowa mind, English, in this case, must be foreign and for all intents and purposes forbidden, unless you allow it to become otherwise. This may be the very reason that Kiowas today are having such a difficult time revitalizing their heritage language. It may be that, ideologically, they also do not wish to write Kiowa or restore Kiowa in any form other than as it is or was once *spoken*, by Kiowa forebears—which in some ways, such as teaching and learning Kiowa, especially for younger generations of Kiowas, cannot be such a good thing (Neely and Palmer 2009).

Many of my Kiowa relatives had and still have reservations about *writing* Kiowa. My uncle Oscar, with whom I did language work in 2000, for example, expressed deep reservations about Kiowa writing. He wanted Kiowa to remain a spoken language and not written, because, as he once said, "Kiowa wasn't meant to be written." He was, you might say, ideologically opposed to written Kiowa, as many Kiowas were and some older ones still are. To talk about language revitalization in terms of constructing writing systems and writing language itself was and still is a source of much anxiety among Kiowas. Many Kiowas resist language renewal in any form, I believe, because Kiowas think committing Kiowa artificially to a written form would be destructive of something innate and sacred. I believe Kiowas are careful not to expose what they believe to be their true Kiowa-ness, which might be figuratively represented by a vessel holding words, truths, expression, wisdom, and—most certainly—stories, as they have come down to the present time by word of mouth. Telling stories in mixed codes, of English and Kiowa, say, as I have experienced Kiowas to do recently, tends to strike one as perhaps an example of this resistance to maintain tribal identity as Kiowas know it.

LANGUAGE LOSS

As one might well imagine, much traditional Kiowa storytelling has decreased enormously in recent years. Among the eleven thousand Kiowa tribal members, only an extremely small number use Kiowa as a code for daily conversation. Most Kiowa speakers living today live in and around Kiowa country in southwestern Oklahoma and are generally age sixty and older. Spoken Kiowa occurs mainly in registers of ceremony and prayer, such as peyote meetings, and in the Christian church where Kiowa is confined to prayers and tribal hymns. Eric Lassiter, along with Kiowa hymn composer and singer Ralph Kotay (2004), collected and published Kiowa Christian hymns. Recorded and translated in Kiowa, these hymns are among the last Kiowa linguistic items produced in Kiowa country. Other places where spoken Kiowa is spoken may be at some social gatherings such as powwows, where elderly Kiowas are sometimes asked to speak or pray. Almost always the speakers are elderly. On rare occasions, Kiowa speakers sit off to one side in small groups of close friends and relatives and talk among themselves, in Kiowa. It is a rare event to find Kiowas talking Kiowa at large public venues and events. At these functions, one might hear only a few familiar Kiowa words or phrases that are known by younger Kiowas, such as *fá:bî* 'brother,' *gà thá:gá* 'It's good,' or *há:chó* (a shortened form of *há:chò gá zándádàu:?* 'How's it [life] shaking?'). Taken altogether, spoken Kiowa is in rapid decline, and with it some ideological beliefs and tribal values.

PLACES WHERE PEOPLE GATHER AND SHARE TRIBAL LIFESTYLES AND STORIES

Even with all of these changes in language and storytelling, many young Kiowas are trying to learn more Kiowa by speaking and attending tribal functions where they feel they can express themselves freely. In many cases, these are intertribal functions. Some of these functions are social events, others are ceremonial, such as at the Native American Church. Many of the young come together just so they can socialize and tell stories. Most appear to be young adults, others are older adults, some married with children. What these people appear to be more committed to are ways they can connect socially in the community. Many if not all in the groups grew up in Indian country somewhere, have come to live and work in the towns and cities, but are still committed to carrying on their lives in tribal and meaningful ways. It is a way in which Indian people, young and old alike, are connecting to what in many cases are tribal traditions.

One such place where many individuals come together is a facility in central Oklahoma. Norman, where the University Oklahoma is located, attracts many young Indians and Indian families, many of whom come from Indian communities across the country. There is a community center in this university town where religious and social activities take place. Planned and constructed with funds generated by individuals representing a good many tribes, the facility attracts many Indian people wanting a place to meet regularly with other interested and like-minded people. Some tribal language classes have been held here. The spirit and enthusiasm with which this dynamic intertribal community is thriving confirm how many Indians living outside the traditional communities are gathering in meaningful ways, because it is the "Indian way," as one individual put it.

I am including what may appear to be inessential to my main topic, but I do so because it is highly suggestive of what many Indian individuals are doing nowadays, in terms of adaptation to Indian lifestyles in the changing world. What is more, many of the activities that often are of Indian interest and value here do include weekly sessions in Native language classes and special events storytelling. Many Indian individuals enjoy the social ramifications that are inherent in talking, playing, and just plain working together. Moreover, many are quite involved in learning tribal languages and telling stories among themselves, "because they believe it to help secure and reinforce what it is to be Indians," as a secretary in our university unit who attends facility activities remarked. "We like to get together and feel like Indians, and we're all different tribes."

I cannot help but add that all these activities lend themselves in one way or another to aspects of Indian tribal ideologies, in the broadest sense; that is, Indian communities, quite innovatively, are actually living out their lives in ways that cannot be called anything more than Indian in the broadest sense. Notwithstanding, these emerging and thriving places have become havens (for lack of a better word) where some Indians can conduct their lives in meaningful ways, including language renewal and revitalization, and to some extent storytelling. For it is in telling stories that people use a powerful resource for finding meaning in their lives and the life around them. To be sure, it is considered the "Indian way," as some would put it: to not only maintain aspects of tribal life wherever one lives but also to endure change one faces. What this means essentially is that, even faced with terrible odds against them, many Indians find ways to endure life in new and often unexpected places. At best, these "survival skills" might be thought of as human activities and actions people employ to invoke deeper values of belief, meaning, and knowledge and knowing, all of which can be categorized as ideological systems of belief, whether demonstrated in living and life in the towns and cities or in the many stories people tell.

STORY MEANING WITH A CONTEXT

In light of the foregoing, I next discuss how the Kiowa language informs and is informed by the stories Kiowas tell. To put it slightly another way, it could also be said that Kiowa stories inform Kiowas about *their* traditions and *their* way of life. I have said elsewhere more or less that without spoken Kiowa there is no oral tradition. This may sound somewhat unfair, however. So let me quickly add that I did not in any way wish to imply that Kiowas who can speak Kiowa are somehow more endowed culturally or tribally than those who cannot speak Kiowa. I am in no position to offer such harsh judgment. I am myself, in fact, more a student of Kiowa, even as I teach Kiowa and have taught it for some time at a major university. What I wanted to do was draw some distinct lines between Kiowa speakers who tell more or less traditional Kiowa stories and Kiowa nonspeakers who do not. The former invoke perhaps some older ideological ideas, the latter may more or less subscribe to newer ones. Even so, we have to admit that much somehow remains Kiowa, however different the language, language mix, or time and place. Something essential remains in the tribal memory and is passed down. Because the Kiowa from an older time evoked and expressed human sentiments and values from that time, something perhaps is missed, if not lost. It is hard to say exactly what or how much is lost. By example, much in the way of ideological beliefs and values in the works of William Shakespeare of Elizabethan England cannot be truly preserved for use by English-speaking people today. We would be hard pressed these days to practice chivalry or honor, for example, in the manner of the seventeenth-century English court.

Though it is fair to say that many things change from the past to the present, it is safe to assume that behaving properly and responding to tribal tradition and ways of living are still pretty much practiced today by Kiowas. By and large, coming down by word of mouth, some essential things that assure the life of the people remain pretty much the same. Words and words in stories are the conduits through which people respond to, reinforce, and extend the way they live their lives. This of necessity requires a competence in language use and communication that in turn necessitates the speaking skill to tell the stories that pass the collective tribal wisdom along. Where Kiowas once used the Kiowa language to speak and tell stories, they now employ English or mixed Kiowa and English.

The Kiowas who assisted my fieldwork in 2000 found little reason to use Kiowa in storytelling because it was simply easier for them to use and express themselves in English. John Tofpi, who was my primary storytelling consultant, often had to be coaxed into telling stories in Kiowa instead of English. Some of the other consultants would state that they knew enough about being Kiowa without having to use the Kiowa language. Moreover, when these consultants did use Kiowa to tell stories, they interspersed it heavily with English. Indeed, every recording, with the exception of my grandfather's, had at least a 60 percent mixed code of English and Kiowa. What Kiowa was recorded often presented problems in translation, in some cases so challenging that attempts to translate were simply abandoned.

We have learned that "communicative competence" involves knowing not only a language code to execute speaking but also what to say to whom, and how to say it appropriately in any given situation (Saville-Troike 2003). As Dell Hymes (1966) has argued, "Speakers who could produce any and all of the grammatical sentences of a language . . . would be institutionalized if they indiscriminately went about trying to do so without consideration of the appropriate contexts of use." However Kiowas were framing their human experiences around and within the language in the past, they did so by utilizing a competency that comes only from the realm of daily living. This includes narratives that invoke unseen powers that surround Kiowa life. Without the linguistic ability to speak the language properly in order to account for and express those invisible powers that were so much a part of life and living, not to mention the ethical or moral instruction, Kiowa storytellers would be at a loss.

The Kiowa language, as it is currently spoken, contains the correct tribal key with which to manage how to live as and be a Kiowa person. Every time a story is told, the listener, through a system of metanarration of cultural voices and cultural values and knowledge, is being brought into the world of the Kiowas. Saville-Troike (2003) argues for a communicative competence that extends to both knowledge and expectation of who may or may not speak in certain settings, when to speak and when to remain silent, to whom one may speak, how one may talk to persons of different statuses and roles, what nonverbal behaviors are appropriate in various contexts, what the routines for turn taking are in conversation, how to ask for and give information, how to request, how to offer or decline assistance or cooperation, how to give commands, how to enforce discipline, and the like—in short, everything involving the use of language and other communicative modalities in particular social settings. Given all these aspects of communicative competency, we can see how important it was and still is for Kiowas to come to storytelling and communication competency prepared to respond and apply whatever comes out of stories to their lives in meaningful ways.

Another way to explain the processes of communication and communication competency among Kiowas is through what Deborah Tannen (1993) terms the "speech frame," a linguistic term applied to the setting in which speaker-message-receiver events occur between message senders and receivers. In the case of the storytelling, we can say that a speech frame of Kiowa storytelling is required to tell stories, a storytelling speech frame. Kiowas bring to storytelling the ideological concepts contained in the narratives that both entertain and inform Kiowas about Kiowa ways, Kiowa ways of living; in short, ways of being Kiowa. Underlying any communication is an aspect of expectation. According to Tannen, in order to function in their home place or environment people cannot treat any new event, person, or object as unique and separate. This is the only way we can make sense out of our world. We have to make connections between the things in our world and the things we are experiencing there. Tannen explains that these connections or experiences help us grow up and live in a given place or culture. When we measure these experiences with the experiences we have previously experienced, we are dealing with expectations (Tannen 1993:15).

These experiences are at the root of theories and studies in a broad range of fields, including linguistics. For Kiowas, oral narratives are rooted in the ideological experiences that come to be expected by Kiowa listeners so that they can learn and by learning reinforce what is meaningful for them as Kiowas. This reproduction of Kiowa tribal ways occurs and is relived every time Kiowas tell stories. Through the speech frame of storytelling, then, expectations of Kiowas telling stories to other Kiowas underlie everything they need to know to live and continue living meaningful Kiowa lives. Even as the Western Apaches produced a genre of place name stories to recapitulate moral teachings and ways for their people to tell and hear stories, Kiowas have made storytelling a central concern for the perpetuation of their Kiowa lifestyle since time immemorial. *Hêjègà*, then, at best, is a dynamic reenactment of Kiowa-ness, fraught with Kiowa experiences of living and the ability to connect these experiences with the expectations contained within the speech frame of storytelling. Every time a Kiowa tells a traditional story, he or she is invoking an older, perhaps more noble spirit that has come down to the Kiowas, by word of mouth. Tannen notes in Hymes's ethnography of speaking, which seeks to analyze language as it is used by people in specific cultures, that frames are included as one of the "means of speaking." Tannen goes on to explain that to interpret utterances in accordance with the way they were intended, a hearer must know what frame she or he is operating in, that is, whether the activity being engaged in is joking, imitating, chatting, lecturing, or performing a play, to name just a few storytelling goals familiar to the culture.

Sometimes the speech frame contains what Erving Goffman (1981) termed a "footing." Footing is the unique quality or aspect of interest that may be communicated directly to a significant person or persons. To illustrate footing, Goffman writes:

> Whenever two acquainted individuals meet for business, professional, or service dealings, a period of "small talk" may initiate and terminate the transaction—a mini version of the "preplay" and "postplay" that bracket larger social affairs. This small talk will probably invoke matters felt to bear on the "overall" relation of the participants and on what each participant can take to be the perduring concerns of the other (health, family, etc.). During the business proper of the encounter, the two interactants will presumably be in a more segmental relation, ordered by work requirements, functionally specific authority, and the like. (1981:125)

Tannen (1993:60) describes the relation between footing and framing: at the same time that participants frame events, "they are also negotiating the interpersonal relationships, or 'alignment,' that constitute those events." If the storyteller is directing his or her story to a group of similar background and interests, then the footing, or its application, is the same for all. In the case of a storytelling session or frame comprising a mixed group of adults and children, the storyteller, for example, might direct communication to the children one moment, then realign the footing and direct communication to the adults. Speakers are always negotiating communication when speaking to mixed listeners as a way to fulfill expectations people have in their linguistic makeup. The core theory of frame analysis, according to the work of Goffman, focuses on the socially constructed nature of reality. When Kiowas tell children about the making of the world after *Zái:dètàlì:* 'Twin Boys,' they would of necessity apply the footing of play, growing up, joking, or teasing. *Zái:dètàlì:* is itself an ideological concept of the split nature of human beings that Kiowas incorporate into storytelling directed to adult Kiowas. The storytelling or speech frame reinforcement features are applied through pragmatic or stylistic language applications understood by Kiowas.

TRADITIONAL STORIES: MEDICINE FOR THE SOUL

As we have seen, much change has come to the Kiowas and Kiowa country.[7] For Kiowa people, the two terms "Kiowas" and "Kiowa country" are synonymous. They are one and the same, because ideologically Kiowas say their birth took place within the womb of the earth. The origin of the Kiowa people is contained within the narrative that says Kiowas emerged from a hole in the earth. Some versions of the origin myth say it was a hole in a cottonwood tree. This origin narrative persists and places the Kiowa people within a framework of belief and outlook. Kiowas know from whence they came and revert back to their origins every time they retell their origin story.

The origin story of the Kiowas is lengthy and elaborate. It is featured pictorially, in a series of ten murals painted by three Kiowa artists in 1984, at the Kiowa tribal office in Carnegie, Oklahoma. The artists, Sherman Chaddlesone, Meric Creepingbear, and Parker Boyiddle, created and contributed three scenes taken from the narrative, beginning with the hollow log incident all the way through the end of the twentieth century and beyond. When Kiowas visit the museum they relive the story of their birth within the earth. Not only is Kiowa origin based on an earthly birth, but it also connects to the stars and cosmos. Indeed, Kiowas have kinsfolk in the sky. In the origin cycle, *Sétàlmà* 'Bear Chasing Woman,' who transforms into a *àunhá:dè* 'bear,' chases her *vyôi* 'sisters' until they come to a *xóêl* 'big rock' upon which they ride into the heavens to escape the bear but also become the stars in the constellation *Já:mátàunjà:gàu* 'Pleiades.' There are several versions of that story. When Kiowas tell the story of the *Já:mátàun* 'Star Girls,' even in English or mixed English and Kiowa, they are transported in their minds and imagination back to a cosmic place long ago.

Traditional *hêjègà*, including the Kiowa origin story, are fraught with cultural meaning and understanding. Without these narratives, Kiowas would be at a loss concerning their birthplace and purpose on the earth. In another narrative in the origin narrative, the mother of *Fái:tálí:* 'Sun Boy' is transported into the heavens where she meets *Fâi* 'Sun,' who marries her when she grows up and with whom she bears *Fái:tálí:.* When they return to earth it is Sun Boy who divides himself into twins, who Kiowas call *Zái:dètà:lì:* 'The Split or Twin Boys.'

These series of transformations are the systems of belief within which Kiowas identify themselves. Throughout the tribal origin narrative various figures make their appearances as markers of the evolution of Kiowas throughout their history. These stories and the beliefs and values are embodied in everything Kiowa and carried across vast time and distances. Kiowas without even thinking about it are connected to ancient figures in the way that Judeo-Christians connect themselves with figures in the Bible. Abraham, the father of the Hebrew people, is the ideological figure identified with the Judeo-Christian people and belief system. Abraham and all of his descendants connect meaningfully to many nations in the way that *Sétàlmà* and *Záidètàlì:* are connected to the Kiowas. Such myths of origin carry powerful ideological meaning for humankind everywhere. Every time these stories are told, they evoke relevant and historical world-views and meaning.

Consider the Kiowa formulaic opening *Cáuigú á cí:dê* 'The Kiowas were camping . . .'. When Kiowas open their narrative with this passage, something magical happens in the mind and evokes, not only an immediate image of the Kiowas camping somewhere a long time ago, but also the sense of having wholeness and being in Time and Place. Every time Kiowas tell an old story, this formulaic opening sends the Kiowa mind on a journey of timelessness and space. To say "they were camping" evokes a sense of wonder that can only be compared to the awe of looking into a night sky full of stars on a clear night. As humans we are limited to knowing only our small place in the vastness of the universe. It is even often more difficult to imagine the purpose and meaning of our ancient birth as human beings. This, we are told, is the stuff of which stories are made.

CONCLUSION

Although it is true that all the ancient voices are silenced, and an awful quiet fills Indian land everywhere, ironically there is still much growing hope and evidence among not only Kiowas but other tribal peoples that some tribal beliefs and values have endured, just as they did in the past.

Many of the old stories cannot be told as they once were, but there remains a resilience and belief within, a metanarrative of events and themes that have been recontextualized in another place and time perhaps. Communicating in Kiowa, English, or mixed Kiowa and English enables many Kiowa young to recontextualize some beliefs and teachings even as their forebears did as a means of reconnecting and continuing in meaningful ways their lives as tribal peoples. Many of the old stories are now being recorded and written in Kiowa and English to reach the widest readership possible. Even as there is a growing urgency to revitalize and renew the Kiowa heritage language, there are also emerging tribal programs in the Kiowa community and in the schools where the youth can access oral traditions in various formats for learning. There are bilingual technologies and aids to help Kiowas gain some use of Kiowa and other tribal practices and customs. A new spirit of pride is growing up in Kiowa country to innovate ways to help more Kiowas learn about their tribal heritage through song, dance, and storytelling.

NOTES

1. Stories often go out into the world and change things. Sometimes stories are good things and not dangerous. So, in order to remember stories, storytellers try to tell them in the same way they were created. They use language and other story devices to keep a story as close as possible to the original one. That is how the language of stories is different than ordinary or everyday speech. First Nations author Thomas King (2005:9–10) wrote that once a story is told it cannot come back in quite the same way as it was first spoken—that is, a story told goes out into the world and makes things either better or worse than they were. In other words, stories are wondrous things but also dangerous.

2. For good examples of recontexualization, see Basso's (1990) work on Western Apache place names, in which moralistic teachings are incorporated into stories from the past.

3. Momaday has since published a book bearing the title of his talk, *The Man Made of Words* (1997). It is a collection of essays on words and language and a valuable companion to other books on oral traditions. Momaday has been writing extensively on the nature of storytelling. His take on oral performance is essentially as a novelist and storyteller. Other books of interest from him are *The Way to Rainy Mountain* (1969) and *House Made of Dawn* (1968), winner of the Pulitzer Prize for Fiction.

4. The *àu:zâithàu:hyòp* story is transcribed in the Parker McKenzie Kiowa writing system, developed by McKenzie over years in the 1920s. See Watkins and Harbour (2010) for useful discussion of the development of this system. Recently, the Kiowa tribal government approved the use of the McKenzie system for writing Kiowa. The system is also used to teach Kiowa at the University of Oklahoma.

5. This is related to Bauman's (1986) discussion of the cornerstones that tie together narrated events, narrative texts, and narrative events. Bauman was exploring larger concerns with the constitutive role in social life. The two cornerstones were the "narrated event" and "narrative event," the "twin social anchor points of narrative discourse."

6. At the AAA meeting in San Francisco in 2008, Lev Michael presented a talk on language ideology and poetic virtuosity in Nanti society (Peruvian Amazonia) that focused on the poetic structure and content of Kasrintaa chants, which are characterized by alterations between fixed refrains and extemporaneously composed verses. The refrains are apparently fixed, we learned, and all members of the performing group may chant the same refrain. What impressed me was the sophistication of these South American verses and how they inform deep rhythms to produce Kasrintaa song.

These poetic renderings are organized around feasts. Older males are responsible for executing performances of the verses. These extemporaneous poems are chanted and have the capacity to create and maintain a form of social inequality among the people, a discursive practice in community. I tried to find something similar among Kiowas and could only offer one example—the Plains Indian hand game—in which mostly adults participate in a guessing game with a rival tribal group, excluding children. Hand game songs are sung accompanied with hand drums. Lyrics are often made up to intimidate or otherwise "shame out" the opponent, in the kind of discursive manner the Nanti people employ.

7. One can get a sense of this change by examining some of the foundational works on the traditional culture and language of the Kiowa. As first documented by ethnologist James Mooney in 1898, the Kiowas are a Plains Indian tribe located in southwestern Oklahoma. In the 1920s, John Harrington along with Kiowa linguist Parker McKenzie worked on Kiowa and eventually published *Vocabulary of the Kiowa Indian Language* (Harrington 1928). More recently, Laurel Watkins collaborated with McKenzie and published *A Grammar of Kiowa* (1984). Bill Meadows (1999) also studied Kiowa warrior societies and has published extensively on Kiowa tribal societies and organization.

CHAPTER 3

YOU'RE TALKING ENGLISH, GRANDMA
Language Ideologies, Narratives, and Southern Paiute Linguistic and Cultural Reproduction

Pamela A. Bunte

For Paiute-speaking adults in the San Juan Paiute community, it is often through traditional myths and legends, as well as through narratives told in everyday interactions, that they create and re-create their identity as Paiute people. Both in traditional myths and legends and in narratives embedded in conversations, Paiute storytellers control metadiscursive practices that reflect and reconstitute their social and political landscape. In this chapter, I use audio- and videotaped interactions to examine the metadiscourse around formal narratives in order to better understand what San Juan Paiute elders are doing through storytelling.

The easternmost of ten Southern Paiute tribes, the San Juan Southern Paiute Tribe, is located in Arizona and Utah in two main communities within their traditional territory on the western part of the present-day Navajo Reservation. One of these two communities is located in the plateau area northwest of present-day Tuba City. The tribal area includes some springs around Echo Cliffs on the western edge of the plateau where they have their traditional farming area. This community also includes the settlement of Hidden Springs at the edge of the Painted Desert in the area west of Echo Cliffs and east of Highway 89. It is sometimes called the Willow Springs community. The other San Juan community is located in the area between Navajo Mountain and the San Juan River—north of

The author (1948–2011) presented versions of this chapter at the American Anthropology Association's 2006 annual meetings and the Society for the Study of the Indigenous Languages of the Americas January 2007 meetings.

44

Navajo Mountain but also including their traditional farming area in Paiute Canyon.[1]

In 1980, when I first visited the tribe for an extended period of time, it consisted of the core members, between six and nine families (depending on how one counts them) that were Paiute-speaking and culturally Paiute, and four to six other families who through particular historical circumstances had become Navajo-speaking. These latter families had varying knowledge of Paiute culture, with most of them practicing Navajo culture exclusively. Nevertheless, the San Juan Southern Paiute Tribe was unique at that time as the only one of the ten Southern Paiute tribes in which some families still used Paiute as an everyday language and some children were still speaking Paiute.

At that time, the San Juan Paiute Tribe was not officially recognized by the U.S. government as an Indian tribe. Therefore, they had no relationship at the tribal level with the federal government and most (at least of the Paiute-speaking families) did not receive any services through either the BIA, the local Navajo government, or the county.[2] Also, no Paiute speaker living on the reservation was employed. They supported themselves primarily through subsistence farming and basketmaking; they were the primary producers in the Western Navajo region of the Navajo wedding basket, a trade basket that the San Juan Paiutes sold to trading posts and individual Navajos who used them for ceremonies (Bunte and Franklin 1987). In addition, in the early 1980s they still gathered many kinds of seeds and berries for subsistence purposes.

Since that time, several events have changed their lives dramatically. Foremost among these is their federal recognition in 1990, which gave them a government-to-government relation with the federal government and access to various programs such as federal funding for tribal administration, leading to employment and programs that serve tribal members, and a written Indian Reorganization Act–style constitution providing for democratic elections, which was very different from the consensus style of governing they had been practicing until then. Also, federal recognition allowed many tribal members to move to trailers, mainly in Tuba City, where their tribal offices have been "temporarily" located for the past fifteen years or so, and where they have access to electricity and indoor plumbing. Simultaneous with pursuing recognition, the Paiutes intervened in the Navajo-Hopi land claims lawsuit, which then became the Navajo-Hopi-Paiute suit in 1983. Their goal was to gain title to at least a part of

their traditional lands. In 2000, this goal came a little closer to being realized when the Paiute Tribe signed a land treaty with the Navajo Tribe that
would give them a small reservation of their own. In 2009, they began
working to have Congress put their land into trust and thereby create a
reservation of their own.

Although the physical and social context has changed a great deal,
some things have remained the same. Stories, especially winter or myth
stories, are still considered to be important and the basis of the Paiute
worldview. In this chapter, I analyze their metadiscursive and metanarrative talk—their talk about discourse and stories—through which they negotiate language shift and the culture and social context, and the ways they
have changed or remained the same. I examine how the storytellers are
using stories to re-create what it means to be Paiute. Specifically, I analyze
the ways these narrative events shape and are shaped by the intertextual
events and how San Juan language ideologies figure into this negotiation
by discussing the relationship between innovation and traditionalization
(Bauman 2004; Briggs and Bauman 1992).

By "intertextuality" I basically mean the relationship between texts.
For example, a person tells a story to a group of people and one of those
tells the story to someone else. We now have two texts: the first text is
the antecedent—the one the second text might be said to descend from.
The second text can be compared to the first "as a structure of multiple
embedded acts of contextualization in which talk is oriented to other talk"
(Bauman 2004:28). Later on in this chapter, Grace Lehi's "linking of [her]
story to the antecedent tellings of [her] father represents the work of traditionalization, traditionalization in practice" (Bauman 2004:26). Besides
being selectively innovative, storytelling is also an area in which San Juan
Paiutes demonstrate a nonpuristic ideology. I briefly describe two potential and two realized storytelling events that illustrate these extremely
pragmatic and innovative attitudes toward storytelling.

FOUR STORYTELLING EXAMPLES: POTENTIAL AND ACTUAL

In the first potential event, the San Juan Paiute Tribe asked graduate student
Nikole Lobb and me to put together a DVD for the tribe of a traditional
Paiute story to be used in an immersion summer camp designed to help
revitalize the language. Nikole and I asked Paiute elder Benly Whiskers to

tell a story for us to use in this project. Mabel Lehi, another Paiute elder, and I transcribed the story and translated the text into English. So that they would not have to use English to teach, Nikole and I made the DVD by coupling the voice of the storyteller with drawings and photos that told the essence of the story. (Nikole did the technical magic while I provided support and direction.) Since we were doing it for a possible language immersion summer camp, we used a story from the legend genre that is approved for all seasons.

As for the second example, one of the Paiute elders, a former president of the tribe, told me he wanted me to do cartoon versions of winter/Coyote stories that were based on the real traditional stories rather than on the mass-media promoted Roadrunner and Wile E. Coyote television cartoon. Since winter/Coyote stories are certainly traditional and DVDs and cartoons are certifiably not, they are mixed and ideologically nonpure.

These two are "potential" storytelling examples simply because they have not yet been deployed to do the revitalization work they were created to do. For example, the DVD would need to be played in an immersion summer camp, a class focused on revitalization, or something similar to fully realize its potential. As the core of this chapter, I examine in detail two other storytelling events that did occur. The first of these is a winter storytelling event, a traditional happening, which took place in 1998 at a nontraditional setting—the tribal health department. The second event was the beginning of a 2006 collaborative storytelling session of winter stories, wherein Paiute elders got together to deliberately revitalize their storytelling tradition. That last event was the catalyst for this chapter because as an event it was completely innovative for Paiutes but was modeled on traditional socialization practices. And for me it highlighted the fact that tradition was present along with innovation in the 1998 session storytelling event. All these events have in common a pattern in which the traditional is leavened with innovative ideas, actions, or techniques.

The reasons Paiutes give for telling the stories are traditional as well. When during a recent conversation I asked the San Juan tribal vice president, "Why do San Juan Paiutes tell stories, winter stories," she responded immediately, "Education!" And then she said, "to teach kids how to act right, and we tell stories so the kids will learn about the animals. We do it because we're Paiute!"[3]

The San Juan Southern Paiute Tribe is presently a community in linguistic, social, and political transition. The status of federal recognition has led to several important changes, including some of the economic, political, and lifestyle changes detailed above. Although these changes have brought benefits to tribal members, the elders are concerned about what is probably another unintended consequence of recognition: a pronounced language shift toward English even within the Paiute-speaking families.

Paiute-speaking elders are themselves now very aware of the impact of the dominant or hegemonic Anglo culture and that it is producing a generation of Paiute children who mostly are no longer speaking Paiute, endangering the language. This is especially serious considering the San Juan community's position as the one place the Southern Paiute language was widely regarded not to be endangered. A Paiute-speaking elder was the first to see this situation as it was and started a class where she taught the children vocabulary. "It was very frustrating," she confided to me. "They told me that they wanted to learn to talk Paiute, but they didn't learn." Then, the tribe received an Administration for Native Americans Planning Grant for language revitalization that enabled the tribe's language committee to travel to see other tribes' programs and to go to workshops tailored especially for them. One workshop especially stood out—it was one with Leanne Hinton and Nancy Steele (Karuk), who are well known for their development and support of the Master-Apprentice program. Nancy performed a storytelling exercise showing how one could use a story to build heritage language fluency.

The process of language shift and endangerment has effectively eliminated the audience (because few children possess sufficient fluency) and produced a generation of elders who have little experience telling traditional stories or even listening to them as adults, causing the Paiute winter stories to become endangered as well. There has even been a similar response to both endangerments, the endangerment of the language itself and that of storytelling; the response to both endangerments is to tell more stories and be pragmatically innovative in how they are told. The Paiute-speaking elders care about being able to tell winter stories, in particular, because they are sacred myths, set in myth time, and are the focus and basis of Paiute cultural beliefs. Coyote, the main character of most of the stories, is a trickster whose deeds and thoughts both helped make the world the way it is today and provided today's people with negative models of how not to act. "Shʉnangwavį," the myth name of Coyote, is what Christian San Juan Paiutes call Jesus when they are speaking Paiute, demonstrating the importance of Coyote to San Juan Paiutes.[4]

STORYTELLING IDEOLOGIES

According to the San Juan people I know, there is a right way to tell the stories. They were traditionally told at night, in the dark, in the winter, and listeners, especially children, were expected to lie down with their legs "folded" or curled up. That is what happened the first time I went out to visit the San Juan in winter. My first experience with San Juan traditional storytelling practice was in December 1981 when we (my late husband, Robert Franklin, eighteen-month old daughter Rebecca, and I) spent several days at the sheep camp home of eighty-year-old Marie Lehi. She was the wife of the late Alfred Lehi, the spokesperson of the tribe in the pre-1980 period, and the mother of the spokesperson in 1981, Anna Whiskers. Everyone at the sheep camp stayed in one house, a largish one-room octagonal house. They had recently built an additional small room off one of the sides where we slept and where the stories were told. Everybody else slept in the large room.

One evening was devoted to telling the traditional winter stories, mythic tales about Coyote and other animals from the myth or beginning-time. Present at this session were Marie, two daughters, two granddaughters, one grandson, one great-grandson, and one male cousin of her grandchildren. The storytellers were Marie Lehi and Anna Whiskers. Although bilingual in Paiute and Navajo, both Marie and Anna always spoke Paiute to other Paiute speakers. That dark winter evening Marie told us in Paiute (not recorded) that we needed to lie down with our knees bent. She told us she had learned the winter story/Coyote tale that she was going to tell us from her mother and then began the story. When Marie was finished, she said she was tired. So, Marie's oldest daughter, Anna, took over the storytelling. After Anna had finished telling another Coyote story, the male cousin, who was in his early thirties, jokingly told us that he would tell us one but it would cost us at least $200. At that time, I was not sure whether he was joking or not. Now, however, I am sure he was; not only was $200 a sum he would not have expected to get from us at that time, but also he was not at the stage of life when it would have been proper, at least in the context of nonfamily members and the elders, Marie and Anna. In addition, I have since had lots more exposure to Paiute joking.

The elders had been remarking before the 2006 sessions were set up that most of storytellers from the 1980s and 1990s had either passed away or were getting forgetful. Normally this would not have been a problem,

since Paiute-speakers in their forties, fifties, and sixties would just have
taken over and started telling the stories. However, this time it was different. All of these younger elders had heard the stories frequently up through
the 1970s and even into the early 1980s, since the telling of these stories
had then been normal winter entertainment. But more recently the situation has changed drastically. During the previous twenty years or so, television and video-type entertainment access has taken the place of the daily
winter evening traditional Coyote stories. These traditional stories have
since then been performed rarely and as a special event rather than as an
everyday occurrence. Although completely fluent in Paiute, the younger
Paiute elders, not having heard the stories as often as any previous generation, often remembered only parts of any winter story, and most of them
did not know the recitatives, or "story songs," well. The exception was
one man in his mid-fifties who knew a great many of the stories but was
generally too shy to tell them.

The fragility of this knowledge was reinforced in a particularly poi-
gnant way: On the first night they had planned to have storyteller sessions
to address this problem, the shy man's brother was taken to the hospital
and almost died. That night they said they realized that they could not
count on the knowledge that only one person had. Thus, these sessions
that took place at Hidden Springs were called explicitly to produce a wider
pool of storytellers mainly in their forties or fifties so that they would each
know several of the stories with the accompanying recitatives.

The ideological importance of storytelling is encoded in statements
such as, "Well, they can't help it, their parents never told them stories/
instructions!" Such statements are repeated frequently both to explain
aberrant behavior and to emphasize the importance of traditional Paiute
teachings normally found in stories, particularly the winter stories, and in
instructions, called *aikupi* 'say (something) + for someone's benefit,' normally given at life crises rituals such as the menarche and first childbirth
rituals (Bunte and Franklin 1987; Franklin and Bunte 1997). There are two
kinds of *aikupi*. Those that generally deal with highly specific ritual situations need to be taken literally: "Some of the best examples of this type
are the sayings associated with life cycle observances. On certain ritual
occasions, elder relatives will talk their younger kin through the ritually
prescribed actions and restrictions on action that must be observed during
times of passage from one stage of life to another. The elders instruct their
younger relatives, explaining how they must conduct themselves hence-
forward" (Bunte and Franklin 1987:222).

The second kind of *aikʉpị* are similar to the proverbs and maxims of Euro-Americans and, like most proverbs all over the world, are to be taken metaphorically rather than literally.

In a previous work (Bunte 2009), I have discussed certain Paiute language ideologies—for example, that words of instruction will be re-activated, that is, "be heard," or, more emically, "words come on the wind," when needed by the child later in life, and that listening or having one's ears open is a persistent theme in Paiute socialization talk. Philips (1983:64–66) discusses a similar conception and notes that Warm Springs Indians give more emphasis "to the child's receptive linguistic compe-tence than to productive competence" (1983:50). Similar cultural empha-ses have also been noted in more recent studies by Nevins (2004b) for the White Mountain Apache and Meek (2007) for the Kaska. We see the consequences of these language ideologies among the San Juan Paiutes over and over again in adults' socializing interactions with children when caregivers provide instructions, warnings, and other advisories but do not expect children necessarily to immediately follow their lead or do what they have instructed. They nevertheless do believe that their words have been heard and may surface as guiding words in future life. We also see the effect of these language ideologies among adults with regard to story-telling; many of the adults at these collaborative storytelling sessions were there just to listen and not to tell stories themselves. The emphasis in Paiute socialization is on the attainment of the knowledge, not the im-mediate reproduction of it. Therefore, they believe that if adults listen to the stories now, the stories will come to these adults later when they need them.

San Juan Paiutes also value innovation and creativity in language highly. Although this seems to compete with another Paiute language ide-ology that values the traditional, San Juan Paiutes actually combine the two, for they are especially in favor of innovation when it is in service of tradition. The two—tradition and innovation—are not usually spoken of at the same time, at least by Euro-Americans. But San Juan Paiutes do not seem to have a problem with uniting tradition and innovation, as attested by the active and highly productive use of their polysynthetic language to create new terms. Just to illustrate a couple of examples, consider the word for "fork," *wǫchʉikamʉats*, literally 'four fingers,' or "computer," *akaxǫkwarʉmpǿǿ*, composed from 'drawing with lightening.' By con-trast, members of some tribes will not innovate new words on ideological grounds—a reflection of a purist language ideology. As mentioned earlier, innovation occurs not only in addition to the creation of new words but also in storytelling.

The first elaborated example is a winter storytelling session that occurred in 1998. The venue was the tribal health department in Tuba City on Main Street, past the trading post. It is an old two-story church building which, at that time, had a kitchen and the health department's cubicle-type offices on the second floor and the tribal gym/workout room and a conference room on the bottom floor. In this health department location, this unprecedented storytelling event took place in the daytime and included an interpreter as well as two video cameras. After the storyteller had finished telling the story, she had the children act out the conclusion of the story. As far as I know it was the first time for winter stories to be told outside of someone's home, and in the daytime. It was definitely the first time that the listeners were told to act out a part of the story. The whole event was especially surprising since it was with a storyteller, Grace Lehi, who five years earlier would consent to be recorded by audiotape only in the dark at her sheep camp home. She obviously felt this time that the story and the storytelling occasion were important.

The story she told was, indeed, an important one for Paiutes. Titled by Sapir (1930:462) as "Coyote and His Daughters," it is about incest and the origin of a constellation they called *Shøøniang*. It also shows why Coyote has the shape he has today instead of being the handsome man he was previously. Furthermore, although Grace did not initiate the acting out, she was not at all an unwilling participant as she actively directed Evelyn James (the interpreter and also the vice president of the tribe) where the children had to go in acting out the chase scene at the end of the story.

Evelyn opened the session with a description of winter night storytelling in the past and then discussed the main audience rules of behavior, such as not lying down with legs stretched out, before she turned the floor over to Grace. As the following transcript demonstrates, Grace also was conscious of conserving as much of the proper way of telling the story as possible. The transcript starts as Grace has just finished the story and Evelyn gives a brief translation followed up by a request to the listening children who were sitting on a blanket (with legs curled up).[5]

Evelyn: and um to this day um Coyote has told those women
           that they going to be nothing but stars and so here's
           the stars. We'd like to let twelve participants up here
           so they can hold the [paper] stars . . . anybody? So we
           will know how *Shøøniang* looks like when you go out
           tonight you will know where they are. You want to?
           Hunh?=
Grace: =*Uru'angwa uruh muan tɨniaxu'ng.*
           My father told that story.
           Muan uvwai tɨniaxu'ng, uvaiyukwɨ.
           My father told it =
Evelyn: =unhhuh.=
Grace: =*Kach, kach mɨyavipɨ'øapai tɨvitsiaxai kuruh.*
           Never, never, lay down with your legs straight [quota-
           tive].
           Nɨnai uruh ya'aikwikain,
           Mɨni uru'avanor tɨniaparɨ ung Shøøniang tɨniɑkat,
           manøni
           When I die, you guys will tell the story about the
           Shøøniang,
           all of you.
           nɨngwɨnakwɨ kɨxɨkw'aivatɨ.
           All you people can take it.
           Nɨxanivatsɨ thap'anga pakw'aivatɨ naka'atɨ tavai
           Something will happen to me and I'll be gone one of
           these days
           Aipɨxa'.
           he said.

In this excerpt, Evelyn goes directly from translating the end of the
story ("and um to this day um Coyote has told those women that they
going to be nothing but stars") to suggesting a major innovation—that
the children act out the story "and so here's the stars. We'd like to let
twelve participants up here so they can hold the [paper] stars." Grace, on
the other hand, is not finished with the traditional story process and interrupts Evelyn with a conventional closing, explaining that she learned the
story from her father. Then, quoting directly she repeats what her father
told them: not to lie all stretched out, that when he died they would be
the ones to tell the story about the origin of the constellation *Shøøniang,*

and, finally, that her father predicted that something would happen to him so that he would be gone. Thus, although Evelyn did the metanarrational work for the introduction—the beginning frame—Grace repeated the part of Evelyn's introduction about not lying all stretched out, in effect framing the end of the narrative in terms of the beginning frame. The mention of her father provided a conventional authorization of her performance, and the quoted phrase "When I die, you guys will tell the story about the *Shǿǿniang,* all of you. All you people can take it" is, as Bauman (2004:26) puts it, "traditionalization in practice"—for by this quote Grace is linking her story to her father's tellings and fulfilling her father's predictions by "taking it," that is, by telling the story. She may also be intimating that she may be gone at some point and that the listeners may have to "take it" (the story) and tell it.

Evelyn elaborated on Grace's conventionalized ending, emphasizing Paiute identity, intertextuality, and the key rule of listener etiquette:

> Well, the old man that um shared this story was—his name was. . . . it was her father, Alfred Lehi. He said, "These stories like this um, ancient stories of the Paiutes, these should be passed on through generation. They should not be stopped just because I am old and I'm not gonna be no longer living. It should be passed on down to the children. So, the children can tell their stories to their children. It should continue on. It should not stop where he is." And then he said . . . when he tells stories like that, he used to tell all his children to obey him, to make sure that nobody is laying with their legs all stretched out and relaxing. They were supposed to always sit with their legs in or lay with their legs in and never have their legs stretched out. So, that was the rule to this story—so, you have to obey. The story to this one is you have to obey the rule and that was to teach the children that they had obedience, that they can obey.

COLLABORATIVE STORYTELLING: THE SECOND REALIZED EVENT

The January 2006 storytelling session in which San Juan Southern Paiutes speakers told several traditional winter stories also demonstrates an ideological commitment to pragmatic innovation in service to the traditional, though it is unlike the previous event in that its purpose was not directly to produce more speakers. Rather, it was to enlarge the pool of storytellers and to help the potential ones know more stories well enough to feel more comfortable telling them. These particular sessions were significant because they were not normal sessions focused on one storyteller at a time; rather, they were primarily collaborative sessions with an innovative agenda. Paiute speakers held these sessions at Hidden Springs because they perceived stories themselves as endangered. I was present, along with a graduate student, Rayed Khedher, and we were asked to record them. The San Juan Paiutes present at these sessions talked during and between stories about language shift, stories they remember and who told them, what comes next in the story, special story words, and the importance of the stories, as they re-created and reenacted what it means to be Paiute.

The following excerpt from the tape is at the very beginning of the session. Tataats is a twelve-year-old girl, Na'aintsits Wᵤn is her grandmother (actual mother's mother), and Matsikw is another one of her grandmothers (Na'aintsits Wᵤn's youngest sister). In addition to these three, there were five adult Paiutes and Tataats' eight-year-old brother, along with two or three other children in their early teens.

Matsikw was the first one to tell a story in this session, which was on day one of the three storytelling sessions. Her three older sisters along with her mother were the major storytellers of this part of the community for the 1980s and '90s. I had never heard Matsikw perform a winter story before, although as the only one of her generation to have been to school and to speak English she has worked with me since 1993 to correct my transcriptions and translations of many of the stories from audio- and videotapes and had been present when many of the stories were recorded. In this tape, she starts out in English.

Matsikw: I'm going to talk about the Rabbit story. I'm going to
            say it in Paiute.
Tataats: You're talking English.
Matsikw: *Payutsivai. . . . Payutsia apaxainaivᵤ.*
            Paiute. . . . Paiute is what I am going to be talking.

Twelve-year-old Tataats has often been told that she should speak Paiute, and here she is implying that the elder should speak in Paiute by stating the fact that she was speaking English—in a Paiute storytelling event. This is significant because it makes clear that she has internalized several important Paiute cultural norms. She has internalized the importance of

Paiute as a special language. She has internalized that storytelling sessions are always conducted in Paiute. In addition, she displays her incomplete knowledge of situation-appropriate norms by correcting her elder, especially in a storytelling session. It is not unusual for juniors to correct elders normally, but it would be unusual in the Paiute traditional storytelling setting. It is unclear whether her unusual behavior helped key the session to be more interactive and collaborative or whether she felt comfortable making the comment because it was already set up, that is, keyed, to be collaborative—not conventional. Notice Matsikw's reaction to her comment: she simply translates "I'm going to say it in Paiute" into Paiute, suggesting that she accepts the comment along with the implied reproach. The excerpt continues with Matsikw starting the story:

Matsikw:	uuumh . . . *Tavutsikwah uni'nipʉxa'* . . .
	uuumh . . . Cottontail was there . . .
	I want to say. //[XXX].
Na'aitsits Wʉn:	*//imia//xwangaxa* (.0)
	In the beginning
Matsikw:	*Imiaxwangaxa, Tavutsikwah uni'nipʉxa'*
	In the beginning, Cottontail was there
	towatsingwʉkaipʉxa' ha
	[and] she had children, right?
	towatsingwʉkaipʉ kiyapʉxa'am
	[she] had children—they had been playing.

Among the San Juan winter stories are those that conventionally begin with untranslatable *Imiaxwangaxa*. I was told that this word means something like "Once upon a time"; in other words, it metacommunicatively marks the kind of story it is. I think it actually means something more like "In the beginning time." In this excerpt Matsikw interrupts her own storytelling with a metanarrational comment, asking for help and continuing the collaborative session. Later, it became even more collaborative with elders volunteering alternate words and information without any invitation.

I emphasize that, although winter stories in general are both socialization tools and just plain fun, perhaps their real value to the people is in the self-portrayal of their Paiute worldview and in their stories' sacredness. Their sacredness was highlighted by a tobacco smoking ceremony, which they had after the first storytelling session. The events took place in a small house that was uninhabited and used for storage. It had one room, and there were boxes of toilet paper, paper towels, and plastic cups stored there. After the stories were told, a prayer was said in Paiute, which intensified the atmosphere of this place. They smoked uncultivated Indian tobacco in (I believe Navajo-made) small pottery pipes, and the four directions were honored. Participants in the ritual told us that they ideally were supposed to smoke four pipe-fulls. Telling the stories is one way that San Juan Paiutes re-create their Paiute identity.

I have never heard a winter story told in English at San Juan or for that matter at Kaibab. I recently asked the president of the tribe if they ever tell the winter stories in English. She paused for a while, thinking, and then said, "Well, it would be OK to translate one that they are telling into English." But the implication was clearly that it would seem strange to tell it as a story in English. So I asked her why not. She again thought for a bit and replied, "It wouldn't sound right." After still more thought she said, "There are a lot of old words in the stories that have to be there or it wouldn't be right."

I think that when she says the "old words have to be there [in the stories]," she is referring to ones like *nʉngwʉvachakway muxuaxatʉ* and *imiaxwangaxa* and words and phrases that are now untranslatable in the classic sense, for they look like they are divided into morphemes, but these "morphemes" are not mapped onto meanings. *Nʉngwʉvachakway muxuaxatʉ* refers to Coyote when he is being a negative role model—as in the story "Coyote and His Daughters," and it means something like "selfish-hearted"; and, as I said above, *imiaxwangaxa* means something like "In the beginning times" or "In the myth times" and is essentially a genre marker that flags the story as a myth.

CONCLUSION

I believe these several storytelling or potential storytelling events are examples of what Briggs and Bauman (1992) call intertextual gaps. Intertextual gaps exist because the fit between a text and the conventionalized genre is never exact. In the cases we are discussing, the gaps are of fairly large amplitude. Bauman (2004:8) suggests that "certain genres may become the object of special ideological focus" and that widening the gap with innovation may lead to "the exercise of creativity, resistance to hegemonic order and openness to change." The Paiute storytelling events have clearly "become the object of special ideological focus." They also could be looked at as examples of resistance to the hegemonic institutions of the dominant society. Paiutes refuse to be pigeonholed into just doing things the "traditional" way if that way will have them lose speakers. We see this innovation in Evelyn's augmented response to Grace's legitimating and certifying language and in Evelyn's call to the children to come out as a nighttime constellation of stars. This is also a language revitalization event. The organizers had commissioned an artist to draw a picture of every animal that was in the set of stories selected by the storytellers. Then Nikole and I wrote down the animal's Paiute name on the picture and handed out the pictures to the children who then colored them.

Paiute storytelling ideologies, like Paiute language ideologies in general, celebrate pragmatic innovation with the intention of language revitalization but not innovation for its own sake. This chapter reviews several cases of pragmatic innovation: the DVD, the cartoon, the children performing the stars' chase scene, Grace's story, and the collaborative sessions. It is important that none of these would ever have occurred had community members not realized that their language was in serious trouble. Language endangerment not only raised awareness, it created an environment in which they were willing to do something to maintain their language and its storytelling traditions.

Today, San Juan Paiutes are not about to let their stories be erased or marginalized—the Paiutes will do whatever they need to retain them. You could say the same thing about their language and their culture—they will do whatever they need to retain them. For instance, the collaborative storytelling sessions were still going on in January 2009. If the Paiutes are worried about the stories surviving, it is partly because stories themselves are so very important. But clearly this concern is, in large part, also about maintaining the local culture and saving the San Juan Paiute language.

NOTES

I want to recognize the support of the Endangered Language Fund for the DVD project on storytelling for revitalization purposes. I especially thank Susan Needham and Rayed Khedher for reading and commenting on drafts of the chapter. I am deeply indebted to the San Juan Paiute people for their thirty years of friendship and active collaboration, without which this research would not have been possible. I especially acknowledge Evelyn James and Mabel Lehi's contributions to the project. I am also pleased to recognize the following people, who in various ways assisted this project: Janet Ogano, Anne Coyner, Nikole Lobb, Rayed Khedher, and Roman Gratreaks. (Note: The volume editor would like to gratefully acknowledge the expert service of Roman Gratreaks, who helped proof the final version of this chapter after the author's death.)

1. For information on the history and land tenure of the San Juan Paiutes, see Bunte and Franklin (1987).

2. An exception to this pattern of nonrecognition is that they did receive health services through the Indian Health Services, if they lived on the reservation.

3. This quotation is from an unrecorded telephone conversation on October 7, 2008.

4. The orthography used here was developed for Kaibab Paiute by me and the late Kaibab elder Lucille Jake and for the San Juan Paiute by the late Robert Franklin and me. It is the official orthography of the San Juan Paiute Tribe and the one used in tribal documents such as the constitution (Bunte and Franklin 2001). Most characters have their International Phonetic Alphabet values. The following are exceptions or are otherwise worthy of special mention. The apostrophe (') is the glottal stop. The letter *x* is the spirantized version of *k* and stands for a (usually) voiceless velar fricative. The letter *y* is the glide. The letter *r* is a short apical trill or flap and is the spirantized version of *t*. The digraph *ng* stands for a velar nasal. Before *k*, however, the nasal is written simply as *n*. The digraphs *ts, ch, sh* are pronounced as they would be in English. *ʉ* is a high back unrounded vowel similar to the *i* in Russian. *ø*, a sound that in Southern Ute and San Juan Paiute replaces Kaibab and other Southern Paiute open *o*, is a mid-front rounded vowel often pronounced with noticeable retroflex approximant *r* coloring (pronounced much like the *-er* in "writer"). Long vowels are phonemic and are written as double vowels, as in *aa*. Three or more identical vowels in a row signal stylistic lengthening. A voiceless vowel is written with a small circle under the vowel, as in *ą̊*. Voiceless vowels are frequently dropped at the end of words. An acute accent on a vowel (e.g., í) indicates word stress.

5. In the transcribed examples, numbers enclosed in parentheses designate the number of seconds of a pause, such as (2) for a two-second pause. A very brief pause is noted by (.0). Latching between speakers is designated by =. Overlapping speech is designated by //. XXX indicates audible speech that is not clear enough to permit transcription.

CHAPTER 4

THE POLITICS OF STORYTELLING IN NORTHWESTERN CALIFORNIA
Ideology, Identity, and Maintaining Narrative Distinction in the Face of Cultural Convergence

Sean O'Neill

Northwestern California has long attracted attention as an area of tremendous linguistic diversity, where speakers have actively maintained profound differences in grammar and vocabulary, even in the face of widespread cultural convergence, intermarriage, and multilingualism (see, e.g., Bright and Bright 1965; Haas 1967; Kroeber 1925:5; O'Neill 2008; Sapir 1921:214). Somewhat subtler are the many small-scale differences in local oral traditions. Though the Hupas, Yuroks, and Karuks tell similar stories based on common themes from their folklore and mythology, these shared tales often appear radically transformed—even inverted—when compared. To take one example, consider the status of Coyote, who plays a central role in creation lore among the Karuks but is usually reduced to the status of a secular buffoon among the neighboring Hupas. Although this difference may seem slight to outsiders, such distinctions are considered very significant within the region, where they potentially serve as badges of ethnolinguistic identity or indexes of community membership, much like the languages themselves.

Earlier versions of several sections in this chapter ("Accentuating Local Differences in the Face of Deep Cultural Parallels," "The Sociopolitical Basis of Identity," and "The Continuing Iconization of Tradition") first appeared in the author's book *Cultural Contact and Linguistic Relativity among the Indians of Northwestern California* (O'Neill 2008) and are reproduced here with the permission of the publisher.

Today, as the languages undergo revitalization, this long-standing concern with local difference is receiving renewed attention in the context of the tribal language programs where speakers are also striving to keep their languages, stories, and worldviews distinct from those of the English-speaking world. In this emerging context, the distinctive Hupa, Yurok, and Karuk versions of these stories continue to be important in the maintenance of social identity, setting the communities apart in publicly accentuated ways and instilling language learners with a sense of pride in the uniqueness of their own traditions. In this chapter I examine the language ideologies and sociopolitical realities associated with the highly localized storytelling traditions of northwestern California, which have been actively maintained as part of the distinctiveness of the respective languages. My findings suggest that the principle of linguistic relativity, whereby speakers of contrasting languages subscribe to somewhat different worldviews, sometimes emerges from conscious choices of interpretation among community members, who actively strive to set their languages and worldviews apart from those of neighboring societies, including the English-speaking world.

ACCENTUATING LOCAL DIFFERENCES IN THE FACE OF DEEP CULTURAL PARALLELS

In my fieldwork in northwestern California, I primarily worked with Hupa speakers to document traditional narratives over a three-year period in the late 1990s. In the process, I was able to translate several Yurok and Karuk tales into the Hupa language, so that multiple versions of a single story could be compared word for word in each of the tongues. It was in this setting that I first became aware of some of the striking differences among some of the area's storytelling traditions, which previous investigators, including Kroeber and Sapir, had taken to be nearly uniform in expression along with the supposedly homogeneous culture of the region as a whole (Kroeber 1925:5; Sapir 1921:214). To my great surprise, Hupa speakers often rejected Karuk stories in the first several lines, even when I read them strictly in English, as subtle departures from their own versions of the same tales began to crop up. Equally often it was the ending, or punch line, that was inverted, marking the story off as a foreign tale only at the very end. "That's a Karuk story," my consultants would announce dismissively, before launching into their own rather different versions of the stories, where the ending had been changed slightly or where one character had been substituted for another similar one.

Later, I learned that one of my consultants sometimes sent out scouts to record the dances of the neighboring Yuroks, so that he could criticize their performances of the songs based on notable departures from the Hupa versions, which were more definitive in his opinion. Soon it became obvious that his own sense of identity as a Hupa speaker was wrapped up in the distinctiveness of the Hupa lore, which was, for him, also tied to the Hupa language. Of course, these minor departures in the content of the stories also held strong political overtones, since the subject matter was largely religious and the vital question of the "truth" was at stake.

As was already documented in the existing ethnographic literature, storytelling had long been crucial in the culture of the region, allowing everything from local family histories to entire systems of mythology to be passed down from one generation to the next strictly by word of mouth. Whether recited in evening narratives at home or celebrated in song on ceremonial dance grounds, the words and deeds of the ancients were regularly brought into the living present through the act of narration. Traditionally, women, for instance, were responsible for learning an extensive body of medicinal formulas, with uses ranging from protecting babies from disease to ensuring long life among adults—something that is again receiving renewed attention as a new generation begins to resurrect this knowledge from the anthropological archives. Traditional healers, for their part, drew upon their specialized knowledge of creation lore to contact spirit beings when initiating the process of healing, creating a living connection among the shaman, the patient, and the religious figure who established the medicine. Since knowledge of these tales was a privilege of specialized religious training, knowledgeable storytellers were inclined to charge a fee for reciting medicinal formulas or healing the sick with song.[1]

As I happily discovered in the course of my research, these storytelling traditions are still very much alive today, having taken on a new life in the context of the tribal language programs. Like most Native languages in the United States, nearly all of them in California are currently classified as highly endangered, meaning that there is serious risk these languages may drop out of use soon if they do not acquire a new crop of speakers in the current generation, while the predominantly elderly speakers are still in a position to pass on their knowledge. Realizing the severity of the situation several decades ago, the Hupa, Yurok, and Karuk tribes all undertook strenuous efforts to revitalize their ancestral languages—a highly visible process that now takes place in such diverse settings as the public school systems, summer immersion camps, and intensive one-on-one Master-Apprentice programs (Hinton 1994:220–47). Under these pressing circumstances, there is a renewed concern with passing on the considerable intellectual heritage associated with learning the traditional oral literature, along with the languages in which they are normally told. It is in this emerging setting that many of the elders have been recruited to tell stories as a way of modeling fluency and generating enthusiasm for learning languages in a "natural" cultural setting. Even during the course of my fieldwork, some of my consultants quickly began to use the stories we collected in their lesson plans, and afterward the materials I gathered were left with the elders who originally told the stories in the hope that they would continue to provide useful learning materials for the language revitalization programs.

Now, as in the past, children continue to be introduced to the storytelling traditions when learning the languages, since even understanding elementary vocabulary requires a deep familiarity with storytelling traditions (O'Neill 2006). To take one example, consider the Water Ouzel (or Dipper), a small local bird whose story is captured in the vocabularies of the Hupa and Karuk languages, though in somewhat different forms. According to the common storyline, the Water Ouzel was a poor father in the ancient past who received an eternity of punishment for turning his back on his children by leaving them to starve as he filled his own belly with the food he caught each day. This much of the story is closely shared among the Hupas and Karuks. It is the ending that accentuates the differences between the communities, even at the level of ordinary vocabulary. Among the Karuks, the Water Ouzel is condemned to eating river moss, as captured in the word *?asaxvanish?ámvaanich* 'the one who sucks moss from the floors the rivers.' Among the Hupas, however, the bird is called *ce·-q'e·t* 'the one who copulates with stones,' reflecting the punishment this figure received in ancient times. The stories and corresponding names each encapsulate an element of natural history, since this bird can still be seen today both hopping about on the rocks (thus appearing to copulate with them) and diving into the water (thus appearing to eat the moss at the floor of the river). Today, as children learn vocabulary, many are becoming familiar with the associated stories, effectively preserving some of the

striking differences between the neighboring traditions even at the outset
of the learning process.

Early scholars like Kroeber and Sapir were certainly correct to observe that many of the core cultural institutions of northwestern California
run closely parallel from one community to the next, something that is
loosely true for everything from the great religious dances to the basic
elements of folklore and mythology. Yet both scholars also overlooked the
many subtle cultural differences that set these neighboring groups apart,
something that took me by surprise when I first became aware of it, since
the anthropological literature did not prepare me for this reality. As we
have just seen with the Hupa and Karuk words for the Water Ouzel, even
the slightest differences in content can be significant at the local level,
and the neighboring speech communities continue to place a premium on
maintaining this sense of distinction, which is highlighted by the otherwise overwhelming similarities between the traditions. Of special interest
to many speakers today are the unique versions of the tales found only in a
specific village or speech community, which provide a source of pride and
instill a further interest in learning the local languages, as the following
examples illustrate.

Across-the-Ocean-Widower and the Origin of Death

Consider the cycle of stories surrounding the local culture hero known as
"Across-the-Ocean-Widower," who stands at the heart of all three Native
religious traditions. Each group sets his autochthonous birth in the Yurok
village of Kenek—at the very center of the universe—where he sprang
spontaneously into existence, without any mention of his parents, as is so
often the case in oral literature. From this symbolically charged location
Across-the-Ocean-Widower embarks on the many adventures that come to
shape the world as we know it.

Almost immediately, Across-the-Ocean-Widower begins preparing
the world for the coming of humans as he institutes the medicines and
dances that people will one day use to fix the earth, for these humans
inevitably stray from the path set down by the ancients, long ago in the
mythical past. Almost as soon as Across-the-Ocean-Widower emerges, a
race of prehuman spirit deities rise up alongside him, together with those
abiding forces of good and evil. At the time, it is said, the world is popu-
lated by spirit beings with features that are like both modern-day animals

and humans, many of which originally have the capacity for thought and speech, which is later given up.[2] As his name suggests, Across-the-Ocean-Widower eventually abandons this world and establishes a home in the heavens at the edge of the horizon, where he continues to lead the spirits there in nightly performances of the religious dances and to watch over humanity from afar. This much of the story is widely shared throughout ethnolinguistic communities of the region, and most of these elements are reflected, in basic form, in each of the neighboring storytelling traditions.

From here the neighboring traditions begin to part ways; despite the similarities, these common threads are often woven into very different tales. Consider the story of how death enters the world. The Hupas, Yuroks, and Karuks all agree, for example, that the original inhabitants of the earth do not know death, and that death emerges as the result of a primal misdeed committed long ago in the ancient past. To a point there is widespread consensus, and Across-the-Ocean-Widower plays a central role in the origin of death for both the Hupas and Karuks. According to a popular Hupa account, death enters the world at the village of Łe·ldiŋ, on the fringe of Hupa-speaking country, as one of the Across-the-Ocean-Widower's orphaned sons is mistreated in the hands of strangers.[3] According to the story, the child is buried alive and nearly dies. Moments before the child's death, Across-the-Ocean-Widower arrives and administers the death as a punishment for all future generations. Here, at this site, the Hupa claim, he also establishes the great religious dances as a way of making reparation for this original wrong. For the Karuks, on the other hand, death enters the world at the mouth of the Klamath River (Thúfip), in Yurok country, as Across-the-Ocean-Widower's father becomes bewildered in his old age and fails to join his sons in the heaven across the ocean downstream.[4] For the Yurok, however, Across-the-Ocean-Widower has no role in the origin of death, which is attributed to other, more minor characters.[5] Instead, the unraveling of life and the emergence of death begin in Hupa country with the first misdeeds of Mole and Jerusalem Cricket, who tamper with important dietary staples and perform nefarious acts beneath the surface of the earth. It is implied that the village of Taʔk'ʸimiłdiŋ, in Hupa country, may have been the site of their first misadventures, which would ultimately result in the emergence of death.[6] In the end, these miscreants must face their acts and make amends on the trails near Weitspus (modern-day Weitchpec), in the heart of Yurok country, where justice is restored. Significantly, each group sets the origin of death far from home, often in the territory of a neighboring speech community, whereas redemption is sometimes found in one's homeland.

The Status of Coyote: Sacred and Profane

Another popular figure in northwestern California is Coyote, whose status, like that of many of the other characters, often shifts quite dramatically from one group to the next. Among the Karuks, for instance, Coyote is absolutely central in the creation, establishing many features of the present world. According to one Karuk story, rivers originally flowed in both directions, making it possible to travel both upstream and downstream without effort—until one day Coyote, in his role as the "lawmaker," announced that the rivers would flow only downstream. Though this act certainly contributes to creation, it also makes life more difficult for the people who come to populate the planet, placing Coyote in the role of both mischievous trickster and powerful creator. In other Karuk tales, Coyote discovers fire and brings salmon and acorns to humans, in a sense creating the conditions for human life by introducing fire and two of the most important dietary staples in traditional times. Sometimes Coyote ventures to the heavens in the sky to participate in religious ceremonies performed there, then often falls back to earth, where his body is said to rest at a sacred site.

Along with creation activities, Coyote often gets into trouble for his sexual excesses, and at times his behavior is even comical—as when he eats his own excrement, marries his own daughter, or tricks women into sex by pretending to be a doctor.[7] In many Karuk stories, Coyote's status appears to teeter between the highly sacred and the deeply profane. Yet the same stories do not circulate in Hupa country, just a few miles down the Klamath River and up the neighboring Trinity River (one of the tributaries of the Klamath). On the contrary, in Hupa country Coyote is more often portrayed as a troublemaker at the fringes of culture and is rarely elevated to the status of even a minor religious figure. Instead, among the Hupas, Coyote is often paired with Frog, his wife, who he sometimes mistreats, even beating her in some episodes.[8] When I presented Hupa consultants with Coyote stories from the neighboring Karuk tradition, they usually recognized the stories as foreign tales; some of them already knew them as the unwelcome stories of the neighboring Karuks. Because these stories went against the grain of the Hupa lore by placing Coyote in a more religious role, no one was willing to help me translate them into Hupa.

The Status of the Spirit Heavens: Cosmological Inversion

Even the traditional religious conception of the universe is far from uniform, showing a great deal of variation throughout the region and often demonstrating a process of inversion, where opposite meanings are ascribed from one community to the next. In traditional times, it was generally agreed, the earth consisted of a roughly disc-shaped expanse surrounded by an enormous, swirling cosmic "river" that circled clockwise around the coast. Although few people today subscribe to this traditional sense of the universe, many aspects of the cosmology are still very much alive, such as the concept of the "upstream" and "downstream" heavens at the edge of the horizon.

By going far enough into any of the rivers, the traveler comes to the edge of the water and eventually arrives at one of several mythical lands said to rest at the fringes of the universe. In folklore and mythology, the concepts of upstream and downstream hold strong religious meaning, and each direction is linked with a particular spirit realm. After death, it is said, the soul of the deceased travels to the spirit heaven, where one's favorite dances are constantly performed.

Yet neighboring groups sometimes hold very different conceptions about where these dances are held within the total vision of the universe. Consider the upstream spirit realm, which takes on nearly opposite meanings from Hupas to Yuroks. In the Yurok tradition, this is the land where the culture hero Across-the-Ocean-Widower fled after abandoning the world he originally prepared for the coming of humans. Here in the upstream spirit heaven, he leads the other spirit deities in a nightly performance of the White Deerskin Dance. The Hupas, however, ascribe different features to this land. It is the Jump Dance that is performed in the upstream heaven, not the White Deerskin Dance, as the Yuroks maintain. Even where this common framework of cosmology is concerned, each group has arrived at its own unique sense of the surrounding universe.

MAINTAINING ETHNOLINGUISTIC BOUNDARIES AND NARRATIVE DISTINCTION

Though of diverse origins, the Native peoples of northwestern California eventually settled on a common way of life as a by-product of ongoing contact and intermarriage. In traditional times, deep affinities swept across almost every aspect of daily social life, beginning with material existence and moving to those more abstract realms of folklore and religious practices—as scholars like Kroeber and Sapir noted long ago. Yet the similarities can easily be exaggerated. Looking back, a century of ethnographic work has revealed that the traditional culture of this region was also surprisingly diverse, as illustrated here with examples from storytelling traditions. Clearly these differences are meaningful today, and the fact that these groups have maintained their differences suggests that these markers of distinction have been meaningful for some time. As my consultants frequently pointed out, these subtle differences in the content of a story are crucial in maintaining a sense of belonging in one's community and, by extension, a sense of distinction from neighboring groups.

The Sociopolitical Basis of Identity: The Eras of the Village and Tribe

Before contact with Euro-Americans in the mid-nineteenth century, daily life in northwestern California largely revolved around the village, which served as the basis for one's primary sense of social identity.[9] In traditional times the village generally consisted of fifty to a hundred people sharing a series of neighboring households on a level area near a river, generally at least a few miles apart from the nearest neighboring village. The traditional homelands of the Hupa, Yurok, and Karuk villagers all converged near the confluence of the Klamath and Trinity rivers, not far from the place that was once regarded as the mythical center of the universe. The Karuks occupied a series of villages along the upper Klamath, reaching some sixty miles upstream from its confluence with the Trinity. A series of Yurok villages extended downstream from this confluence to the coastline. The Hupas, on the other hand, occupied dozens of villages along the neighboring Trinity, and in this traditional social setting larger groups of Hupa speakers came together only for collective social rites, including the calendrical religious ceremonies such as the White Deerskin Dance of late summer or the Jump Dance in fall or early winter. Otherwise, everything from daily subsistence activities to local political leadership revolved almost entirely around life in this home village; beyond the village, no larger political units existed. Instead, all property belonged to individuals and their families, but not to tribes or larger corporate entities. A few villages along the boundaries between the major speech communities may have been bilingual, but this was not the norm throughout the region as a whole.

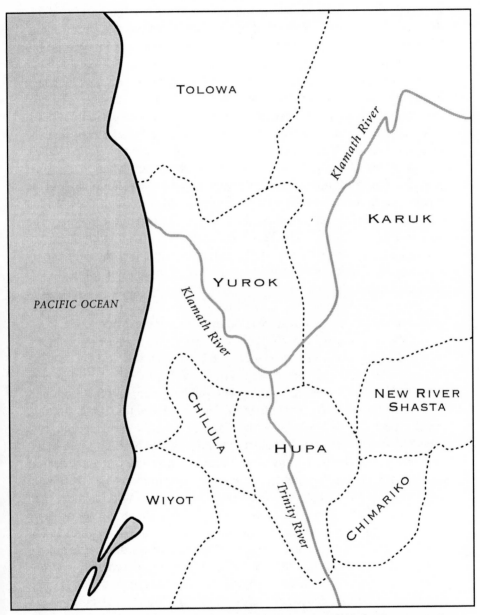

Map 1. Map locating Hupa, Yurok, and Karok in northwestern California. Reprinted with permission from *Cultural Contact and Linguistic Relativity among the Indians of Northwestern California*, by Sean O'Neill (Norman: University of Oklahoma Press, 2008).

In this traditional social setting, each village was home to a single dominant language, which served as a powerful marker of in-group status. To speak this language outside its homeland was generally considered improper. Since intermarriage was common (Waterman and Kroeber 1934), spouses from distant villages generally needed to master a new language before gaining full acceptance into their new home community. To take one example, consider the case of Mary Marshall, whose personal life history as the daughter of a Yurok mother and a Hupa father meant that she grew up speaking both languages. As a lifelong resident of Hoopa Valley, she rarely had the opportunity to speak Yurok, except when visiting her extended family in Yurok country or when speaking with her mother in the privacy of the home. In the summer of 1927, Edward Sapir drew on her expertise as a bilingual consultant, since she spoke two of the languages he was then investigating.[10] The Yurok she spoke in her work with Sapir was unusual in many respects, giving rise to the suspicion that she deliberately spoke faulty Yurok out of respect for the strong prohibition on using this alien language in Hoopa Valley. Of course it is also possible that her Yurok had simply gotten rusty from lack of regular use, since, as an outside language, it was not spoken in Hoopa Valley with any great frequency.

Howard Berman (Sapir 2001:1028–33) attributes many of these anomalies to Sapir's relative inexperience with Yurok, but it is equally possible that his sole informant, Mary Marshall, spoke faulty Yurok, or that both Sapir and Marshall were struggling with the language, and that both partially contributed to the anomalies in Sapir's field notes. Most striking, s and $š$ are collapsed in Sapir's records of Marshall's Yurok speech, two sounds that an experienced linguist like Sapir would have no trouble distinguishing had she been consistent. Furthermore, there is a great deal of inconsistency regarding the presence of glottalized stops and the glottal stop, which is more likely an indication of Marshall's faulty memory than a mistake on Sapir's part. Otherwise, Marshall appears to violate many of the regular morphophonemic rules in Yurok, as when she substitutes an l or w for an initial h following a vowel in the preceding word; the rule among other speakers is to substitute a g for an h in this phonological environment. Other rules she extended beyond their normal range, which is often a mark of an inexperienced speaker; for example, Marshall often appeared to drop a final h before a neighboring word starting with a consonant, though this rule is far more restricted among other Yurok speakers. Given Sapir's well-known ear for field languages, it is unlikely that all of these inconsistencies can be attributed to him alone, especially considering that some of the features he supposedly "misheard" in Yurok—such as glottal stops and glottalized stops—were also present in other languages he elsewhere documented with tremendous accuracy, including Hupa.

The past century has brought many changes to these peoples, and today their economy has turned from traditional practices like salmon fishing and acorn production to modern professions like logging, business, and forestry. In response to these dramatic changes in lifestyle, many of the smaller villages were gradually abandoned, and the populations are now concentrated in and around small towns. As a consequence, the traditional sense of village identity has gradually given way to a more embracing sense of community, rooted less in place than in other salient markers of group membership such as participation in local politics and cultural events. So, in contemporary times, it is tribal membership, rather than village membership, that generally serves as the primary criterion for belonging in the Native communities of northwestern California, and for some time this has largely been approached in terms of the language one's ancestors spoke.

Professional anthropologists and government officials alike were quick to group the peoples of this region on the basis of language, while ironically doing little to preserve these languages and sometimes even actively discouraging them, as was the case during the era of the boarding schools in the early to mid-twentieth century (Hinton 1994:173–79). This grouping according to language of course reflected a hallowed European tradition of correlating speech with other features of the surrounding society, including race, culture, and nation. As Fredrik Barth (1969:11) once noted, the supposed unity of language, race, and culture represented an "ideal type" to generations of European thinkers, including Herder and Humboldt, who often suggested the significance of language in the development of "national character."[11] Yet this traditional European understanding of language was not completely out of place in northwestern California, where language had long served as a badge of social identity—once as a marker of village membership and, more recently, as an index of tribal membership.

The Continuing Iconization of Tradition

One obvious area of continuity appears at the level of ideology. Given that language and storytelling are so strongly tied to identity among the Native peoples of this region, there is reason to believe that both underwent a process of "iconization" in Native consciousness long before the arrival of Euro-Americans, potentially calling up idealized images of ethnicity among those familiar with the distinctions between the communities. As Judith Irvine and Susan Gal (2000:37–38) point out, any feature of language (or society) can potentially function as an iconic representation if it conjures images of ethnicity within a community. Once this idealized "picture" of ethnicity is linked with a given social trait (such as the sound of a language), this trait has come to act as a sort of "icon," since meaning is conferred through the use of imagery (as with religious icons). The underlying process of attributing ethnic differences to distinctive features of language or culture has deep roots in the related process of symbolism, which allows one object of consciousness, such as the mere sound of a language or the content of a story, to stand for something else to which it is not intrinsically related, such as an associated ethnic identity. Though the language one speaks is not intrinsically related to one's village or tribal affiliation, through long association these languages—and related storytelling traditions—have come to serve as badges of community membership.

From informal conversations with speakers of the northwestern California languages, I have learned that caricatures circulate about the sounds of the neighboring tongues, much like the ones that English-speaking Americans spread about New Yorkers speaking too rapidly for comprehension or about Southerners speaking in a slow drawl that matches the pace of life there. From a Yurok speaker, for instance, I once heard the slightly deprecating claim that Hupa speakers talk "in the front of their mouths," a remark based on the conspicuous presence of front velar stops and palatal sounds in Hupa phonetics. For this consultant, the very sound of the Hupa language called up images of Hupa speakers and their distinctive ways, including their dances, language, homeland, and storytelling traditions.

Once set into motion, this process of association can be repeated indefinitely, allowing the oppositions between the communities to be "recursively" projected onto almost any symbol of the differences, including language (Irvine and Gal 2000:38), storytelling, or even community-based stylistic preferences. The resulting process of assigning ethnic differences to minor departures in the content of a tale was certainly very much alive when I was doing my fieldwork in the late 1990s, given the way my consultants consistently responded to the stories of the neighboring communities by rejecting them outright, despite the apparently overwhelming similarities to their own narratives. At the same time, there is an abiding sense that each language is most welcome in its homeland, and much less so outside of it.

On ideological grounds, it is clear that the Native communities of this region have long celebrated the distinctiveness of their languages, a deep-seated tradition that continues to this day. In traditional times the languages were sometimes regarded as artifacts of creation stretching back to the beginning of time.[12] According to one report, collected by Sapir, the neighboring peoples were warned not to bother Hupa speakers in times of war because of the power this language was said to hold. This power, it is said, stretched back to the time of creation, when the Hupa language was first established, presumably alongside Yurok and Karuk.[13] From my own fieldwork I learned that Hupas were warned, for religious reasons, not to speak their language on the coast, especially in Yurok country. In Hupa folklore it is said that the ocean would get jealous of the power held by Hupa speech, a problem that Yurok speakers presumably did not face when speaking their own language in the coastal portions of their homeland. Of course, this story also conveys a subtle denigration of the Yurok language, which apparently does not have the same effect on the ocean, while providing further testimony to the awesome powers of Hupa speech.

When one hears the sound of Hupa speech, it is said, the ocean will rise up and sweep the speaker away to his or her death. Clearly it is dangerous, according to the wisdom related in this story, to speak the Hupa language so far from its homeland, though certainly some amount of multilingual was regularly observed at the great religious dances, where it was the norm.

Localist Ideologies and Syncretic Realities

Considering the strong religious values associated with these highly localized forms of speaking and storytelling, it is not surprising that the Hupas, Yuroks, and Karuks take such great pains to set their traditions apart from those of their closest neighbors. As I often sensed when talking to my consultants, the words and stories of one's home community serve multiple symbolic functions, allowing speakers to assert connections with other members of an in-group while setting themselves apart from any neighboring communities. Given the pervasive focus on maintaining distinct traditions to mark the many sharp ethnolinguistic boundaries, there is reason to believe that a pervasive ideology of localism continues to persist among the Native peoples of northwestern California. As Jane Hill

(2001) has observed, such strong ideological preferences for local forms of speaking—and, I would add, storytelling—are common in areas where resources are relatively secure, suggesting that ecological factors are often decisive in determining the type of language ideologies that take root in a particular social milieu.[14] Certainly, northwestern California, with its rainforest ecology, has long been home to a world rich in material resources (Conathan 2004:151), though today any sense of security is probably rooted in the social benefits of tribal membership (e.g., land, rights, and financial support) rather than traditional economic resources (salmon, acorns).

This pervasive ideology of localism, which my consultants frequently echoed with claims about the uniqueness of their languages and storytelling traditions, exists in stark contrast to the reality of syncretism, given the obvious history of swapping stories and borrowing from one another over the course of many centuries. Though my consultants often insisted on the differences among the traditions, obviously these groups have been exchanging stories for some time. This process of combining elements from multiple sources—and blending them along the way—is a familiar one in many parts of the world, especially in situations of sustained contact and multilingualism, as has been the case in northwestern California long before contact with Europeans.

In one extreme form, the distinctions between these traditions can be temporarily collapsed, resulting in a kind of syncretism where elements from the neighboring groups are freely combined in some settings, as Jane Hill and Kenneth Hill (1986) observed in the Malinche volcano region of central Mexico. After centuries of contact, speakers of Mexicano, an indigenous language, have come to intersperse their speech with the colonial language, Spanish. As a result, Mexicano, which descends from classical Nahuatl, has absorbed some features of Spanish, including nouns, verb roots, grammatical affixes, and syntactic templates. This type of blending opens up a variety of ideological strategies to the speaker, who can claim some of the power associated with the Spanish-speaking world or, just as easily, create a subtle parody of the Spanish colonial heritage. The Hupa, Yurok, and Karuk languages show little evidence of mixing, but this familiar process of syncretism is certainly at work in their storytelling traditions, as seen in the many parallel stories surrounding the religious figure known as Across-the-Ocean-Widower. Like Abraham of the Middle East, who stands at the heart of Judaism, Islam, and Christianity, this ancient figure institutes many of the religious traditions of the region.[15]

In some settings, there are reasons for emphasizing the parallels, since highlighting the similarities allows for a more inclusive sense of identity.[16] In this setting, the reality of syncretism is sometimes allowed to come to consciousness, and the oppositions can be briefly collapsed. On a historical basis, it is clear that the Hupas, Yuroks, and Karuks have at times emphasized their common cultural ground as part of a concerted effort to avoid conflict on a daily basis. These efforts to maintain smooth relations reach their height at the religious dances, where the local differences are partially overlooked in the interest of "repairing the world" or "fixing the earth" and, in doing so, restoring harmonious relations among the groups.

On a daily basis, offending a neighbor, even far upriver, has long been taken as a very serious matter, and even the most minor breaches of politeness can be punished with stiff fines. Among the most common offenses are using insulting words or mentioning the names of the dead. Yet, at times, wars broke out between the neighboring speech communities, with one famous incident occurring between Hupa and Yurok villagers shortly before the California Gold Rush of 1849 (Sapir 2001:515–30). Painful memories of these bloody wars have led the peoples of this region to value peace at any cost, which, on a daily basis, amounted to avoiding any hint of interpersonal conflict, since in traditional times the offended party had a right to impose a stiff fine on the person who injured them; this fine, in turn, had to be paid off before purifying the world during the religious dances, and an apology had to be extended so that the conflict could be left in the past.

In contemporary times, highlighting similarities between the communities also allows for a wider regional sense of identity that sets the Native communities apart from the outside culture of contemporary America. My consultants often defined their identity first in terms of tribal membership and second in terms of being "Indians" of northwestern California, to be counted among their Yurok and Karuk brethren, with whom they, for the most part, shared a common religion and material culture. As still another more recent source of identity, many of the Native peoples in this area are very proud to be Americans, simultaneously resenting the atrocities committed by Euro-Americans against Native Americans and taking pride in their kin who have often served in international wars to defend their homeland.

Just as the oppositions can be glossed over—or even temporarily erased—in the interest of claiming a broader sense of identity, so these differences can also be accentuated, in the interest of claiming separate local

identities.[17] Despite the obvious parallels, a lingering sense of difference
always rests beneath the surface, ready to be drawn out according to the
situation at hand, as I observed repeatedly when my consultants reacted to
episodes from the neighboring storytelling traditions. Under these conditions, an ideology of localism prevails over the reality of syncretism. This
process of maintaining boundaries, even in the face of intense contact and
multilingualism, is common where speakers regularly cross the borders
imposed by even the slightest ethnic or linguistic differences. Rather than
level out these differences through a general process of regional diffusion,
boundary crossing often heightens the sense of ethnic distinction.

A particularly striking case of this phenomenon occurs among the Arizona Tewas, who have maintained a strong sense of linguistic distinction
despite living as an ethnic enclave among the Hopis for centuries (Kroskrity
1993). Though the Arizona Tewas came to embrace much of the Hopi way
of life, including the tradition of the ceremonial kiva speeches, they have
also remained fiercely purist in their attitude toward their own language, in
large part because of its ideological status as an icon of ethnic distinction.
Though most Arizona Tewas also speak Hopi fluently, Tewa is largely reserved for settings that highlight their membership in the Tewa community,
which makes it the primary language of the home and village; otherwise,
Hopi is the standard language of daily life elsewhere on the Hopi Reservation. As in the case of northwestern California (O'Neill 2008:276–84), a
strong ideology of indigenous purism (Kroskrity 2000a:337) has largely
prevented obvious mixing between the languages, so that Arizona Tewa
has absorbed relatively little from Spanish and Hopi, despite centuries of
intense contact and multilingualism. Yet, largely below the threshold of
consciousness, the languages have influenced each other, particularly at the
level of convergent semantic drift, though much less so in terms of structure or sound patterning. Similarly, despite the scale of the cultural convergence and multilingualism, the speakers of the Hupa, Yurok, and Karuk
languages have actively maintained highly distinctive grammars, phonol-
ogies, and vocabularies, with very minimal borrowing between traditions
(O'Neill 2002:87–88).

Under such conditions, where daily contact results in widespread convergence, any remaining differences can become powerful symbols of
ethnic distinction—almost as if their significance has been amplified under the circumstances, despite their apparently trivial objective appearance
to outsiders. Barth (1969:31) once called these minor symbolic differences "*diacritica* of ethnicity," like the subtle diacritical marks that can be

assigned to a letter to modify the pronunciation and meaning of a word, since they often function as powerful markers of ethnic distinction despite the apparent triviality of their appearance.

Multilingualism and the Compartmentalization of Tradition

If the languages and storytelling traditions of the Hupas, Yuroks, and Karuks have resisted convergence, it is certainly not because people are unfamiliar with the stories of neighboring groups. On the contrary, daily social life continues to provide members of each group with frequent opportunities to interact with members of neighboring groups and swap stories. For instance, intermarriage has long been common in the region (Waterman and Kroeber 1934), so it has not been unusual to grow up around speakers of several languages. To this day, a woman often moves to her husband's village, so female speakers are often especially multilingual. Traditionally, many children grew up in the presence of bilingual mothers, and some children continue to be exposed to several languages in the context of the school-based language programs. In the context of the extended family, a person's full circle of relations often encompassed several neighboring speech communities, providing frequent opportunities to visit with speakers of unrelated languages. Given the degree of intermarriage and multilingualism, knowledge of the neighboring languages and storytelling traditions has probably always been common—making the task of setting one's language apart all the easier to accomplish, however unconsciously this has been carried out.

Returning to Mary Marshall, Sapir's bilingual consultant in Hupa and Yurok, it seems significant that she consistently switched repertoires, telling separate stories in each language. The absence of mixing and overlap is remarkable. Instead, she told completely different stories in the two languages, suggesting that multilingual speakers observed a relatively stable rule of compartmentalization (Kroskrity 1993:210; 2000a:338–39), reserving some stories for delivery in Hupa and others for Yurok, without obviously blending the traditions or blurring the ethnolinguistic boundaries.[18] In part it was her style of delivery that changed as she passed from one language to the next. When performing Yurok stories, for example, she consistently introduced the characters by name at the outset, explicitly informing the audience that the story was about Coyote or Crane in the very first line. In fact, in the sample of texts Sapir collected, she begins all three of her Yurok narratives by identifying the main characters at the outset. The first narrative, "Coyote and Crane" (Sapir 2001:1017–22), opens with the following words: *šegep* 'Coyote' *me* 'past' *kʷeget* 'visit' *koohci* 'once' *mʌkʷtikš* 'Crane.' In this sentence, which loosely translates as "Coyote once went to visit Crane," she clearly introduces both of the main characters. In a second narrative, "Coyote Tries to Kill the Sun" (Sapir 2001:1022–25), she also mentions Coyote (*šegep*) in the first line. In the third Yurok narrative, "Medicine Formula to Get Wealthy" (Sapir 2001:1025–28), she introduces a maiden (*weʔyon*) and a young man (*cinomewoš*) who was her lover in the first and second lines, respectively.

In contrast, when telling stories in Hupa, Marshall would often launch into the tale without identifying the characters, leaving the audience to infer the actors' identities based on the storyline to follow; the pattern is common among Hupa storytellers, and it is significant that Marshall did not transfer this familiar Hupa convention to the stories she told in Yurok. For example, one of the central narratives in the Hupa creation pantheon opens with the following words (Goddard 1904:96): *Č'ixolčʷe·diŋ* 'Creation Place' *ʔe·na·ŋʔ* 'it was' *naʔtehɬdičʷe·n* 'he grew up,' which loosely translates as "He grew up at Creation Place." This narrative, which was told by Emma Lewis in 1901, does not even mention the protagonist by name for quite a while, though anyone familiar with the traditional creation lore would immediately recognize this character as Across-the-Ocean-Widower, the myth figure who emerged at this site. Here it is an event (growing up at Creation Place, *Č'ixolčʷe·diŋ*) that identifies the character, though his actual name rarely appears in these narratives. In a sense, it is parallel to the way Christians sometimes refer to God through the use of mere pronouns like "He" or "Him" or "His."

Indeed, Marshall's Hupa narratives, in contrast to the ones she delivered in Yurok, often appear more mysterious in structure, since she does not immediately identify the characters, relying instead on the audience to infer their identities through their actions. In the opening line of her narrative "The Origin of the Jump Dance" (Sapir 2001:72–75), for example, she says: *Taʔk'ʸimiɬdiŋ* 'At Hostler Ranch' *čin* 'they say' *k'ʸixinay* 'a spirit being' *c'isleʔn* 'one became.' This first sentence, which loosely translates as "they say someone became a spirit deity at the village of Taʔk'ʸimiɬdiŋ," provides little specific information about the identity of the character, though anyone steeped in the local lore would instantly recognize this figure as the Hupa Indian who originated the Jump Dance. Later, when introducing a Hupa story called "The Rival Wives" (Sapir 2001:438–45), she opens with the words *nahxi* 'two' *xoʔad* 'his wives,' which loosely translates as "He had two wives." Significantly, no specific information is provided about the identity of either the wives or the husband until much later in the story.

At the same time, the content of her storytelling also underwent a dramatic shift as she passed from Hupa to Yurok. Two of the Yurok stories she told Sapir feature Coyote in a starring, quasi-heroic role, something that is rare in Hupa lore. Though there is some overlap with Karuk oral literature, neither story is present in the Hupa tradition, in which Coyote is more often known for his licentious behavior or portrayed as a buffoon.[19] The one story that contains some overlap with the Hupa tradition is a medicine formula for securing wealth, a common theme in local lore. Yet Marshall's Yurok version differs in substantial ways from the usual Hupa versions, which tend to glorify the Hoopa Valley by setting the origin of wealth there and referring to the great beauty of this land.[20] It seems significant that her Yurok formula for procuring wealth is set, not in Hoopa Valley, but in Pekʷtuɬ—near the traditional center of the universe and in the heart of Yurok country.[21] I observed a similar insistence of compartmentalization during my fieldwork, when my Hupa consultants quickly rejected Yurok and Karuk versions of the tales.

In a similar way, much of the traditional lore was never completely translated into English and given modern adaptations, almost as if this established tradition of compartmentalization had been partially extended to the English language, which had no established connection with the Native oral literature. Curiously, many of the stories had not been transmitted in English in any regular way, starting with the era of the boarding schools in the early twentieth century when there was an abrupt shift away from the Native languages and a move under the then-dominant ideology of assimilation. Though, in principle, the stories could be easily translated into English, just as the Hebrew Torah had been translated into so many European languages, something was blocking the transmission of the Native stories into English. By the mid-twentieth century, or within the span of little more than a generation, the Native languages were no longer a major part of everyday life, a result that was sadly consistent with what many in the U.S. government planned when the boarding schools were engineered as part of a deliberate ideological mission to denigrate the languages and break the regular lines of transmission between the generations.

During the course of my fieldwork in the late 1990s, the impact could clearly be witnessed even at the level of ordinary vocabulary, where there was a conspicuous absence of Native words for modern concepts beyond the era of the Great Depression of the 1930s, when most people, including children, stopped speaking the languages on a daily basis; this sudden shift to English, of course, meant that most of the fluent speakers were over seventy at the time of my fieldwork. Under these circumstances, many of the traditional stories had also largely dropped out of circulation, though many of the elders who retained the languages also remembered the traditional oral literature, which they were equally eager to pass on to a new generation. Owing much to the efforts of linguists such as Victor Golla, Leanne Hinton, and William Bright, who offered an alternative ideology of pride in this considerable ethnolinguistic heritage, the situation was gradually starting to change by the late 1990s, during which time the languages were undergoing almost a renaissance of renewed interest among a dedicated group of young language enthusiasts within the Hupa, Yurok, and Karuk tribes.

Compartmentalizing Contemporary Worldviews and Revitalizing Native Traditions

This long-standing concern with maintaining the boundaries between traditions is all the more pressing today in the context of revitalizing the languages and preserving the Native storytelling traditions, alongside the new waves of American national culture.[22] I close this section on a note that captures some of the struggles Native communities are facing today as these groups strive to preserve their languages and keep their local cultures distinct from the constant encroachment of contemporary American society. One day, early in the course of my field experience, I asked an elderly Hupa speaker what seemed like a fairly straightforward question. In the context of documenting a traditional religious narrative, I simply wanted to know how to translate the short English phrase, "He landed the boat or canoe" into Hupa. This was part of a story Pliny Earle Goddard had originally collected at the turn of the twentieth century, though one that had largely slipped from memory as the community shifted to English over the previous several generations. At the time, during the late 1990s, we were working on preparing a contemporary version of the story for use in the classroom. The text was a religious narrative about safely navigating the area's rivers, which was partly accomplished by paying the proper respects to the sprits who presided over the waters.[23] Though this elder was fluent in both English and Hupa, he had largely compartmentalized the two traditions, insisting on keeping the worldviews separate while actively working to maintain the boundaries in his approach to teaching his native language.

This elder, who has since passed away, thought about the English phrase for a moment, then chuckled, realizing, as I now believe, that there was no exact Hupa translation.[24] As I came to learn, he worked hard to retain the original phrasing of these stories, so that they would not be too heavily influenced by assumptions based on English translations or American cultural ways. After some reflection, he gave a very complex form, which I could not immediately understand, one that sounded something like *xoł=me·nandiɢe·d*. Since I recorded the interview, I took it home and listened to this mysterious construction several times before attempting to transcribe it. As I wrote out the word, it quickly dawned on me that the elder had reformulated the entire construction. Strangely, from the point of view of English, the topic of the construction was not the one paddling the canoe, but a long object, as indicated by the final syllable in the word, namely, the stem, *-ɢe·d,* which refers to a single sticklike object, in this case a canoe, since it is both made of wood and relatively long like a stick. Yet it was also clear that the canoe was in control of the situation, since this stem was preceded by the reflexive prefix *di-*, which indicates that this object was acting upon itself—that is, the reflexive marker *di-* and the verb stem *-ɢe·d* join together to form a unit (*di-ɢe·d*) loosely meaning "a sticklike object propels itself." At the same time, the person who was in charge of the situation in the English construction was demoted to the role of passenger in Hupa, as indicated by proclitic *xoł=,* which loosely translates as "with an animal or person (as passenger)."[25] The Hupa construction also made explicit one element that was not present in English: that the canoe was in fact returning to solid land, having left the shore at some earlier point. The concept of a return was indicated by the iterative marker *na(·)=*, and the shore was abstractly referenced by the directional marker *e·=*, which refers to spatial contiguity and means something like "up to a point," here specifically an inanimate point of contact (the shore), as indicated by the prefix *m-* at the beginning of the construction. In the middle of the form, the conclusive marker *n-* indicates that the event comes to a point of termination, as the sticklike object reaches its destination, namely, the shore. Instead of saying "he landed the canoe," what he actually said was something like this: "A sticklike object propelled itself conclusively back to some inanimate point (the shore) with an animal or person as passenger."[26]

When I returned the following day, first I asked about the form, then meaning, just to see if my analysis was accurate. Afterward, he repeated the form several times, exactly as I had heard it, and proceeded to tell me that my sense of the meaning was essentially correct. For him, it was a kind of quiz, I think, which allowed him to test me, since the construction departed in significant ways from the original English phrase. Yet that is as far as I could have gotten with the linguistic meaning alone, since there were also several unstated cultural assumptions implicit in the semantics of the Hupa construction. To give background on these unstated cultural references, he started by whipping out a small model canoe he had built from wood and proceeded to ask me whether this model was "dead" or "alive." To loosely paraphrase, he said, "You probably think the canoe is dead, but for us it is alive, since it is made of wood and the wood came from living being—that is, a tree." He then asked me to name the parts of the canoe, such as the seat or the prow, and asked me to reflect on their meaning. There was nothing to lead me to believe the boat was animate as far as English was concerned. In Hupa, on the other hand, all boat parts were named after parts of the body, drawing attention to the deeper cultural assumption that the boat was a living being. In Hupa, the prow was called the "nose" and the two seats at the back were called "kidneys," since they were said to resemble those organs. At one time European sailors also partly conceived of ships as living beings, calling them "she," naming them after women, and often placing a female figurehead at the prow. Yet I am not aware of any English ship terms based on animal or human body parts.

My consultant then explained that since the boat is animate it could rightfully be in control of the situation, guiding itself through the water, despite the fact that an animal myth figure was paddling it.[27] At this point, it appeared that the boat held more control than the figure who was apparently guiding it, just the opposite of what the English phrase "he paddled the boat" suggests. He told me that the same form could be applied to a person guiding a boat or canoe on the river in contemporary times, so this expression was not confined to the myth times or to animal protagonists. From the point of view of this Hupa expression, the boat was animate and had more control than the person paddling it. The experience is probably familiar to anyone who has ever boated on the Trinity River in a small vessel, since the river's many eddies cause considerable turbulence, frequently taking the boater off the expected course. In this sense, the Hupa expression may in part capture the capriciousness of the rapid river waters. But there is more; there are also religious reasons for thinking that the person guiding the boat was not completely in control, since the spirit of the boat is also considered to play an important role in guiding the passenger to safety.

But there was more to his story. My consultant also explained that there are prayers that should be said before boating on the dangerous rivers, which might appear harmless enough in calm stretches but have swirling "holes" in places that continue to sweep people away to their deaths each year. All of this meant that my consultant conceived of the boat as living in a world where human fate was to some extent in the hands of spirits that needed to be properly contacted and respected before venturing out into the water. None of this was conveyed in the English formulation, and the Hupa construction made sense only once all of these background assumptions were fully explained.

As this exercise in textual exegesis illustrates, the age-old principle of relativity takes on new political relevance in the emerging context of revitalizing languages that have suffered a history of oppression. Here it is not the case that language is simply guiding speakers to certain unconscious observations or culturally prescribed choices of interpretation, as both Sapir (1929) and Whorf (1956) keenly observed long ago. Rather, in the context of language revitalization, speakers are often consciously insisting on maintaining distinctive choices of interpretation, especially those that contrast with the views of the dominant culture. Though these language-borne worldviews and storytelling traditions often resonate with deep-seated religious beliefs, the local perspectives also continue functioning to maintain ethnic boundaries between communities, which today include not only the neighboring tribes but the English-speaking world.

CONCLUSIONS

The ethnolinguistic situation in Native northwestern California is close to what Mikhail Bakhtin once characterized as "polyglossia," a condition where multiple languages come into association with a single national culture, supposedly freeing the mind from the tyranny of any single ethnolinguistic tradition while opening up the possibility of a broader of type of multilingual and multicultural consciousness. Bakhtin described polyglossia as follows: "Language is transformed from the absolute dogma it had been within the narrow framework of a sealed-off and impermeable monoglossia into a working hypothesis for comprehending and describing reality. . . . But such a full and complete transformation can only occur

under certain conditions, namely, the condition of thoroughgoing polyglossia. Only polyglossia fully frees consciousness from the tyranny of its
own language and its own myth of language" (1981:61).

In historical times there was no "national culture" in northwestern
California but speakers of a dozen or so languages who participated in a
regional cultural orientation—one that simultaneously bridged these linguistic differences and created many internal divisions based on subtle local distinctions in both language and storytelling. Today, in sharp contrast
to the past, it is certainly possible to speak of a "national culture," one
that has brought with it a shift to the English language in most settings,
adding still another language and culture to the complex ethnolinguistic
blend that has long characterized northwestern California as a region. Today, as in the past, the Native peoples of northwestern California continue
to practice a shared way of life while retaining many distinctive features
of language, culture, and worldview at the local level. Like Bakhtin's
(1981:272) concept of "centrifugal forces" in language and society, where
variation continues to arise despite efforts to impose a single, uniform
standard, this study suggests that this pervasive insistence on local differences is deeply rooted in the human condition. Despite the rash of changes
brought by the onslaught of Euro-American culture, the Native communities of this region have maintained strong ties to the past, at the levels of
both ideology and practice. Today, as in the past, the strong localist ideologies of northwestern California continue to provide a powerful motivation
for accentuating differences between the neighboring groups, something
that is largely achieved through the practice of compartmentalization,
which is powerful today in differentiating between Native and non-Native
worldviews.

NOTES

1. The established tradition of paying storytellers has taken on new relevance in the context of conducting linguistic fieldwork and paying consultant
fees.

2. Some characters, such as Dog, pledged to speak no more; if he should
ever speak again, it is said, the end of the world would be at hand. For this reason,
the Taco Bell commercials of the late 1990s, featuring the talking Chihuahua,
held additional meaning for the Native peoples of this region, generally causing
laughter but sometimes real concern.

3. For a full version of this story, as told by McCann, see Goddard's *Hupa Texts* (1903:220–25).

4. For a full version of this tale, as told by an otherwise anonymous consultant named little Ike's mother, see Kroeber and Gifford's *Karok Myths* (1980:32–36).

5. For the full version of this tale, as told by Lame Billy of Weitpus, see Kroeber's *Yurok Myths* (1976:47–54).

6. The Yurok name for this village is Oplego, according to Kroeber (1976:50).

7. For an extensive collection of Karuk Coyote stories, see Bright (1957: 162–207). Bright's survey of Karuk oral literature opens with seventeen Coyote stories. As legend has it, Bright (personal communication, 2003) once crashed a car into a tree on his return home from a recording session with a Karuk speaker who had told a particularly riveting story about Coyote. Apparently the young scholar could not keep his mind off the narrative afterward; he was not hurt in the incident.

8. See the story "Coyote and Frog," told by Emma Frank (Sapir 2001: 408–11).

9. European contact came relatively late to northwestern California. Though the coastal Yuroks had occasional contact with early explorers, the Hupas and Karuks had scarcely seen Euro-Americans before the gold rush of 1849 and subsequent annexation of California to the United States (Buckley 2002:7–12; Keeling 1992:27–32).

10. In the span of about eight weeks, Sapir managed to collect an impressive body of seventy-seven narrative texts in Hupa and another three in Yurok. Given the harried nature of his academic schedule, he was unable to set aside time to complete his work on the languages of northwestern California. So, upon his death in 1939, his notes were eventually transferred to one of his early students, Harry Hoijer. Toward the end of his own career, Hoijer passed Sapir's materials on to Victor Golla, whose dissertation on Hupa grammar he was supervising during the mid-1960s. Starting in 1996, I was fortunate enough to collaborate with Dr. Golla on the task of preparing Sapir's materials for publication. With the exception of a single article on tattooing (1936), Sapir himself was unable to see any of these materials to print during his lifetime. As a result, years of work were required before the raw field notes could be converted into an edited volume. Sapir's (2001) work on the languages of northwestern California was published in Volume 14 of the *Collected Works of Edward Sapir* under the joint editorship of Dr. Golla and myself.

11. It was precisely this type of naïve thinking that Franz Boas (1966 [1911]) took great pains to deconstruct, eventually embarking on a long intellectual

campaign to show that the variables of race, language, and culture could be easily isolated from one another. It is well known that his student Edward Sapir (1921:214) drew upon the case of northwestern California to show that the variables of language and culture could be easily teased apart and were, therefore, not "intrinsically associated," given that the Hupas, Yuroks, and Karuks shared a culture but spoke completely unrelated languages. Such cases, which are by no means rare, posed a major stumbling block for those who wanted to argue for an original unity between language, culture, and race, as Barth (1969:11) noted in his own day.

12. This process is part of a widespread pattern in Native American societies, where language is often closely linked with place, family, and creation mythology on both ideological and emotional grounds (Basso 1996; McCarty and Zepeda 1999).

13. This report comes from Sam Brown, who in turn learned the story from his great aunt (his maternal grandmother's sister). He maintains that the Hupa language is capable of reaching out into the water, perhaps a reference to casting a curse that spreads into the very depths of the earth. From the story, "A War between the Hupa and Yurok" (Sapir 2001:522–30).

14. On comparative grounds, Hill (2001) has recently uncovered a fundamental correlation between material resources and related attitudes about neighboring linguistic varieties, an insight that was based originally on her work with the Tohono O'odham of southern Arizona. Where local resources are fairly secure, Hill has found that speakers tend to maintain close-knit social networks in the immediate area while resisting external linguistic influences; here, as is the case in northwestern California, linguistic and material resources are managed in a similar fashion, so that speakers maintain strong ties within the group and have no strong need for outsiders. Where resources are widely distributed and less secure, speakers tend to cast a wider social network and are more open to external linguistic influences, including the dialects of neighboring groups.

15. To take a broader look at the subject, consider the Near East, where throughout much of history Jews, Muslims, and Christians have all regarded themselves as God's favorite people based on ties to the legacy of Abraham, either through Isaac, Ishmael, or Christ. It is well known that Jews and Muslims, for instance, hold conflicting versions of the story of Abraham, the first monotheist. According the Judeo-Christian telling of the story, God commands Abraham to sacrifice his beloved son, Isaac. The neighboring Muslim version, which emerged in the seventh century C.E., agrees in most details, except for the part about the beloved son, who is Ishmael, not Isaac. For Christians, the story of Abraham is echoed in the sacrifice of God's own son, in the person of Christ, who is also in the

line of Isaac. Here subtle variation in the common story makes all the difference, and bitter wars continue to be waged under the banner of each of these religions.

16. To continue the Middle Eastern comparison, Muslims, Jews, and Christians have, for example, at times regarded each other as "fellow people of the book," reflecting the fact that all have subscribed to similar tales popular in the Near East for millennia, as echoed in the Koran, the Torah, and the Bible. Yet the balance is often precarious, with members of each group sometimes fighting bloody wars against one another based on the assertion of separate identities, only later to align, at times, based on their wider parallels.

17. Here I draw on the concept of "erasure" (Irvine and Gal 2000:38–39), an ideologically driven phenomenon in which one blocks out any information that does not conform to one's immediate cultural expectations. The force is powerful in human relations, and in the history of professional linguistics many scholars "blocked out" sociolinguistic variation that did not conform with the standard grammar or vocabulary of a given language—effectively erasing many so-called nonstandard forms from the supposed science of human speech.

In a less stable way, there is evidence that the Native peoples of northwestern California sometimes temporarily erased (or merely glossed over) their differences in the interest of emphasizing their common ground and creating a broader regional identity. The anthropological concept of erasure was probably inspired by the work of Jacques Derrida, who used the term "erasure" to refer to dubious though commonly accepted terms that should be questioned, even if they cannot be completely replaced. In his writings, Derrida drew a line through terms he was erasing, thereby placing them in doubt and granting them only a quasi-reality. In this state of erasure, the terms thus take on a kind of quasi-consciousness, occupying a precarious middle ground between the accepted and the unacceptable—present to the mind and absent from consciousness. In a similar way, the differences between the Hupas, Yuroks, and Karuks were probably never truly erased and probably took on a status of quasi-awareness even in situations where speakers sought to minimize the differences, such as at the religious dances.

In grappling with this complex ethnolinguistic situation, it is possible that Sapir (1921:214) and Kroeber (1925:5) partially erased some of the cultural differences among these groups, perhaps in part as a response to the indigenous ideologies that sometimes stressed the similarities in an effort to maintain smooth interpersonal relationships among members of the various ethnolinguistic groups.

18. Some amount of compartmentalization is probably universal, due to the fundamentally social nature of human language, which represents still another reflection of the pervasively context-driven nature of speaking. Given that nearly everyone is capable of producing multiple forms of speech, it follows that the

process of selecting a suitable variety (language, dialect, genderlect, etc.) is largely
governed by context, a general condition which, in turn, leads to the compartmentalization of the speaker's overall repertoire. In monolingual communities, there
is a strong tendency to compartmentalize variation at the level of dialects and
other ideologically charged forms of speech, which often sound curiously comical or even offensive outside their usual domain. In multilingual communities, it
is the languages themselves that often become compartmentalized according to
salient features of identity.

   19. As Howard Berman points out (Sapir 2001:1016), the story "Coyote
and Crane," which Marshall delivered in Yurok, bears striking similarities to the
Karuk story "Coyote and Great Blue Heron" (Kroeber and Gifford 1980:186–87),
and both are in fact about the same bird, despite the different English names. In
a similar way, the story "Coyote Tries to Kill the Sun," which Marshall also told
in Yurok, is parallel to the tales discussed in *Karok Myths* (Kroeber and Gifford
1980:342); Stephen Powers (1887:39–40) recorded a similar Karuk tale. No recorded parallels have been documented in the Hupa tradition, however.

   20. See, for instance, the following Hupa narratives from Sapir's fieldwork in northwestern California: "Medicine Formula for a Man Who Desires
Wealth and Success in Love" (2001:362–65) and "Medicine Formula for Wealth"
(2001:366–70).

   21. According to Kroeber (1976:203n28), Pek\u02b7teł (also Pekwteu) is located
near the confluence of the Klamath and Trinity rivers, across the river from Weitspus (modern-day Weitchpec). Kroeber notes that it was also a wealthy village in
traditional times.

   22. In a similar vein, Lisa Conathan has recently uncovered evidence of
extensive regional variation or emergent dialects within many of the area's languages (2004:113–38).

   23. Goddard (1904:314–15) once recorded the tale as "Formula of Medicine
for Going in Dangerous Places with a Canoe," and in the story it is a mythical bird
(called Snipe) who paddles the vessel, which is a redwood canoe.

   24. It is not proper, in the Native culture of northwestern California, to use
the names of the dead, and in traditional times a fine could be assessed for violat-
ing this taboo, since it was believed that doing so could disturb both the living
family members and, more important, the spirit of the one who had departed. For
this reason, I refrain from using this speaker's name here.

   25. This unit is itself composed of the third-person animate possessive prefix *xo-* and the positional element *-ł* 'with it'; the combination loosely translates
"with him or her."

26. To translate the English phrase directly into Hupa, one could say *me?niłɢe·d,* which loosely translates as "one brought a sticklike object back to shore; one landed a boat." Yet this is not the standard construction in this type of situation, and though grammatically plausible this form is at the same time culturally unacceptable, given that it does not resonate with the assumptions made by traditional Hupa speakers. In this alternative construction, the boat is not explicitly in control of the situation. It is also based on the verb stem *-ɢe·d,* which signals the presence of a sticklike object. Yet in this case the transitive valence marker (or classifier) *ł-* indicates that the verb takes both a subject and an object, here meaning that the sticklike object is explicitly guided by an external source of agency, not by itself as was the case in the previous form where the reflexive marker *di-* was present. The subject is clearly stated by the animate third-person marker *č'i-,* here occurring in its reduced form as a glottal stop (?), the expected contraction where *č'i-* closes a syllable. Otherwise, the same grammatical machinery indicates that the sticklike object (the canoe) pushes up against the shore, where it comes to a halt; again, the inanimate third-person possessive marker *m-* signals the shore, the adverbial marker *e·* = signals motion toward this shore, and the conclusive marker *n(i)-* signals the termination of the action.

27. Two similar constructions provide further insight into this situation. When speaking of the birth process, the traditional Hupa construction is *xoł-xitinaw,* which loosely translates as "(the baby) moves around with (the mother)." Here the mother is placed in the role of accompanying the unborn child as it moves around inside her, completely of its own volition. Significantly, the baby, who is certainly animate, retains a measure of control in the situation, though this type of perspective is not suggested in the English term "labor." Similarly, instead of saying "he smoked himself" to describe a sweat, one says *xoł-te·lid,* which literally translates as "one accompanies (the fire) as it burns along, here and there." The fire is the active one in the situation, while the person undergoing the sweat is merely accompanying the event—the burning of the fire.

CHAPTER 5

TALES OF TRADITION AND STORIES OF SYNCRETISM IN KIOWA LANGUAGE REVITALIZATION

Amber A. Neely

"The language of one's birth is a priceless gift. To lose it would be to lose one's self and one's uniqueness. To withhold it from others would be to waste and lose, in selfishness, this priceless heritage; a gift from our Creator specifically for us." So begins the acknowledgments in *Thaum Khoiye Tdoen Gyah* by Alecia Gonzales (2000), a Kiowa textbook dedicated to teaching language and cultural traditions in tandem, through extensive use of stories and traditional tales. This trio of statements illustrates language ideologies relevant not only to the Kiowa situation but to ideologies of language and culture on a broader scale (Hinton 1994), as the driving force behind many language revitalization efforts today. Yet realization of intricate connections between culturally appropriate language use and identity does not immediately translate into cooperative efforts for language continuance. Nor does this ideological trio fit seamlessly together for all community members.

Focusing on the use of story by one well-known, yet somewhat controversial Kiowa teacher, I take an exploratory look at how teaching Kiowa language by emphasizing cultural values is meant not just to preserve those values but also to highlight commonalities among Kiowa people. This ideological "erasure" of difference (Irvine and Gal 2000) is meant to bridge divides that have hindered language renewal efforts to date in

This chapter is a revised form of a paper originally presented in the session "Telling Stories in the Face of Danger" at the 105th annual American Anthropological Association meeting, San Jose, California, November 15–19, 2006.

the Kiowa community. Using story as a vehicle to bridge Kiowa language and culture of yesteryear and ways of speaking and meaning today is part of an effort to incorporate younger learners and older speakers in a more tightly integrated and mutually engaged community and, some hope, a community of speakers. The aim is noble and, though steps toward it have not gone uncontested, efforts can and will continue.

INTRODUCTION TO KIOWA LANGUAGE AND REVITALIZATION EFFORTS

Language revitalization efforts within the Kiowa community, a respected elder Kiowa woman tells me, have been going on for at least fifty years as far as she can recall. "And nothing's changed yet," she says. Reasons for this are manifold. Of the eleven thousand enrolled Kiowa tribal members, between twenty and two hundred speakers remain, nearly all above the age of sixty.[1] Beyond the symbolic use of a few words of greeting or phrases to index one's identity as a member of the Kiowa community, opportunities to speak Kiowa are limited: prayer (public or private), ceremonial situations, powwows, and some conversation with or among elders (Neely and Palmer 2009; Palmer, this volume). The danger of losing the language completely is real and immediate, with potential consequences for tribal identity, cohesion, and perhaps even some aspects of culture. Some Kiowa people maintain an ideology similar to what Nancy Dorian (1998) has described as a "linguistic social Darwinism," displaying resignation to the idea that the era of spoken Kiowa is meant to pass, perhaps even has already passed. Few can understand the lengthy speeches or prayers given at public events by elders and tribal authorities, and even fewer can actually still give extensive benedictions in Kiowa. Others claim that children are not interested, or that Kiowa is too complicated. These attitudes certainly do not hold for everyone, as ongoing language teaching efforts attest. Yet teachers do face many material, ideological, and logistic hurdles.

Kiowa language teachers are active in at least five different geographic areas in Oklahoma. Most teachers use materials they have created, since no standardized writing system has been established (Neely and Palmer 2009). Although the teachers have mutual respect for each other, the majority of classes still operate independently, often because of distance but also because of divergent writing systems. Some teachers operate within the public school system, as does Alecia Gonzales. Others put together community classes or work in small groups on language preservation projects, often without compensation. Yet community reactions are not always uniformly supportive. Kiowa society is quite heteroglossic in the Bakhtinian sense, and language ideologies such as those mentioned above (including attitudes of resignation and language purism) combine with intratribal politics and linguistic complications to tighten the already constrictive sociolinguistic vise in which most endangered languages are caught.[2]

On one level, Kiowa teachers aim to resist these macrosocial factors, to stimulate local loyalties and produce speakers. But on another level, they realize that attempts to teach language have another purpose: maintaining and reaffirming Kiowa cultural identity in the face of multiple divisive factors. The historic composition of the Kiowa tribe of loosely joined bands often divided by geographic and conceived distance still operates today, though less strongly than the relations between bands observed by Field for the Kumiai (this volume). Further contributing to a watering down of tribal cohesion is the long-running, fairly common practice of Kiowa people to marry outside the tribe. Historically captives were sometimes married into the tribe, and today Kiowa people often choose spouses from other tribes as well. Similar to the Cherokee situation reported by Sturm (2002), some young people avoid dating other Kiowas, dreading the rebuke, "You can't date her, she's your sister—in the Kiowa way!"[3] As more and more Kiowa people become bilingual, it becomes ever more expedient to use English in marriages, even if the marriage partner is also Native American, as opposed to encouraging the partner to learn Kiowa.

These practices have throughout decades past continuously reduced contexts for spoken Kiowa, particularly in the home, a major site of intergenerational mother tongue transmission (Fishman 1991). Even when Kiowa people married within the tribe, in some families the language was used exclusively among adults. For many years, the children were not expected or even encouraged to learn Kiowa; this is not surprising, given the boarding school experiences of many of these children's parents, who were punished for speaking Kiowa. Some from the baby boomer generation have noted that adults often spoke Kiowa to discuss things that the children were not supposed to hear, or children were sent out of the room when the adults sat down to discuss business in Kiowa. In this way these people got the feeling that Kiowa was something reserved for adults, something that they would learn when they got older and became full-fledged Kiowa adults. Yet, in a situation seen time and again throughout Native North American groups, as Kiowa began to be used in fewer and fewer domains, possibilities for learning decreased and the generational break between those who speak and those who understand became apparent. The relocation of Kiowa people from southwestern Oklahoma to major cities across the nation, sometimes voluntarily and sometimes less so, to take advantage of wage labor and improve their standards of living, also contributed to the fading of Kiowa language networks among members of the society.

As the language became more and more infrequently used in the home, some parents and communities expected that children would just "pick up" the language along with the culture at community events, or they increasingly placed their hopes in classes for language learning when these were available. Although these hopes have proved to be in vain since classes or textbooks alone are not the most effective type of language transmission for stimulating endangered languages, still the benefits of these means for maintaining presence and prestige of the language should not be underestimated. The fact that Kiowa is taught in at least two secondary schools in Oklahoma as well as at the university level to fulfill foreign language credits helps significantly in establishing its validity as a worthwhile pursuit. Use of story in the classroom is a significant component, helping bring home the inherent value of the language in transmission of cultural values and traditional knowledge.[4]

STORYTELLING, SONG, AND CULTURAL EMPHASIS AS TEACHING TOOLS

As University of Oklahoma Kiowa professor and Kiowa scholar Gus Palmer emphasizes, storytelling for the Kiowa people is an entertaining and yet also functional art form, as identity is performed through storytelling and story listening (see Palmer 2003 for vibrant examples). Teachers such as Mrs. Gonzales are using both story and song in the classroom for "cultural reproduction," a general maintenance of culturally appropriate language use: knowing words, internalizing values and proper types of behavior, understanding stories and history. But they are also using it for reasons of unifying the community and strengthening family ties. Thoughts of rescuing "intellectual treasure" (Hill 2002a) as well as of moral obligation indicated in the opening quote are also used as rationale to bring linguacultural traditions to youth who may no longer be hearing it as told by Kiowa families in decades and centuries past. It is true that there are other teachers in the Kiowa community who also use story in the classroom to teach Kiowa and also focus on customary values, identity, and the importance of community. Yet Mrs. Gonzales's situation is particularly striking because of the extent to which she builds her lessons around traditional stories and also because of the controversy her work generates in some parts of the community.

The pursuit of cultural reproduction for community maintenance is one of Mrs. Gonzales's primary motivations in seeking to teach Kiowa language through use of story and song. She sees her role as one not just of language transmission but of socializing her students in both communally agreed-upon traditional Kiowa cultural ways and contemporary bicultural values and lifeways. Stories provide a valuable backdrop for education in important cultural values and means of behavior, by both the material content (behavior of characters and consequences these entail) and the way the storytelling event is constructed. Stories, particularly traditional tales, are in fact the key rubric Mrs. Gonzales utilizes in her approach, forming the framework for vocabulary learning, transmission of cultural understandings, and proper behavior for young people, as Kiowa and as good citizens.

Even though there is a central focus in some classes on storytelling as a vital means of emphasizing cultural values and teaching language, the value of song in language teaching is not to be overlooked. The importance of song among the Kiowa people has been extensively explored by Lassiter and colleagues (Lassiter 1998; Lassiter, Ellis, and Kotay 2002), and it is evident whenever one attends a Kiowa ceremonial event. Many elders lament that the words to some Kiowa songs are "lost" and have been replaced by generic vocables, or that the youth do not sing them correctly. Song, in connection with both prayer and other traditional and entertainment functions, can be a motivational medium for those wishing to learn and use Kiowa. One aim is to gain sufficient language skills in order to be able to sing traditional songs properly around the drum at ceremonial events and powwows, and the ability to sing Kiowa hymns at church and pray in Kiowa forms a central reason for others.

Since motivation is one of the key factors in successful language acquisition, encouraging students in their aims is one of the most significant roles of language teachers and others in the community. Mrs. Gonzales focuses on songs connected with stories, bringing forth the enthusiasm for song to embrace story as well.[5] She told me with quiet pride of a young man she knows who was sitting in the back seat of his grandfather's vehicle singing a song. His grandfather heard that it was a Kiowa song, and he asked if the young boy knew what the words meant. The little boy not only knew the meaning of the words but could retell the storyline too. Although he retold the story in English, these are steps along the way to being able to retell the story in Kiowa and eventually being able to compose his own stories in the language. This type of progression is illustrated in Mrs. Gonzales's textbook, which outline the progression of the student's Kiowa proficiency. Early stories are largely in English, with a few Kiowa words, whereas most later stories are in Kiowa with line-by-line English translations.

Designed with public and home educational settings in mind, Mrs. Gonzales's Kiowa books use both form and content to integrate more traditional understandings of language and culture and values with contemporary realities of teaching and learning. One of the foundational aspects of her approach is her classroom philosophy's focus on giving students the tools to survive and thrive. By telling both "tales of tradition" and "stories of syncretism," she aims to teach children not only to speak the Kiowa language but also the value of maintaining and actually constructing their cultural identity—not just in the Barthian (e.g., Barth 1969) sense of ethnic identity as oppositional differentiation but in a more integrative fashion. Her design illustrates the syncretism of necessity, of cultural maintenance, survival, and revival, and an erasure of divisive forces within the Kiowa community, the result of resistance and persistence, strategies of cultural survival.

COMBATING DIVISIVE IDEOLOGIES BY EMPHASIZING CULTURAL VALUES

Mrs. Gonzales's works actively combat divisive ideologies within the community through two primary means that both emphasize cultural values, but in complementary ways. Her strategies speak to competing discourses within the Kiowa community that are related to numerous language ideologies Neely and Palmer (2009) describe as discourses on tradition, power, and authority. One strategy is extensive use of what I call "tales of tradition" to address questions of identity and authenticity: what "real" Kiowa is and who should speak it, particularly who is authorized to use it in public situations or to teach it. A central concept is that of language as symbolic capital (Bourdieu 1982), seen as a limited good and wielded by some in the community as proof of authenticity and used as a form of power. Related concepts are the Andersonian role of language in nation building and the effects of acculturation theory (and assimilation policies) discussed in Kroskrity (2000a:331), macrolevel structural forces that have had a significant impact on local identity in terms of tribal power structures and boundary maintenance.

Attempts to maintain and build upon a degree of cohesion and centralized authority within the Kiowa community are buttressed by both cultural and linguistic means. Although attempts in the past to centralize this authority have tended to break down, they nevertheless continue, as is evidenced by the recent shift in focus of one tribal committee to encompass preservation and maintenance of both culture and language. Because of the continuing influence of the divisive factors mentioned above (including familial and political affiliation), however, these efforts often have both inclusive and exclusive effects. This aspect of identity and authority is particularly salient not only for classroom context and the identities of the students learning it but also for the identities of teachers themselves.

The second major narrative strategy is "stories of syncretism," referencing the rift between ideas of "traditional" and "contemporary" spheres and the fit of Kiowa language into this customary but false dichotomy.[6] This strategy addresses in which *domains* it is proper for Kiowa to be used, and what *kind of* Kiowa should be spoken there. Language ideologies common to language endangerment situations such as language purism and linguistic social Darwinism (Dorian 1998) are wrapped up in this debate. Language change is seen both as something inevitable and already evident in the Kiowa community and something to be feared, avoided, and even reversed if at all possible, similar to the ideologies Kroskrity refers to for the Arizona Tewa (this volume).

Traditional stories, with their trusted format and standard discourse-marking phrases, provide one means of accessing both older and more recent Kiowa structural forms. One can also relate to this dichotomy the growing generational gap between youth and elders, a relationship traditionally important in the Kiowa community. Throughout the past, Kiowa children were raised by their grandparents, and many grandchildren still stay with their grandparents when school is not in session. But as children become more and more engulfed by American pop culture, from Disney to rap music, it can be difficult for their grandparents to relate to these contemporary aspects of their grandchildren's lives. Storytelling can help bridge this gap, and we can see how Mrs. Gonzales's integrative use of both traditional tales and syncretic stories works to bring the Kiowa language into a shared space in which both the traditional and the contemporary can coincide, and to which both grandparents and grandchildren can relate.

TALES OF TRADITION: CONTESTING IDENTITY AND AUTHENTICITY

The Saynday and other Kiowa stories that I refer to as "tales of tradition" are central to all of Mrs. Gonzales's language teaching efforts, in addition to serving as her main battleground for mediating identity and authenticity. Eleven traditional Kiowa tales and songs form the backbone of her textbook. Each traditional tale is accompanied by a song, and students are expected to sing along to the songs just as they read along with the stories. The traditional tales are the centerpieces around which vocabulary and dialogue exercises are framed and from which cultural lessons are drawn. The Grandpa Rabbit tale (see appendix 1) illustrates the consequences of disregard (lines 1–9: the old man is banished), the value of honorable conduct and compassion (lines 10–14: the rabbits take compassion on him), and the vital nature of family (lines 15–17: he learns their language, and the rabbits become his family) and responsibility (lines 29–32: the rabbits are honored through duty). Many of these concepts are interwoven throughout Kiowa social praxis, particularly the significance of family and responsibility. The key moral of this story seems to be that one can redeem oneself from dishonor only by honorable conduct, but the recurring motif is clearly the interdependence of humanity and, by extension, all of nature. The old man could not have redeemed himself, or even have survived, on his own without the compassion, affection, and assistance of his adopted rabbit family. This tale emphasizes the necessity of cooperation, the need for Kiowa people to stick together and to help each other out. It is a timely lesson that exemplifies Mrs. Gonzales's mindset: we are most effective when we are united. Cultural and linguistic survival will be much more easily accomplished together, and a unified community is much more likely to thrive.

Another interpretation emphasizes the value of alliance. The Kiowa oral history is distinguished by events of alliance and peacemaking with other tribes; they have lived in close association with the Plains Apache (formerly Kiowa Apache) tribe for as long as oral history recalls, and with the Crows in particular they have maintained a long-standing alliance. There were also important peace accords accomplished with the Cheyennes around 1840 and the Comanches in 1790 (Mooney 1979). The alliance with the Crow people provides perhaps the most thorough parallel to Grandpa Rabbit and Kiowa children's association with the Rabbit family. Mooney's report describes cultural exchanges in which Kiowa children were sent to live with the Crows for extended periods of time, in order to learn their language and their ways, to help "preserve the old friendship" long after the Kiowa people had moved on southward (Mooney 1979:156). This friendship is maintained even today through the biannual handgame tournaments that take place in the spring and fall, for which people from each tribe subsequently travel many miles to the others' homeplace. Many Kiowa people also travel north for the Crow Fair, held in the fall.

The ties with the Crows go even deeper when it comes to dance and religion; the Kiowa *tai-me* and accompanying rituals originally came from the Crows and were associated with the Sundance. When the Kiowa children learn to dance with the Rabbits, it seems to signify much more than simple enjoyment and companionship—a deeper tie of mutual respect and spiritual unity. The sharing of responsibility and maintenance of the ties between the Rabbits and the Kiowa children were renewed each year during the Sundance and still are today during the Gourd Dance ceremonial celebrations in July each year, where Grandpa Rabbit sings the children's songs and the children fulfill their traditional obligations and dance (receiving treats in return).

Cultural concepts are also embedded in the vocabulary used in the story. The word *ayedle-kxee* (*élqì*) used in line 2 to identify the protagonist as an "old man" can also refer to a "big man" or an "important man."[7] This linguacultural concept illustrates the importance of elders in Kiowa culture, since the word *ayedle* (*él*) 'big' or 'old' is also used as a term of respect for important and powerful people. The word for "rules" in line 20, *kxee-khaum-gyah* (*qíkàumgà*), is derived from two noun stems, *kxee* (*qí*) 'man' and *khaum* (*kàum*) 'together,' plus a nominalizer. Rules are things made by people together, for people together; rules of conduct are meant to regulate how people behave in groups and toward each other. As can be seen from the core message of the story, these rules are also requisite for community solidarity, to ensure peace and prosperity.

In addition to illustrating important concepts topically and lexically, use of the traditional tales pragmatically teaches linguistic structures specific to storytelling while providing a model for Kiowa sentence and narrative structure. Throughout the narrative one repeatedly finds a traditional form in the reported speech verbal suffixes, also called "storytelling" or "hearsay" markers: -hayle (-hèl) (e.g., lines 2, 5, 9, 10, 13), -may (-mè) (e.g., lines 1, 3, 7), and –day (-dè) (lines 6, 10–16). Other storytelling markers can be found in openings and closings, such as the common introductory phrase found in line 1: Ha-gyah gyah daw-may (Hágà, gà dáumè) 'It was somewhere, that it happened . . .' and the concluding line 33: Oh-day haw yehn hi-gyah daw (ó:dèhàu yàn hâigàdàu) 'That is all I know.' Field (this volume) aptly identifies such formulaic framings as acts of "authentication." Throughout the tale itself one finds useful discourse markers such as hay-gaw (hègáu) 'well,' 'then,' or 'now' (lines 3, 6, 13); geah-gaw (gágàu) 'and then' (line 9); and ah-gaw (áugàu) 'so,' 'well' 'anyway' (lines 15, 26) that help organize the narrative. These terms are useful and continue to be some of the most consistently heard structures in Kiowa discourse today. Many Kiowa elders, speakers, and partial speakers use them in daily conversation, even code switching and using them while speaking English, because they are so useful, being relatively easy to use (sometimes as placeholders or fillers in conversational exchanges) and because they serve as valuable markers of Kiowa identity. Furthermore, since these are terms the students may have heard their grandparents use, they are easily recognizable in further communication with elders, family, and other Kiowa speakers.

Story fulfills a similarly unifying purpose in Mrs. Gonzales's five storybooks (e.g., 2005a, b) for younger children (including CDs that feature recordings of her telling the tales in Kiowa), which she produced individually as part of a series but are recently available as a full set. With this five-storybook series, Mrs. Gonzales brings the stories to a younger audience, acknowledging the home setting as a primary site of learning for Kiowa children. In addition to the aural benefit of traditional Kiowa storytelling for young ones, the storybooks emphasize the importance of visual art in Kiowa culture, with beautiful illustrations contributed by Shaun Dae Chaddlesone, the daughter of a noted Kiowa artist and a talented artist in her own right. The illustrations are full of color and depict traditional scenes, such as a mother with child kneeling by a tipi and Saynday (Séndé) the trickster beating his drum for the prairie dogs (so he can trick them into becoming his supper). In each book introduction Mrs. Gonzales paints a quaint picture of grandchildren gathered around a grandmother in the home to hear stories as "models, values, moral conduct, and traditions learned and enjoyed for the future." The introductions also provide important framing devices for the storybooks and textbook. Through them Mrs. Gonzales positions herself clearly as a Kiowa woman, raised with Kiowa traditions, intimating to her audience that "these tales were told to me."

In the textbook introduction she traces in herself the path the language has been taking in the community, from "not wishing to share" to "beginning to lose the working dictionary" to a realization of what the consequences would be for her people if she kept the "precious gift" of language to herself. She then goes on to thank her family members, for she considers this work not solely her own but also her family's lifetime achievement. She also expresses appreciation to prominent Kiowa educators who all reviewed the manuscript, including Pulitzer Prize–winner N. Scott Momaday. In these ways she emphasizes her Kiowa identity and stresses that hers is a work of and by the community, for language and cultural perpetuation.

IDENTITY AND CONTESTATION WITHIN THE DISCOURSE OF POWER AND AUTHENTICITY

Despite the demonstrated value of the type of work Mrs. Gonzales is attempting, despite her solid positioning and detailed traditional emphasis in her endeavors, the validity of her efforts and her authenticity are nevertheless contested by some members of the Kiowa community. There are those who take issue with how she speaks the language, indicating that it is not "real" Kiowa, providing a veiled (or not so veiled) reference to inauthenticity. Others protest that the children are not learning anything in her class, that she is not producing speakers. The most common rebuke is a direct attack on her identity, assertions that "she's not even Kiowa." Though it is true that she has both Kiowa and Apache ancestors, this sort of bicultural identity is quite common. More to the point, these responses together constitute part of the competing discourses within larger discourses of power that dispute her right to teach Kiowa, to be considered an expert on the language. Mrs. Gonzales certainly has pedagogical credentials, having long taught and advised at all educational levels in addition to serving as a speech pathologist and even a college dean. Yet some credentials exacerbate rather than reduce such perceived distance between Mrs. Gonzales and the community, inasmuch as time spent in a university setting means not only time spent outside the community but becoming an "outsider."

Mrs. Gonzales did return to the community quite a few years before starting to teach and is well respected in many Kiowa circles. She has been teaching in Anadarko now for more than twenty years and is highly regarded there. Much of the critique comes from Kiowa people in other parts of Oklahoma, who are often affiliated with different families or groups that are consistently active in more specifically Kiowa cultural activities and social organizations. Some Kiowa speakers remark that they rarely hear Mrs. Gonzales speaking Kiowa in public, even though it must be noted that many Kiowa speakers rarely speak much Kiowa in public these days. Though the value of the language is acknowledged in certain domains, in many others, even visiting in public, it has fallen into disuse by the majority of speakers. Perhaps the inertia of switching from the English that has become habit to Kiowas, or even the fear of being called out for mistakes while speaking Kiowa, is too great. The tide may yet turn.

With an attitude typical of many strong Kiowa women with whom I am acquainted, Mrs. Gonzales takes the critique in stride. She is an admirable role model in terms of an integrated identity, as an elder woman successful both in Native American and in wider educational contexts. It is no simple matter to negotiate multiple identities, especially in Anadarko, where no fewer than seven tribes represent nearly half of the total population and there are white, Hispanic and African American populations as well. A one-time Plains Apache tribal princess, Mrs. Gonzales welcomes all students, many of whom are also of mixed descent. Though she gives them the opportunity to identify with other tribes (she gives the Kiowa names for other tribes early on in the textbook), the dialogues and practice sentences are oriented toward a Kiowa identity. In multiple word lists are the such phrases as *"Khoiyematawn ah daw"* (*Cáuimátàun à dáu*) 'I am a Kiowa girl'; *"Haw Khoiyetahlee aim daw?"* (*Háu Cáuitàlí èm dàu?*) 'Are you a Kiowa boy?'; and *"Haw aim Khoiyekawn?"* (*Háu èm Cáuikáu?*) 'Do you have a Kiowa name?'. Mrs. Gonzales gives the children a sense that everyone is welcome, that the children should be proud of their heritage, especially if that heritage is Kiowa but even if it is otherwise.

The usage of the stories themselves is traditional yet contemporary. Mrs. Gonzales's relationships with all of her students, Kiowa and non-Kiowa alike, seem more like those of a grandmother and grandchildren. She addresses them affectionately in Kiowa-appropriate ways, giving them orders to come here, sit down, and close the door in Kiowa. She expects them to behave themselves and to participate, as all Kiowa children must, during the storytelling event (Palmer 2003, and this volume). Instead of just telling the story as elder and having the children passively listen and say "*hàu*," the communally accepted traditional scenario, Mrs. Gonzales changes the discourse practice to better suit a contemporary public school context. The established Kiowa tradition differs slightly from the situations described by Nevins for the White Mountain Apache or by Meek for the Kaska in that the children are expected to listen more actively (Meek 2007; Nevins 2004). Mrs. Gonzales's students take turns reading lines aloud, either in English and supplying the Kiowa word, or completely in Kiowa if the class is more advanced. One of the Mrs. Gonzales stories is printed in the form of a play. This in itself is both traditional and contemporary, in that many traditional Kiowa tales feature significant amounts of dialogue by the characters, frequently punctuated by the narrator's intonation of "*tdonay*" (*jóné*) 'he (supposedly) said,' indicated by a hearsay marker. Mrs. Gonzales also uses playwriting as an exercise, encouraging students to convert stories into plays and act them out, sometimes with puppets.

One similarity does exist between Mrs. Gonzales's classroom story-telling practices and the pedagogical efforts undertaken by the White Mountain Apache teachers (Nevins and Nevins, this volume): the peda-gogical focus on extremely active language learning does indeed differ from the situation that one would expect to encounter in homes. Ideally el-ders would take the lead, as opposed to children coconstructing the learn-ing context. In fact, the expected situation rarely exists today, since this Kiowa language storytelling context is not often encountered, so com-munity resistance to this teaching methodology seems to be reduced in comparison to the Apache context, although it certainly does still exist. Mrs. Gonzales does endeavor to balance these Western language teaching strategies with long-standing Kiowa social and cultural teaching practices, for she also engages in the more typical "elder speaks, children listen" for-mat on occasion as well as focusing on topics relating to Kiowa culture.

Mrs. Gonzales emphasizes Kiowa values and traditional knowledge in other parts of her textbook through historical description. She describes their travels as known through oral histories and written accounts, listing names of the warrior societies and the Kiowa social organizations as well as dedicating an entire section to food and eating that gives a set of proper rules for Kiowa social eating etiquette, which are important in Kiowa so-ciety. Palmer (this volume) discusses the focus on food in Kiowa social gatherings and even in the storytelling event itself. Students also learn the proper way to set up and take down a tipi and make a travois, and they make models of campsites and beaded moccasins to supplement the lessons.

Clearly the emphasis in such experiential practice is not just on understanding and pronouncing Kiowa but particularly on strengthening a sense of belonging via cultural values found in each story. These values (including respect, honorable conduct, the importance of family, the value of song and spirituality, appreciation of art and tradition) are not all in danger of being lost; they are used as a means of emphasizing what Kiowa people (and in a broader sense, all people) have in common. The unifying aspect is critical for language revitalization purposes; it takes at least two people to have a conversation, but it takes a community to revitalize a language.

STORIES OF SYNCRETISM: TRADITIONAL VS. CONTEMPORARY

While emphasizing tradition for strengthening community ties via identity, Gonzales also connects the Kiowa language to contemporary times in order to make it more relevant to her students' daily lives. This is a key to any language revitalization project; the language has to be deployable in multiple domains. This remains one of the most pressing questions for language revitalization: in which domains is Kiowa meant to be used? A large number of Kiowa people believe that "real" Kiowa is "Old Kiowa," that it is sacred. As indicated above, Gonzales believes that the language is a sacred gift, but she also believes that it is an issue of stewardship not to let it go to waste, especially to the extent that it is no longer used. Although many emphasize the importance of Kiowa in religion, few believe that it is so sacred that it cannot be utilized in other domains. Yet there are many in the community who seem reluctant to use the language, perhaps for fear of "getting it wrong" and somehow being disrespectful by doing so (see Neely and Palmer 2009). These ideologies are a form of language purism, sometimes referred to as "elder purism" (e.g., Loether 2009), which holds that change to a language should be avoided at all costs, since it might threaten the language's integrity. Although such ideologies veil their negative impact as a valorization of elders, traditional speech, and traditional contexts of speaking, they effectively deauthenticate language learners, linguistic change (including adaptation to the present), and new contexts of language use (e.g., schools) (Gomez de Garcia et al. 2009; Meek 2007; Nevins 2004).[8] There are many in the community who resist such an

ideological stranglehold on adaptive linguistic change, but they are generally of the younger generation and hesitate to challenge elders.

Gonzales, after carefully reinforcing her position, has pragmatically
taken a few bold moves to counteract conservative ideologies and bring
the Kiowa language into the grasp of today's students. She does this in two
important ways: by including vocabulary for items used daily, such as hot
dogs and hairbrushes; and by including mini-stories, practice dialogues
that relate what I call "stories of syncretism." These dialogues often focus on modern values, including the importance of reading, studying, doing well in school, working hard, achieving some degree of affluence and
stability, and becoming contributing members of society. Some of these
values overlap such traditional values as working hard and contributing to
the community.

Teaching words for contemporary things does not go uncontested in
the community, however. Some elders are even hesitant to utilize words
their parents' generation had coined, if they do not represent "traditional"
Kiowa things or activities. The reasons these words may invite scrutiny
by peers are that others may not remember them, that they have not been
used for a long time, or that they have no tradition of use in their families. By encouraging the use of new words, Mrs. Gonzales is defying not
only ideologies of the elder purism but also conservative ideas that restrict
language to certain speakers and contexts. In any case, the number of vocabulary sets provided for traditionally practical concepts, such as family
and food etiquette, largely outweighs the number of contemporary themes,
pointing to the values that still matter most.

The mini-stories or dialogues are sometimes just pairs of question-
and-answer sets, but others are more extensive. Some dialogues highlight
culturally relevant topics, and others include discursively useful phrases
such as "Where is she working?" But the majority of these dialogues highlight a syncretic type of identity, with phrases like "Bow your head," useful in religious settings, alongside exchanges on the order of "Look, I am
reading!" and "It's good, you are reading," which are useful for teaching
younger siblings. Mrs. Gonzales's entire approach also argues against the
so-called traditional ideologies that relegate Kiowa to a purely oral sphere.
Dialogues such as these reemphasize Kiowa mores such as the value of
spirituality (in a nondenominational way) alongside more contemporary
achievement in school and literacy, not only in English but in Kiowa, the
heritage language, as well.

One particular dialogue (see appendix 2) discusses the professions of the participants' parents. One participant's father is a teacher, another's is a manager. The interrogating child probes the others for further information (lines 1, 3, 5, 7, 9, 11) about where their fathers work, what they do for work, how long they have been doing their jobs. This dialogue extols not only the value of hard work but also of doing what one enjoys (line 15). The speaker whose father teaches comments on the benefits of "doing one's job well," adding that "it must be so because you have a beautiful home and a good car." The curious one invokes his wise grandfather: "Grandfather said that you can tell about how people are by what they have. Some are poor because they are inept." The teacher's child produces the seemingly relativizing statement, "I guess that is the way people see you."

This exchange not only highlights certain cultural values that are part of the integrated American socioeconomic life that many Kiowa people lead today but also gives the materialist ideology a bit of a twist that registers in at least two distinct ways. Public honor based upon acquisition of fancy material goods can be beneficial and can influence people's thinking about the owner of said goods. On the other hand, the interpretation is somewhat ambiguous. The dialogue does not seem to be passing value judgments in the conclusion; it is not asserting the justification of people making such judgments, simply stating that such judgments are sometimes made. It is an astute and politically savvy approach that these young fictitious speakers are taking, one that shows that Kiowa students should be well versed in considering the thoughts of others and, when appropriate, just taking them in stride. One might surmise that Saynday the trickster (and Kiowa cultural hero) would be proud.

DISCUSSION: CONTESTATION AND PERSISTENCE

Mrs. Gonzales faces many challenges in attempting to provide high school students with storytelling resources. These students, from economically depressed areas, need these resources in order to forge syncretic identities from traditional and contemporary values. Another of her many challenges is her goal of contributing to the unification of the community while teaching its severely endangered heritage language. Still other challenges include the lack of widespread community support, her contested identity as a Kiowa/Plains Apache woman, and her use of "modern" words. People also question whether her efforts, which have been ongoing for three generations (around twenty years), have been or are capable of producing new speakers of Kiowa. Given her dual goals of cultural and linguistic transmission, accomplished to a large extent through telling stories, she certainly seems to have some important elements for success.

Generally speaking, however, taking a language course (particularly a high school–level course), even for semesters or years, is not sufficient in itself to make one fluent in the language. This is particularly true if one is not using the language much outside of the classroom. One needs a strong motivation to learn and to practice, and, most important, one needs opportunities to speak and hear the language in a variety of settings before becoming comfortable with it. If students do not have domains where they can use the language, the acquisition of linguistic skills does not just slow but fades before they actually can reach a reasonable degree of communicative competence, let alone fluency. For most students of Kiowa, as for many Native American languages, these conditions are simply not readily available; they must be created.

It is not difficult to create opportunities to practice a language, for young and old alike. For example, more and more youth have been attending the Oklahoma Native American Youth Language Fair each year. In its fifth year, more than seven hundred students participated. Some schools, tribes, and nations have begun planning to institute their own local language fairs. Another example is the Choctaw Nation's Annual Storytelling Festival, where many gifted storytellers share their stories, some in English and some in Choctaw. Perhaps a storytelling club could be arranged, effectively bringing together elders and youth, or older and younger kids, to give them opportunities to share and further their learning of the language and culture together. There are some youth-oriented clubs in other areas, such as the Kiowa Mini-Indian Club and the Kiowa Young Men's Association, both based in Carnegie, but membership is limited compared to the number of Kiowa youth statewide.

In a situation of endangerment where the language is not being heard enough, the main question remains: what is Kiowa being taught and learned for? If the intent is to revitalize the language, storytelling may be a good place to start, but it cannot end there. Which domains do the majority of Kiowa people feel remain important for speaking Kiowa today? Does the community really want widespread revitalization, or would they be satisfied with making sure traditional ideology (via stories, songs, and concepts) is secure? These are key questions that need to be addressed before any type of language revitalization effort on a broader scale can be attempted. Further areas of research include such questions as which ideologies are more prevalent in the community: conservative ones of language purity or of the benefits of a reified language/culture interface? Each response would entail a different type of language preservation effort, although storytelling could play a key role in either, using recordings of traditional stories or materials such as those of Mrs. Gonzales. The answers to questions like these will remain vague suppositions until a large-scale effort to reach as many Kiowa people as possible is accomplished. In the meantime, teaching efforts and storytelling continue in the Gonzales classrooms and in others, in community buildings, meeting halls, and perhaps private homes. As long as they do, at least part of the culture of Kiowa language use among the Kiowa people will continue to breathe new life.

APPENDIX I. STORY

Poe-lah-yee Kone-tday hane-tday gyah aim
The Story of Grandpa Rabbit

1 *Ha-gyah gyah daw-may, kxai-hehn. Ayedle-kxee daw may.*
   Hágà gà dáumè, qáhì. Élqè dáumè.
   It was somewhere, there was a man. An old man.

2 *Khoiye tdoen gyah, gyah tame haydle.*
   Cáuijògà, gà témhèl.
   He broke a law of the Kiowas.

3 *Khoiye aim hay-gaw haun ahn tane-tsoe daw-may.*
   Cáui ém hègáu hàun án ténchò dáumè.
   He was banished and was no longer considered a Kiowa.

4 *Khoiye-goo ah maw haydle ha-gyah tsoe.*
   Cáuigù à máhèl hágàchò.
   The Kiowas moved away from this place.

5 *Gaw ah aiye-say toe-day haydle.*
   Gàu à áisèjòdèhèl.
   And they left him abandoned.

6 *Hay-gaw gyah-gehn aum-day haydle, aun-gaw ahn-day.*
   Hégàu gàgí áumdèhèl áugàu áundè.
   It became night, and he sat alone.

7   *Gaw khoe-doe maw-khaw p'hayle-tdaw-daw may.*
    Gàu còdó máucàu féljàu dáumè.
    He was very sad and depressed.

8   *Khoiye-goo ah-goon! An-koe maw-khaw hehn thaw.*
    Cáuigù à gún! Ànkó máukàuhẹ́thàu.
    The Kiowas have banished me! I will just die.

9   *Geah-gaw ahn p'hay-gyah p'oiye haydle.*
    Gágàu àn fégà vóihèl.
    And then he lost consciousness.

10 *Ahn oiye p'hay-gyah tsahn haydle naw poe-lay-yope a maw-*
    kone doe day.
    Àn áuifègà chánhèl nàu pòlá̱:yòp á máukò̱jòdè.
    He came to, and saw he was surrounded by rabbits.

11 *A Kaw-on than p'haydle-doe-day.*
    Á káu:àun thá fèljòdè.
    They had compassion on him.

12 *Gaw a own p'haydle-doe-day.*
    Gàu á ó̱:fèljòdè.
    And they loved (or cared for) him.

13 *"Hay-gaw haun aim hame-maw thaw," a tdaydle haydle.*
    Hégàu hàun èm hẹ́:màthau à jélhèl.
    And they told him, "You will not die now."

14 *P'ehn-gyah gaw tohn, gaw tdoe, ate-ee aum haydle Poe-lah-*
    yee kaw-on than p'hay-doe.
    Fị́:gà gàu tó̱:gàu jó étjè ạ́uhèl. Pòlá̱:yì káu:àn thạ̱: féljòdè.
    They gave him food, water, and shelter, because they had
    compassion on him.

15 *Ate-ee than aun haydle. Ah-gaw poe-lah-yope a khee-day*
    ain, a tiye doe day.
    Étjè thạ̱ áunhèl. Áugàu pòlá̱:yòp á cídè èn á tájòdè.
    And he lived where the rabbits lived.

16 *Poe-lah-yee tdoen-gyah, gyah maw-hame haydle, gaw a own*
    p'aydle doe-day.
    Pòlá̱:yè jó̱:gà gà máuhèmhèl gáu à ó̱:fèljòdè.
    He learned their language and he loved them.

17 *Khoam hane daw-may, poe-lah-yope gaw Khoiye sahn-daw*
    day khee aw khoam-daw may.
    Còm hàun dáumè, pólá̱:yòp gàu Cáuisà̱:dàudè cí áu
    còmdáumè.

He had no friends, only the rabbits and the Kiowa children
were his friends.

18 *Khoiye sahn-daw tdoen-gyah bet toe awn haydle.*
Cáuisâ:dàu jó̲:gà bét jó̲:áunhèl.
He sent the Kiowa children a message.

19 *P'aw haw-baw ah keel ain bah ahn.*
Váu háubàu á cíl, én bá á̲.
Come to where I live by the river.

20 *Khoiye sahn-daw a tsahn haydle gaw kxee-khaum-gyah ate
aum haydle.*
Cáuisâ:dàu á chánhèl, gàu qícàumgà ét áumhèl.
The Kiowa children came and they made the rules for the
Rabbit Society.

21 *Poe-lah-yee kone-tday a kxai-tdai aum haydle.*
Pòlá:yì Kó:jè á qáijè áumhèl.
They made Grandpa Rabbit their chief.

22 *Oiye haw Poe-lah-yee Khoon-gyah gyah aum day haydle.*
Áui hàu Pòlá:yì Gúngà gà áumdèhèl.
That is when the rabbit dance began (or originated).

23 *Poe-lah-yee tsoe ate khoon maw-hame haydle.*
Pòlá:yì chó ét gúnmáuhèmhèl.
They learned to dance like rabbits.

24 *Gaw Poe-lah-yee khoon daw gyah a aum haydle.*
Gàu Pòlá:yì gúndàu gà á áumhèl.
And that is when they composed the Rabbit Dance Songs.

25 *Oiye haw ayedle-kxe khaun-gyah ahn p'aw haydle, Poe-lah-
yee Kone-tday.*
Áui háu élqì kàugà àn váuhèl, Pòlá:yì Kó:jè.
That is the time that Grandpa Rabbit was given the official
name 'Grandpa Rabbit.'

26 *Tahle-yope aw-gaw kxai-hehn aim, ah maw-than aum day
thaw aim bate khaum haydle.*
*Tá:lyòp áugàu qáihè̲ èm, á màuthàn áumdèthàu èm bét
káumhèl.*
He taught the boys about manhood and how to become great
for their people.

27 *Khoiye kxai-tday poe-lah-yee yee-gaw aim bate hiye day haydle.*
Cáuiqáijè pòlá:yì yígàu èm bét haídèhèl.
The chiefs learned of this society.

28 *Kyoiye poe-lah-yee-gaw, kxai-tday, aw gaw, ah kheiye kxai-*
    tdai yee-daw aim ate ee tane-tsoe aum haydle.
    Cáuipòlá:yígàu, qáijè, áugàu, à ká qáijài yídàu èm ét
    ítènchò áumhèl.
    The rabbits with the chief made him an honorable leader of
    the now [official] Rabbit Society.
29 *Gaw poe-lah-yee gaw ahlesaw-tday gyah bate aun haydle.*
    Gàu pòlá:yìgàu élsàujè gà bét áunhèl.
    And they gave the little Rabbits duties or tasks.
30 *Kxaw-tdoe ain tahn-aum gaw bate saw-tday than-aun daw*
    may.
    Qáujò én t̠á:àum gàu bét sáujè th̠á:áundàumè.
    They gave them duty as helpers for the Sundance.
31 *Ain-haw tdai p'ay khoon ayn ate saw-tday ate than-aum-*
    maw.
    Énhàu jé vái gún én ét sáujè ét th̠á:áumàu.
    Now they helped clean the gourd dance grounds.
32 *Maw-p'aydle ahn ate tdoe tdope.*
    Màu vél àn ét jójòp.
    They pick up the trash at the gourd dance grounds.
33 *Oh-day haw yehn hi-gyah daw.*
    Ó̠:dèhàu yàn hâigàdàu.
    That is all we know of this story.

APPENDIX 2. DIALOGUE

1   Speaker One: *Ha-gyah ah tdaw-tdaw gyah saw-tday tdaw?*
    Hàgá à jáujáu gà sâujèjàu?
    Where does your father work?
2   Speaker Two: *Khoot-tdoe yaw gyah saw-tday tdaw.*
    Cutjóyàu ga saujejau.
    He works at the school.
3   Speaker One: *Haun-day saw-tday gyah yah doe?*
    Hàundá sáujè gà yado?
    What kind of job does he have?
4   Speaker Two: *Maw-tae kxee daw.*
    Mâutèqí dàu.
    He is a teacher.

5   Speaker One: *Haun-day khoot sahn-daw bate maw-hame*
      maw?
    Háundé cútsàu:dàu bét màuhę̂:màw?
    What does he teach the students?

6   Speaker Two: *Paw-ah-tday-gyah gaw thaw-koye toden-*
      gyah aun bate khaun-maw.
    Páuàjègà gáu Thàucáuijògà aù bét cáumàu.
    He teaches them how to play ball and English.

7   Speaker One: *Ha-oh-day siye gyah saw-tday tdaw ain haw?*
    Háòdè sáugà sáujèjàu èn háu?
    How many years has he taught here?

8   Speaker Two: *Ain haw day siye, hay-gaw yee-kehn siye gya*
      saw-tday tdaw.
    Èn háudesau, hègáu yí:kì sau gà sáujèjàu.
    At this year he has been working for twenty years at this
      place.

9   Speaker One: *Naw ahm, ha-gyah ah tdaw-tdaw gyah saw-*
      tday tdaw?
    Nàu àm, hàgá à jáujáu gà sáujèjàu?
    And you, where does your father work?

10 Speaker Three: *P'ehn k'aun-tdaw-tode yaw gyah saw-tday*
      tdaw.
    Fí:câunjaujo yau gà sáujèjàu.
    He works at the grocery store.

11 Speaker One: *Haun-day saw-tday-gyah ahn-daw?*
    Háundé sáujègà àn dáu?
    What job does he have?

12 Speaker Three: *Kxai-tdah-kxee daw.*
    Qáijàqí: dàu.
    He is the manager.

13 Speaker Two: *Ah kxai tdai aum day thaw day haw gyah*
      khoat?
    À qáijái àumdè thàudè háu gà cót?
    Is it difficult to become a manager?

14 Speaker Three: *Mahm-gaw khoot ahn ha-gyah daw, gaw*
      khoat tday gyah saw-tday tdaw doe kxai-tdai daw.
    Máugàu cút àn hâigàdau, gàu cótjègà sáujèjàu dò qáijàidàu.
    He completed a lot of schooling and worked hard to be able
      to become a manager.

15 Speaker Three: *Tdaw-todye tdoen gyah saw-tday-gyah*
     baht own p'aydle-doe tdaw ain saw-daygyah yen thai-
     gyah thaw.
     Jáu jói jò:gà sáujègà bát ó: féldojàu èn sáudègà yán
     thágàthàu.
     My father said that if you enjoy your work or job it will be a
     job done well.
16 Speaker Two: *Mauntsaw gyah daw doe tdoe maw hee-tday*
     gaw kxaw dial maw thai-gyah.
     Máunsáu gàdàudo jó màu hí:jé gàu qáudál màu thágà.
     It must be so because you have a beautiful home and a good car.
17 Speaker One: *Kone-tday tdoen gyah ahn p'ah-hehn ahdaw*
     p'ah ah boe-own tsain ahn ah kaw-on.
     Kó:gí jó:gà àn fahí:ádàu. Fáà bóò chè àn á cáuò.
     Grandfather said that you can tell about how people are by
     what they have. Some are poor because they are inept.
18 Speaker Two: *Maun tsaw ahn aim thaw-ban.*
     Máunsáu àn èm bòtháu.
     I guess that is the way people see you.
19 Speaker One: *Maun tsaw gyah oh-bioye daw.*
     Máunsáu gà óbáuidàu.
     I guess that is true.

NOTES

I express my immense gratitude to those who have supported me in this research, by contributing suggestions, critique, and encouragement: Darlynn Dietrich, Jason Jackson, Michael Jordan, Mary Linn, Paul Kroskrity, Sean O'Neill, Gus Palmer, and, most important, Mrs. Alecia Gonzales.

1. Although this range seems broad, it depends on how one defines the term
"speaker." Estimates from different people in the community vary widely: some
base their estimates on age, assuming that anyone above a certain age should
be able to speak Kiowa; others base their estimates on the ability to hold a brief
conversation in Kiowa; still others, particularly of the older generation who are
speakers or partial speakers themselves, estimate that there must be fewer than
forty, and more likely only fifteen or twenty, who have a thorough enough command of the Kiowa grammar to tell stories.

There has been no systematic measurement of Kiowa usage among Kiowa youth, though some minimal usage has been reported to me. Truly, it seems that more of this usage by younger people is heard among graduates of the University of Oklahoma classes, but of course that is the youth population with whom I am more closely acquainted.

2. I use Woolard's definition of language ideologies as "representations, whether explicit or implicit, that construe the intersection of language and human beings in the world" (1998:3). By "linguistic complications" I refer to the effects of increasing language obsolescence and accompanying structural attrition, as well as to orthography disputes; see Neely and Palmer (2009).

3. The complexity of navigating between two different kinship systems— the long-standing Kiowa lateral kinship system and the Western bilateral system—has made it increasingly difficult to find potential partners from within the community to whom one is not related. The lack of knowledge among young people regarding traditional Kiowa kinship relationships considerably contributes to the frustration.

4. Throughout this chapter I refer to "traditional" knowledge and "traditional" stories, contrasting them with "contemporary" tales or "modern" values. The traditional stories form part of the standard canon of Kiowa oral literature and have been told and retold through generations with the characters and plot relatively intact. In terms of traditional knowledge, one must recall that processes of traditionalization are continuously working to redefine what exactly constitutes the types of knowledge Kiowa people have passed down and should be valued as "truly" Kiowa; traditionalization is "the creation in the present of ties to a meaningful past that is itself constructed in the act of performance" (Bauman and Braid 1998:112). Detailed descriptions of the processes of traditionalization can be found in Bauman (1992), Glassie (1995), Jackson (2003), and Mould (2005).

5. The practice of joining song to stories is common in Kiowa stories, similar to what Kroskrity (this volume) observes in Tewa culture.

6. The use of "syncretism" here is meant to denote the careful thought and planning that goes into constructing one's identity, integrating ideology maintained from times past with that developed or acquired in more recent times. In this I follow Hill and Hill (1986:1), who speak to the "definitions, attitudes, and techniques" that are "symbolic resources which are critical in the struggle of the people of the Malinche to construct for themselves a useful identity and to organize their world in order to survive and prosper in it." It is the agency I see in Mrs. Gonzales's work that I wish to highlight as a similar type of "syncretic project."

The juxtaposition of "traditional" and "contemporary" is seen by Mould to be an essential element in the process of traditionalization (2005:257). Although I

114 STORYTELLING AS CULTURAL RESOURCE

see validity in his analysis, I am not convinced that the traditional must necessarily be posited directly counter to the contemporary. In fact, here I argue that, although Mrs. Gonzales makes some of what one could label traditionalizing moves, she is also attempting to relate long-standing values to what are considered contemporary ones through use of cultural syncretism.

7. Throughout this chapter, the Kiowa words and phrases are written first in Mrs. Gonzales's writing system and thereafter in the Parker McKenzie orthography, used by Palmer in his work, by Watkins in her *Grammar of Kiowa* (1984), and by researchers and students at the University of Oklahoma. The McKenzie orthography more closely approximates IPA (with the exception of eight consonants, ejectives, and unaspirated, voiceless stops), whereas Mrs. Gonzales's orthography is a "transphonic" type of alphabet. A key to differences between the many orthographies for Kiowa as well as an explanation of their difference can be found in Neely and Palmer (2009).

8. The type of language purism particularly present among some elders in the Kiowa community (outlined more extensively in Neely and Palmer 2009) not only involves acknowledgment of respect for elders and the cultural practices of one's ancestors but also ties into discourses of power and intratribal politics and of religion, both Native and Christian—a phenomenon also mentioned for Cochiti Pueblo in the case of writing (Pecos and Blum-Martinez 2001:76). The concept of ideologies of "purism" in general among other indigenous communities has been documented in many cases, particularly a well-known study of Nahuatl (Hill and Hill 1986) but also for the Arizona Tewa (Kroskrity 2000a), the Western Mono (Kroskrity 2002), and even in "most" Native American communities (Hill 1983:269).

CHAPTER 6

KUMIAI STORIES
Bridges between the Oral Tradition and Classroom Practice

Margaret C. Field

In this chapter I examine oral tradition from the Kumiai community of Baja California in the form of a traditional folktale about Rabbit and Frog. This story, like most forms of oral tradition, has much to say about traditional Kumiai social relations and cultural norms. I emphasize the point that oral tradition, including folktales like this one but also other genres such as mythology, sacred texts, historical tales, and song, not only represents important forms of traditional knowledge but also helps constitute group identity. In other words, traditional stories may be viewed as forms of linguistic structure, or interactional strategies, through which identity is discursively produced (Bauman 1992; Bucholtz and Hall 2005; Jahner 1999; Sekaquaptewa and Washburn 2004).

More specifically, I suggest that the story discussed here indexes traditional Kumiai identity linked to "localist stance" (Hill 2001). Localist stance is reflected in social organization, which may be described as closed—characterized by sharp insider-outsider boundaries and dense social networks—as well as by a connection between group identity and "environmental rights and opportunities," or access to resources (Hill 2001). This description fits many indigenous speech communities of California.

BAJA CALIFORNIA KUMIAI COMMUNITIES, DIALECTAL VARIATION, AND IDENTITY

Baja California Kumiai communities are related to U.S. Kumeyaay, or Diegueño, communities both linguistically and culturally. Historically, many Kumeyaay/Kumiai villages covered what is today southern San Diego County as well as part of Mexico, extending fifty miles both north

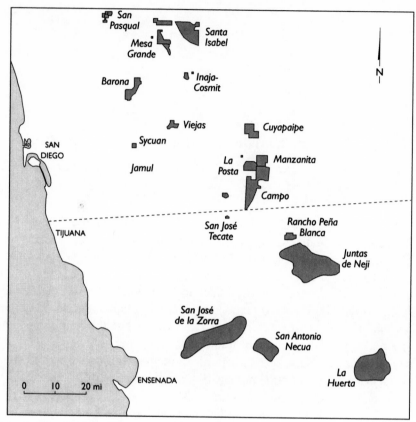

Map 2. Map of Kumeyaay and Kumiai communities.

and south of the international border. Today there are twelve federally recognized Kumeyaay tribes (some of which prefer to be called Diegueño)
north of the border and six Mexican Kumiai villages.

Kumeyaay ("Kumiai" in Spanish orthography) is a Yuman language
consisting of several overlapping dialects, which differ largely in terms of
their lexicon (Langdon 1991).[1] Dialect differences are so great that Langdon proposed that there might even be three separate languages, although
Kumiai speakers insist that all varieties are mutually intelligible (Smith
2004; Meza Cuero, personal communication). From a Kumiai perspective, there are two main subgroupings of Kumiai people (and dialects),
one northeastern, known as 'Iipay, and the other southwestern, known as
Tiipay (both terms meaning "people"). This two-part division is apparently

at least a century old, given that it was reported to Waterman in 1910. However, dialectal variation across and within the many Kumiai communities today is more complex than a simple dual division. Especially among Baja Kumiai communities, there is a great deal of dialect variation, which is only now being systematically explored.[2] Initially at least, it appears that the dialect known as Kwa'alh, spoken in the southernmost Baja community of Santa Catarina, which is shared with many Pai Pai speakers, may be only partly mutually intelligible with other Tiipay dialects.

Here is an example of contemporary dialectal variation across several Baja Kumiai communities, for the word "father":

Juntas de Neji	*netaat*
Santa Catarina	*nyetaat, keniitat*
San José Tecate	*neku*
San Antonio Necua and La Huerta	*nyeku*
San José de la Zorra	*nekuy, kuy*

As discussed by Langdon (1991), variation across Kumiai dialects is mainly lexical. Lexical dialects are found in much of Native California (Golla 2000) as well as in indigenous Australia (Evans 2001; Hill 1978; Smith and Johnson 1986; Sutton 1978). For example, Golla (2000) has suggested that in the great San Joaquin Valley of Central California, traditional Yokuts territory, there may have been as many as forty distinct dialects of Yokuts, with a shared vocabulary seldom greater than 50 percent, and some sharing as little as 25 percent. Cultural mechanisms leading to this kind of intense lexical replacement may include tabooing of everyday items linked to certain animals or food sources, as well as death (Conathon 2004), but also may be connected to group identity and language ideologies. In his discussion of possible motivation for lexical dialects in aboriginal Australia, Evans makes the following observation:

> Speech communities in Northern Australia are traditionally characterized by extensive personal multilingualism and a societal emphasis on both language knowledge and language "ownership" as a means of demonstrating clan membership and affiliation to land and sea territory. . . . affiliation to language is primarily a matter of social group membership rather than actual competence. As many anthropological linguists have argued . . . the reigning social model over much of Australia posits a direct relationship

between land and language, as well as between language and particular social groupings [i.e., patrilineal clans]. (2001: 253)

This situation is very similar to that found across Kumiai communities, where traditionally Kumiai and other neighboring tribes' (Pai Pai and
Kiliwa) social organization took the form of small, exogamous, patrilocal and multilingual bands with clear attachments to particular territories
and geographic resources (Owen 1965; Shipek 1982). Owen argues that
Baja California bands were traditionally multilingual (due to intense bilateral exogamy) and that, although bands shared some ecological resources,
each also was clearly identifiable on the basis of its attachment to a unique
geographic region and particular local resources: "The highly variable
landscape of Northern Baja California . . . ensured that the general ecology
was not identical for any two bands. . . . sea coast, lower Sonoran desert
at 2000 feet, upper Sonoran desert at 4000 feet, semi-alpine conditions at
7,000 feet, regionally distributed stands of oaks, highly variable coverage
of agave, and other such variety ensured that the ecology of any one band
would be significantly different from that of any other" (1965:678).

Baja Kumiai communities typically referred to each other through
directional or geographic association. For example, people from Neji,
Tecate, or coastal areas refer to themselves as "Tiipay Kumiai," or "Western People,"[3] whereas people from the La Huerta and Alamo plain region
refer to themselves as "Tiipay Kuwaak" ("Southern People"). Likewise,
Neji inhabitants use this term to refer to people from La Huerta, which
is south of Neji. These ethnographic descriptions (and others, e.g., Spier
1923; Shipek 1982) of Baja Kumiai social organization accord well with
Hill's (2001) description of localist speech communities as linked to environmental rights and access to resources. Hill's description of localist
speech communities also includes the attributes "closed" and "dense," two
qualities that often coincide in speech communities (Milroy 1980; Milroy
and Milroy 1985). A speech community in which members all know each
other is a closed network; closed networks are typically "dense" in that
communication between members consists of multiplex ties (i.e., the connections between them encompass multiple roles, such as relatives, friends,
and neighbors.) Closely knit, or closed, speech communities with dense
networks typically reinforce linguistic norms more so than open networks,
which are more susceptible to change within the network.

Language ideologies also are at work in maintaining norms (or changing them) within speech communities. Localist speech communities ap-

parently embrace a language ideology that values local speech norms and dialect and link it to local identity. Quoting Evans on how this dynamic works in Australia, "In many areas there is also an ideology that each distinct social group, down to clan level, should have some distinct linguistic features, and there are known to be cases where the fission of one clan into two leads to the emergence of two distinct 'clan lects' . . . even though the difference between them is confined to a few key vocabulary items" (2001: 254).

Kroskrity (2002, 2009a) has termed this form of language ideology, which is seen in multiple regions of indigenous America, "variationist":

> In contrast to standardizing linguistic regimes that either seek to eliminate or supplant variation due to region, ethnicity, class, etc., Western Mono communities have promoted a language ideology of variationism in which dialectal variation is not hierarchized but is instead naturalized as the expected outcome of family and individual differences. This emphasis has historically valorized such forms of variation even to the point of honoring family and individual differences rather than adopting a singular, or orthodox, vision of what is linguistically correct or sociolinguistically prescribed. (Kroskrity 2009a:193)

To summarize, traditional Kumiai speech communities may be described as relatively close-knit or closed, with dense social networks or multiple ties among members, and linguistically distinct in that local dialects are marked by a certain degree of lexical variation. Local dialects are linked to localist as well as variationist language ideologies, which value local variation and link dialect to group identity, location, and geographic resources.

ORAL TRADITION, LOCALIST STANCE, AND KUMIAI IDENTITY

In this chapter I argue that oral tradition, or genres of narrative and song that may be construed as cultural property within cultures lacking a tradition of literacy, serves as a linguistic structure that helps reinforce cultural values and group identity (Bauman 1992; Bucholtz and Hall 2005; Jahner 1999; Sekaquaptewa and Washburn 2004). The story presented below is an example of this kind of cultural property; it belongs not only to the storyteller but to his speech community, in that it is old and familiar to the community.[4] The content of this story indexes cultural values that support the previous description of Baja Kumiai communities as closed and local-ist in orientation. This story is also told in Kumiai, so it indexes Kumiai group identity twice—through the code used and through the content of the narrative itself. Kroskrity (2000b) discusses this kind of "multiple in-dexicality," in which membership in a larger speech community is indexed through traditional storytelling yet local dialect indexes membership in a subcommunity within that larger speech community. The storyteller, Jon Meza Cuero, grew up in the vicinity of the contemporary community of San José de la Zorra and learned this story from his father. He begins with an example of what Bucholtz and Hall (2005:601) term "authentication" (building on Bauman's 1992 notion of "traditionalization"). As these au-thors state, authentication is a social process that is played out in discourse, as in formulaic openings and closings of narratives.[5] This is exactly what the storyteller does here, "authenticating" his story as well as providing some background contextual information for the naïve listener:[6]

Ke'nápa nyuuches.	It's an old story.
Nyúuchesa.	It's old.
Nyuu,	It's old,
nyuu yus 'i,	it's old, I say,
ke'nápa nyuuch yus	it's an old story, but
'ematt 'ekurr,	long ago,
tipay,	people,
tipay pii tenyewaay,	people were here,
matt pii tenyewaay.	they were in this place.
Tipay máwa,	They were not people,
chiillyich.	they were animals.
Chiillyích pes	they were animals, but
tipay llywíicha.	they were like people.
Tipay Aa chuuwaay,	They spoke the People's Language,
peyii neyiw,	they came,
peyii naa,	and they went,
matt cham naach,	they went all over the world,
Tipay Aa shin chuuwaay.	and they spoke the one People's Language.
Chiillyich yu,	They were animals,
cham chiillyich,	all of them were animals,

chiillyich pes	they were animals, but
Tipay Aa—	the People's Language—
tipay llywii Tipay Aa chuuwáaya.	they were like people and they spoke the People's Language.

The rest of the story is presented here in a slightly simplified fashion; the complete version may be found in Kozak (forthcoming). Prosody is reflected in punctuation. Words inside parentheses have been added for clarification (mainly to clarify speaker, since this was accomplished through voice quality).

Rabbit and Frog

There was a Rabbit. He had a house, Rabbit did.
There he was, and Frog passed by.
Rabbit was in his house, and was warm.
Frog passed by the house, hop, hop, hop! hopping by the house.
Frog peeked inside.
Rabbit was sitting inside. He was eating.
Frog passed by and went away.
A few days later, Frog came passing by. He went up to Rabbit's
    house.
"Hi! How are you?" he said as he arrived.
"I'm fine, and you?" (said Rabbit.)
"I'm fine. Gee, it's very cold outside!" (said Frog.)
"It's cold? It's nice and warm in here." (said Rabbit.)
"I'm really cold." (said Frog,) rubbing his hands together. "Gee,
    it's really cold."
"Oh?" (said Rabbit.) "Walk around and you'll be alright."
"Maybe you'll give me another chance" (to come in, said Frog.)
"No," (said Rabbit.) "You are from outside and you must stay out-
    side. God made you so that you would live outside. I do not,
    I'm a rabbit, and I must stay in my house."
"Alright, see you soon," said Frog. "I'm going now."
And he went hopping away—hop! hop! hop!.
In two or three days, he came back.
"Hello Brother!" he said. "How are you?"
"I'm fine. How are you?" (asked Rabbit.)
"Oh, I'm really cold." (said Frog.)

"It's cold?" (asked Rabbit.) "You are someone from outside! It's
    not cold for you!"
"Still, I'm really cold." (said Frog.) "How would you feel if you
    were outside?"
"How can you be cold? You belong outside." (said Rabbit.)
"My body is cold." (said Frog.) I'm shivering—brr! Shivering a lot!"
"He's lying to me, making himself shiver." (said Rabbit.) "Okay,
    alright! He wants to come in for a little bit. (But) on another
    day, not now." (thought Rabbit.)
(Frog) sat there awhile and then he left, hopping away.
Rabbit sat there thinking. "It must be very cold for my poor brother.
    Maybe if he comes back, I'll say 'it would be good if you came
    in.'"
On another day (Frog) came back.
"Hi Brother!" (Frog said.)
"Hello! What's up?" (asked Rabbit.)
"Oooh, It's really cold." (said Frog.) Outside, the ground is wet. It's
    snowing too! It's really bad." (said Frog.)
"Come on in!" (said Rabbit.)
Then (Frog) hopped in, and he just sat there on the floor.
"I'm nice and warm here" (said Frog.)
"Okay." (said Rabbit) After sitting awhile, "Bueno, Hermano,[7] I'll
    be back soon." (said Rabbit.)
"Where are you going?" (asked Frog.)
"I'll bring some food." (said Rabbit.)
Rabbit went out looking for food.
He came back much later.
"What's up?" (Rabbit) said. (Frog) was his brother.
"Nothing, I'm fine here." (said Frog.) "Oh, I'm fine."
(Rabbit) gave him food, and (Frog) just sat there eating.
"Oh, the food is really good! Good food!" (said Frog.) They both
    sat there eating.
Then one day went by. Two days went by.
(Rabbit) went out again looking for food.
When it was late he came back.
When he came back, Frog was just sitting in there, big and puffed up.
"Hello!"
"Hello! How are you? Are you sick or something?" (asked Rabbit.)
"No, I'm fine" (Frog said.)

"Why are you so big?" (asked Rabbit.)

"Why am I big? Every day you bring me food! I get really full, and
     I'm just going to sit here getting fat!" (said Frog.)

That Frog he just kept getting bigger, really, he was the biggest!

"You are big," (thought Rabbit.)

Rabbit went out looking for food again.

Three days later, Frog was even bigger, and most puffed up.

When Rabbit arrived, (he said) "Hello brother! Your belly really is
     very big!"

"Oh? (said Frog.) "It's alright. So what if it's very big?" (said
     Frog.)

"If I am to fit in the house, you have to leave!" (said Rabbit.)

"No, no, it's my house!" (said Frog.) "It's really, really, really good,
     my belly is very big." (said Frog.)

"Okay then, you stay here, and I'll go away." (said Rabbit.)

He did it very reluctantly.

Frog stayed in the house.

He stayed, and Rabbit went away, looking for another house.

Frog stayed in the house. Rabbit just left him behind in there.

That'll be the end of it, this thing that I've been telling.

This story may lack final overt evaluation by the teller, as is customary with most Native American storytelling (Beck et al. 1977; Toelken and
Scott 1981), but, as Toelken discusses for the very similar genre of Coyote
stories, the moral of the tale is communicated indirectly, through word
choice, prosody, intonation, and other contextualization cues (Gumperz
1996). For example, Frog's tone of voice suddenly changes when he
responds to Rabbit's question, "Why are you so big?" He sounds more
forceful and dominating, telling Rabbit in no uncertain terms, "I'm just
going to sit here getting fat!" Just a few lines later he informs Rabbit that
it is now his house. As Toelken states, "Causing children to laugh at an action because it is thought to be weak, stupid, or excessive is to order their
moral assessment of it without recourse to open explanation or didacti-
cism" (Toelken and Scott 1981:106). In this story, Frog's actions are, like
Coyote's, both weak and excessive. Frog begs to be allowed in, showing
weakness, and he is also a glutton; both traits are typical of Coyote in
American Indian literature.

     It is easy to discern the moral of this story. After inviting Frog into his
home, industrious Rabbit loses his home to the ungrateful and selfish Frog,

who refuses to leave. What did Rabbit do to deserve this fate? He acted against his initial better judgment (concerning frogs belonging outside) and embraced Frog, a relative stranger, as a kinsman and brother. Notably, Frog is the first one to call Rabbit "brother."[8] Following traditional Kumiai protocol, Rabbit feeds Frog as well, but Frog "just sits there" getting fatter and fatter until there is no room for Rabbit in his home and he has to leave. One can infer from this tale that it is important to be selective about whom one allows into one's home, as well as to be suspicious of strangers who are quick to claim a kinship relation.

This story thus reinforces localist ideology and values. It is an example of a traditional text with moral significance. Traditional stories such as this one form an important body of knowledge that not only represents cultural values and philosophical orientations but continues to imbue these things in their listeners. As Jahner (1999: 20) states, oral traditions constitute educational systems. Communities view their oral traditions as public evidence of communal identity, and it is incumbent upon academics who work with traditional texts and oral communities to find ways to build more bridges between existing bodies of scholarship and the needs of traditionally oral communities to assure the future of their identities.

ORAL TRADITION AND LANGUAGE REVITALIZATION IN THE BAJA KUMIAI COMMUNITY

In the spirit of bridging scholarship and community needs, this story and others are being incorporated into ongoing collaborative language revitalization efforts in the Baja Kumiai community.[9] The goals of this project are multiple: (1) to document the multiple dialects of Kumiai spoken in Baja California; (2) to create a discourse-based lexicon and grammar detailing the extent of this variation and representing each of these dialects; (3) to create pedagogical materials for teaching Tiipay that reflect this dialect variation, in both paper and multimedia formats, as well as in Spanish and English;[10] (4) to assist Tiipay speakers in learning to write their language so that they may be actively involved not only in creating teaching materials but also in learning how to use literacy as a teaching tool for the future; and (5) to archive all of the audio and video data collected across these communities for future research and use by Kumiai communities at the Archive of Indigenous Languages of Latin America (AILLA) housed at the University of Texas, Austin. This last goal is definitely not the least, for paper versions of field notes too often "languish on metal storage shelves in the archives of various research institutions, as well as among the private papers of individual scholars" (Evers and Toelken 2001:7).

Obviously, the initial creation of paper teaching materials must take precedence over multimedia ones for use in Baja Kumiai communities, many of which are still without electricity, let alone computers. Still, the development of multimedia materials serves important purposes; it not only allows the learner to hear the language being spoken but also works to bridge preliterate languages with contemporary contexts: "A central concern for the use of lesser-used languages in electronic mediation is . . . achieving a transformation of ideological valuations of the language so that the lesser-used language is viewed as part of the contemporary world and as relevant for the future of a particular group" (Eisenlohr 2004:24). It helps to overcome perceptions that may exist in the dominant culture (as well as indigenous ones) that the lesser-used language is somehow lacking and works to promote the language while confirming indigenous identity and culture (Hornberger 1996:361). On the other hand, as Eisenlohr makes clear, it is important to work collaboratively with indigenous communities in creating electronically mediated language materials, especially when linguistic differentiation such as multiple dialects are a concern. This is especially the case in communities that are localist in orientation or variationist in language ideology; academics need to take care to avoid any type of privileging of one dialect over another that might, even accidentally, lead to the development of some type of hierarchization of dialects. In other words, they need to observe a "policy of strict locality" (Hale 2001), and we intend to observe this caveat throughout the duration of the project.

How this story and others are specifically used in language teaching materials remains to be seen; we have not yet reached that point in the development of the project, and this decision will have to be made in collaboration with community members. The storyteller Jon Meza Cuero envisions a live puppet show as the best dramatic representation for his story. Perhaps the final decision concerning how to use this story as a language teaching tool will ultimately be made by individual teachers in the community. No matter how this story and others that we document are used by Tiipay teachers, they will be traditional Tiipay educational materials, which impart more than just linguistic information. In this way, we hope the teaching materials generated by this project acquire the pragmatic edge needed to assist Baja Kumiai communities in maintaining not only their language but their culture and identity as well.

NOTES

1. Because this chapter deals mainly with Baja Kumiai communities, I use the Spanish spelling henceforth.

2. A three-year project funded by NSF's Documenting Endangered Languages program is currently under way at San Diego State University.

3. This is Hohenthal's (2001) translation of the word "Kumiai"; I have not yet found confirmation of this meaning from any contemporary Baja Kumiai speakers, but it is possible that it is an archaic term for a westerly direction or possibly an association with the coastal region.

4. This is in spite of the fact that no evidential quotatives (e.g., "so they say,") were used in the telling of this story; none have been deleted.

5. In fact, the first five lines contain archaic forms that are not easily translatable (Amy Miller, personal communication).

6. Many thanks to Amy Miller for help with this transcription and translation.

7. Here Rabbit briefly lapses into Spanish. It is possible that this is a typical communicative code switch indexing familiarity or solidarity, but it is too soon in our research project to say this with confidence.

8. The Kumiai word used here, *iirrmaans*, is a borrowing from Spanish *hermano*—which perhaps is important as well, connoting an insincere relationship with an outsider rather than the traditional kinship relationship connoted by the Kumiai terms for "younger brother" and "older brother."

9. See note 2.

10. English-Kumiai versions are necessary for language teaching north of the border, where there are seven Tiipay-speaking communities (Viejas, Cuyapaipe, Manzanita, Campo, La Posta, Sycuan, and Jamul).

PART II

STORYTELLING TROUBLES AND TRANSFORMATIONS

CHAPTER 7

THEY DON'T KNOW HOW TO ASK
Pedagogy, Storytelling, and the Ironies of Language Endangerment on the White Mountain Apache Reservation

M. Eleanor Nevins and Thomas J. Nevins

This chapter investigates the perception among residents of the Fort Apache Reservation that traditional storytelling is in decline, along with the implications of this perception for our understanding of the contemporary speech community. The question of how researchers and language professionals can best assist indigenous communities with the problems they confront often informs research agendas for those studying Native American communities. We argue that understandings of the decline in traditional storytelling, like understandings of language loss (Nevins 2004), are formulated differently from different social and institutional positions within Native American speech communities. Further, if researchers do not look for diverse perspectives, they can easily allow the structural collusion between academic agendas and museum- and school-oriented approaches to language maintenance to drown out competing voices.

The larger volume of which this chapter is a part focuses ethnographic and analytic attention on storytelling in relation to crises of cultural and linguistic reproduction. The volume title, "Telling Stories in the Face of Danger," implicitly casts storytelling as an attempted corrective in the face of language and culture loss. We argue that, if an answer to the problem of Apache language and culture endangerment lies with stories, then we ought to be clear with ourselves what kinds of questions we are asking. To

---

Earlier versions of this article were presented in a session organized by Paul Kroskrity and Margaret Field at the 2006 annual meetings of the American Anthropological Association and to the Anthropology Department at the University of Nevada, Reno.

what extent is our model of a crisis in cultural reproduction, and the role
stories might play in addressing such a crisis, mirrored in discourses and
practices within Native American communities? Is the problem of story
and language decline simply a failure to transmit stories from those who
know them to those who do not? Or is the problem more subtly constituted
than this?

SHARED TERMS, RELATIVE MEANINGS

Some chapters in this volume suggest that there are contending versions
of what Kroskrity here describes as "the story of how stories should be
told" circulating in many Native American speech communities, with implications for language and cultural maintenance efforts. We attempt to
illuminate this issue by exploring interpretations of the decline in traditional storytelling offered to us by older and younger Apache speakers
outside bureaucratic educational contexts. We argue that, despite obvious
differences in the way younger and older people diagnose the problem of
contemporary narrative reproduction, they share the assumption that what
is at stake is not simply the transmission of stories but a kind of reciprocity
between generations.

These reciprocity-oriented discourses contrast with the way storytelling is defined in institutions such as the tribe's Culture Center and Museum.
In the latter, Apache stories and songs are incorporated into the museum's
mission to document, preserve, and display Apache cultural objects. This
orientation to languages and stories casts them as components of a body
of authentic cultural knowledge that can be (with various degrees of accuracy) documented, displayed, and reproduced. Storytellers are authorized
in this setting as cultural experts whose authority inheres in their reputa-
tion for knowledge of stories and their skill in performing them. Here an
idiom of accreditation, expert knowledge, and evaluative criteria focused
on accuracy in rendering details predominates (see Keane 2007:255–69
for a parallel contrast). University-affiliated language and culture experts,
such as anthropologists, linguists, and other heritage professionals, tend to
frame Apache language and stories in terms that echo these. The same is
true of school programs that include Apache stories as part of an Apache
culture curriculum.

These two broadly contrasting sets of assumptions speak to what we
have argued elsewhere is a relativity in the meaning of ostensibly shared

terms like "language loss" and "heritage," a relativity with implications for the way that programs intended to promote Native languages, cultures, and identities are received within the communities they are intended to benefit (Nevins 2004; Nevins and Nevins 2009). Often, efforts to utilize the resources and organizational apparatus of historically introduced institutions like schools or museums to teach Native American languages and cultures are shaped by a fundamental limitation: the authority structure, language ideology, discourse genres, and pedagogical practices already in place in these institutions tend to be taken for granted and naturalized because they are already explicitly articulated in the curricula taught in most public schools in the United States. Native American language maintenance programs, because of time and funding constraints, often use existing English curricula as the template for creating indigenous heritage language materials and frame traditional indigenous language stories as "culturally appropriate" analogues to the literature children encounter at school (Sarris 1993). By contrast, forms of learning that take place across generations in extended families can be invisible (Philips 1983) to those formulating maintenance efforts, because in many cases these are tacitly held, enacted through practice, but not talked about directly and codified.

With this chapter we hope to contribute to making visible those competing discourses and the process of translation and mediation involved in attempts to utilize storytelling in the service of cultural documentation and reproduction. We first approach the problem of storytelling from a different vantage point, focusing instead on talk about storytelling outside of school, museum, and similar institutional contexts. Then we explore the role of idioms of reciprocity in the process of translating stories from their locus in extended family and ceremonial contexts to a different status as items of cultural knowledge in schools and museums.

Many members of minority speech communities seem to agree with linguists and anthropologists on matters such as the problem of language endangerment or the relative importance of stories to the maintenance of the linguistic and cultural lifeways. However, we contend that this agreement is more apparent than real. Speakers of minority languages may attribute significantly different meanings and entailments to terms such as "language loss" or "language maintenance" than those attributed by linguists and other credentialed language experts (see also Collins 1998a, b; Hill 2002a). In fact, the assumption of agreement is itself a problem, since it promotes a false sense of common cause while obscuring differences in the direct and metacommunicative meanings attendant to terms

like "endangerment" and "maintenance." These differences can have implications for the meaning and viability of programs designed in response
to language endangerment.

In other words, we must consider what speakers of minority languages
mean when they say they are concerned about language and culture endangerment. Are they referring to the loss of language as an objective system
for communication? Are they concerned about the reproduction of inventories of oral narrative? Ultimately these questions force us to explore the
articulations of terms and concepts like "language endangerment" with
a set of associated Western objectivist meanings—the implication being
that these communities are losing "things" and the remedy prescribed for
maintenance is to put these "things" back into the community. Again, we
need to ask if members of this speech community discuss language loss,
or culture loss, in the same terms? Or are we in fact addressing ourselves,
perhaps unwittingly, to contested discursive terrain in which our maintenance efforts can figure importantly within negotiations among differently positioned stakeholders in the local community (see also Kroskrity
2009b)? We suggest that this is an important question to grapple with if
we are going to cooperate with communities such as the White Mountain
Apaches in formulating responses to the issues that confront them.

WESTERN APACHE STORYTELLING TODAY

This chapter draws upon our experiences during three years of research on
the White Mountain Apache reservation in eastern Arizona from 1996 to
1999. At that time the reservation population was growing rapidly, somewhere between ten thousand and fourteen thousand people, with a near-
majority under the age of twenty-five. Western Apache language could
be heard in most public venues in the main town of Whiteriver, including
grocery stores, banks, government offices, workplaces, broadcast from
the tribe's radio station, in traditionalist ceremonies, Apache evangelical
churches, and many Apache homes. Older women at home and in public
ubiquitously wore camp-dresses, homemade voluminous dresses trimmed
with ribbons and rickrack, which provided a constant visual reminder of
the differences between this reservation community and surrounding non-
Apache communities. A casual visitor to the reservation would likely be
struck, as we were, by the apparently robust vitality of Apache language
use, particularly compared to many other Native American communities

in the United States. However, many reservation residents, upon learning we were there to research how Apache language is used today, or how people today use stories in everyday life, expressed a sense of concern about the prospective loss of their language and culture.

Many expressed concern that young people, in unprecedented numbers, did not seem to be learning to speak and understand Apache. Some older people complained that, because young people were not learning Apache, there were things that older people could not say to them, including some traditional stories. For example, here is a statement we recorded with Rebeckah Altahah, an elder and the wife of a *diyiń*, or ceremonial specialist, as we were translating a story performed by her husband: "Then now we try to talk with our kids and we have to talk English and that's hard. And we can't tell stories like this to them because it loses the meaning or the fun part in it, the joke in it, you know, it loses that as you try to speak it in English because it's meant to be told in Apache, I guess. It had more meaning in Apache."

The phrase "loses the joke in it" indicates something more than failure to decode Apache grammar; it identifies a problem with how stories are interpreted when they are told. This concern about loss of interpretive competence among the young echoes an observation also made in 1956 by Tsinabąąs Yazhi (Little Wagon), a monolingual Navajo storyteller, to Barre Toelken that because of schooling many young people did not know how to listen to stories (Toelken and Scott 1981:94–95).

A concern for stories and storytelling informed the design of several Apache language maintenance efforts ongoing at the time of our research. We eventually became involved with an Apache language maintenance program, a component of which involved enlisting Apache artists to construct narratives set in local scenes with familiar characters for inclusion in the tribe's Internet-distributed curricular resources (Nevins 2004). Storytelling figured importantly in other Apache language and culture classes that we were not involved with but which were run through different reservation schools. These programs relied upon older teacher's aids for storytelling and would also invite selected elders from the community to whom they offered a modest stipend to tell stories deemed appropriate for the classroom.

As storytelling enters into language maintenance efforts, then, it is useful to consider the status of both storytelling as well as the teaching of stories in the contemporary speech community more broadly. Are stories, like the traditional Apache language stories whose use in the community

of Cibecue has been famously described by Basso (1984, 1988, 1996), still
being told? The answer to this question is a conditional yes, with the pro-
viso that, although stories are being told, there seems to be some concern
within the community that they are not being told often enough. Many
young people have some exposure to "traditional" narrative practices, particularly in the context of the Sunrise Ceremony, but some believe that
telling stories about the ancestors is no longer as pervasive and important
as it once was.

Obviously, storytelling as a locus of pedagogy and socialization for
Apache youth competes with English language–based media—television,
radio, the Internet, movies—and opportunities for storytelling are limited by the fragmentation of the intergenerational family. Stories are the
province of elders, and it is common today for grandparents to see their
grandchildren only periodically. Parents are busy with work, and children
with homework or the social necessities of watching popular television
programs and editing their online social networking accounts. From any
perspective, whether that of the "outsider" linguist or concerned speaker
of the Apache language, it is easy to see that traditional narratives and
storytelling practices have a lot to compete with.

A question for us here is whether Apache speakers represent the problem of storytelling in terms of a crisis of cultural reproduction, a seem-
ing zero-sum battle with new media for the limited time and attention of
the family. And the answer is a limited yes, with important reservations.
Sometimes people point the finger at media, but they also represent the
problem in an alternate form. What we found is that the idiom of narrative decline is articulated in terms of a larger breakdown in the terms of
reciprocity—acts of giving and receiving—that link the elder and younger
generations to one another.

NARRATIVE DECLINE AS FAILED RECIPROCITY

We worked over the period of two winters with a well-known *diyiń* named
Jerry Altahah and with Rebeckah Altahah, his wife. Both worked with us
to record and translate, among other things, traditional stories. Many of
our sessions prompted Mr. Altahah to comment upon how he learned the
many songs, stories, and ceremonies he knew. His father had been a *diyiń*
and had taught his own ceremonies to his son. Upon noticing his child's
gift for singing, as well as his capacity for near-perfect memorization, he

had commissioned several other *diyiń* to teach his son the songs and stories that are necessary to conduct ceremonies properly. Aside from his formalized training in the ceremonies, Mr. Altahah learned many traditional stories and songs from older family members during the winter months when such storytelling was considered safe.

At the time of our fieldwork, Mr. Altahah was seventy-two years old, a prominent *diyiń* as well as a widely acknowledged authority on traditional knowledge. In addition to performing several traditionalist ceremonies, he was often called upon by various offices of the tribe's bureaucracy to serve as a cultural expert. In this capacity he regularly visited some of the schools on the reservation to perform songs and short traditional stories that he deemed appropriate for that context. He shared with us some of the stories he performed for the schools. He also performed for us longer, more involved stories that were appropriate to extended family settings and not associated with particular ceremonies. He termed these "legends," or *nłt'éégo nagoldi'e* 'good story.'[1] In a translation session devoted to one of these legends (Nevins et al. 2004), Mr. Altahah remarked that, until recording it with us, he had not told that story in fifteen years. As we were wondering why, he gave us this account of how his family would go about getting an elder family member to tell their stories: "If we wanted a story from my dad or my mom, we usually get together and make arrangements for what day we should get together and let my dad or mom tell us a story. It would be a legend. And, we have to pay them to do that too, so that way they are willing to do it. So, that's how we used to do it."

The implication here is that he had not told the story because no one had asked him to tell the story, or at least had failed to ask in a manner recognizable to him as morally in keeping with appropriate relationships between generations. Here Mr. Altahah casts the sharing of stories and the learning that goes along with it within an idiom of reciprocity that is properly initiated by the learner's act of giving.

That storytelling is an exchange of sorts is underscored by some of the formal characteristics of stories. For example, the storyteller marks the end of a story with the phrase *shigoshkan dasjah,* 'my yucca fruit lie piled up.' This metaphorical framing of storytelling as "piling up yucca fruit" underscores the fact that telling a story is work that the storyteller performs on behalf of the listeners. Like the Tewa stories described by Kroskrity (1985, and this volume), this casts storytelling within an idiom of nurturance and growth. Yucca fruit was once a primary subsistence item, and piling it up is work carried out for the sustenance of listeners. So storytelling is cast

as analogous to other situations in which a family member, or groups of
family members, labors to produce something discrete and momentous
that contributes to the sustenance of the family. Just as senior members of
a family host a big dinner to feed an extended family so that they willingly
engage in various punctuated forms of work (that do not occur every day),
including harvesting and roasting corn, butchering a cow, or building a
Sunrise Ceremony camp (more on this below), so a storyteller should be
presented with sustenance-oriented gifts to make him happy about performing the work of storytelling. The storyteller gives back with a similar
act of sustenance by "piling up yucca fruit" for his audience.

Goodwin (1994) describes an extension of the idiom of nurturance in
the practice of feeding each child a kernel of corn for every line of a story
the teller hopes they remember. Tracing relations of reciprocity in the opposite direction, Opler (1996) describes Chiricahua storytellers presenting
listeners a gift of food or other objects of exchange at the end of a long
night of storytelling to repay them for having "taken their night away." The
point here is that storytelling is not reducible to the transmission of a text;
it is also an idiom of mutual obligation (minimally) between listeners and
teller.[2] So from this perspective, today's grandparents are not telling stories because their sons and daughters, now with children of their own, are
not asking them to, and perhaps do not know how to ask appropriately.

From our experience it seems likely that fluency in the metacommunicative idioms of traditional storytelling is less common among the young
adult generation than fluency in what counts more broadly across school
and other contexts as "Apache language." While working with a tribal
educational office on a language maintenance program, we sat at a table
with several Apache speakers in their thirties and forties looking at previously documented traditional narrative texts (Goddard 1919). Though
all could decode the literal meaning 'my yucca fruit lay piled up' from
the Apache phrase *shigoshkan dasjah,* they puzzled over its significance.
They similarly puzzled over the use of *ch'idii* 'people say,' at the end of
nearly every sentence.

The dominant connotation of *ch'idii* for young and middle-age speakers during our fieldwork period was translated as "gossip." It was often
used both to qualify something being circulated as possibly untrue and to
index the fact that there are numerous people without firsthand knowledge,
nonetheless talking about, and causing others to imagine, something they
claimed to have happened to someone else as if it were true. This meaning did not harmonize for these young to middle-age Apache speakers,

as they pondered incorporating traditional stories in a language and culture program, with the orientation to the traditional storytelling texts such
programs imply, as authoritative items of Apache cultural tradition. It is
perhaps ironic that engagement with educational institutions intended to
define and valorize traditional culture can present impediments to interpreting texts according to other, previously broadly established, community conventions.

As we discuss below, although many young people still associate
learning with intergenerational reciprocity, some of the important idioms
of this reciprocity are no longer widely known. This confusion speaks
to a shift in the understanding of the social context of stories as well as
in the reciprocal framing of intergenerational Apache pedagogy. Some
older people comment upon the fact that the Apache language spoken by
younger people is not the same, and that this makes it difficult for younger
and older people to understand one another. It is likely that the differences
they refer to consist as much in different metacommunicative idioms as
in differences of code. Older people describe the fact that many young
people do not follow them in their manner of speaking as a consequence of
young people not "listening." Here "listening" refers to a quality of awareness and participation in relations of sustenance that define family life
(Nevins 2004). Addressing changes in orientation to traditional stories,
ceremonies, and place names, some elders explain the decline as resulting
from a lack of respect for them and, by proxy, for the ancestors.

What about the perspective from the generation of today's parents?
Jerome Benally is a member of an extended family with whom we worked
for over three years. At the time of our research, Mr. Benally was forty
years old and a father of two. He was also the oldest of his siblings. As
such, after their parents, aunts, and uncles, Mr. Benally was the person
to whom all his brothers and sisters (young adults in their thirties) would
defer on matters of Apache language and culture. He worked with us as an
informal consultant to the Apache language project mentioned above.

One day while driving along a backcountry road on the reservation,
Mr. Benally was discussing the difficulty of bringing Apache traditional
knowledge to bear on their contemporary problems. He said: "The problem is that today elders are stingy. This land has many stories. All these
plants [gesturing to the land around us] have names and uses, and most
people don't know them. Today if you took away the reservation, most
people couldn't survive. They wouldn't know how to live. Maybe there is
an elder who knows a plant that will cure diabetes. Maybe someone knows

a plant that cures cancer. But they won't tell about it. They will take it with them."

Here Jerome points to the same problem Mr. Altahah addressed (the breakdown of narrative pedagogy between grandparent and parent generations), but from the perspective of today's generation of parents. The older people are described as "stingy," they fail to share, preferring to take their knowledge with them when they pass on.

So what is being discussed in the contrasting interpretations offered by Mr. Altahah and Mr. Benally? Both of their comments are informed by the idea that learning implies mutualistic obligations that link young and old in a kind of intergenerational reciprocity. However, despite these shared assumptions, their interpretations of the current decline in storytelling differ in important ways. Depending on which of their perspectives you take, storytelling is in decline because either the young people are not asking as they should or the elders are not giving as they should. This is paralleled in discussions of the stories, songs, and ceremonies controlled by *diyin*. Cosmological stories concerning *ᵐBa' Ts'ǫsé* (Coyote), *Isdzą́ń Nadleeshé* (Changing Woman), *Nayenezghą́ą́né* (He Overcomes Evils), and others are largely the province of *diyin*. In part this is because learning such stories, along with songs and ceremonies associated with them, are part of the secret and specialized training a *diyin* must undergo to command a ceremony. However, in informal conversations among adults in their twenties and thirties we encountered a recurrent complaint and ambivalence about relying on *diyin* for help. On the one hand, they complained that *diyin* give stories or songs only if you pay for them, and that some "get greedy" and ask too much. On the other hand, when an occasion came up that posed the prospect of engaging a *diyin* with the requisite payment, which involves what is termed "giving a feather," young people we knew stepped back from it. One woman in her early thirties said, "To do that you have to really believe." She went on to explain that to do so would enact a commitment not only of money but also of personal exposure to the agencies involved in ceremony that very few take lightly.

For their part, more than one *diyin* who worked with us complained about young people attempting to learn the songs of ceremony, and attempting to do the work of a *diyin*, without going through the requisite series of exchanges and training. The latter includes the presentation of a ceremonially prepared feather and other gifts in order to treat the powers appealed to through the ceremony with a form of respect they can recognize. To take a song or attempt a ceremony without this presentation was described as dangerous and likely to have ill effects on the false *diyiń* as well as on the people he or she is singing for.

What is also at stake here is a sense of respect and value. Elder and younger see their generationally opposite numbers as either failing to express proper respect or failing to value the common good adequately. Mr. Altahah uses the term "respect" to indicate both an affective stance and specific actions. Respect is understood not just as a subjective orientation but also as a specific form of communication. Adherence to the conventions of asking—which takes place in part through informal labor as well as ceremonial payments—is the material embodiment of respect. The issue raised by Mr. Benally, which concerns the labor of storytelling that is the responsibility of the elders, articulates the memory of the ancestors with the emerging experiences of the young. In this view storytelling is the material embodiment of the elder's authority and is ideally motivated by a sense of value that is complementary to the one that motivates the young to work on their behalf.

An additional complaint addressed to intergenerational communication more broadly comes from teenagers, spurred on by their Apache language teachers in school programs. This takes the form of problematizing the teasing they receive from older family members, particularly when older people tease younger people as they attempt to speak Apache. Representatives of more than one language program on the reservation admonished parents and grandparents not to tease young people in their language efforts because this makes them embarrassed and less likely to try to speak the language (see also Loether 2009).

This warning makes sense in relation to school discourses about building children's self-esteem and fighting stigma, but it does not make sense in relation to extended family pedagogical practices. Teasing, like storytelling, is an indirect way of teaching that avoids directly telling a person what to do or think but puts that person in the position of becoming sharply aware of how others view his or her behavior (Nevins 2004). It is applied to people of all ages, but older people most frequently tease younger people. Storytelling, the "shooting with arrows" described by Basso (1984, 1988, 1996), as well as the use of metaphors described as "wise words" (Basso 1976), are pedagogical practices on a continuum with teasing, since all involve bringing a person into self-awareness through suggestion of how his or her behavior is viewed (sometimes with amusement) by others.

During our fieldwork the multigenerational households we visited were enlivened every day with teasing, much of it directed to ways of speaking (see also Basso 1979). Speaking inappropriately, including mispronouncing a word (English or Apache), especially if it involved accidentally evoking an unintended meaning, was met with teasing and laughter. Two women in their twenties told me stories about accidentally saying a word with sexual connotations when they intended to be talking about putting dumplings in a stew, or, worse, referencing a brother. In each case the young woman was embarrassed enough to flee the house in the face of the laughter that quickly spread among everyone present. It might be noted that both young women are now fluent speakers, who can dish out teasing as well as anybody, and that the teasing they received motivated both to never make the same mistakes again.

The broader point we are making is that front and center in Apache discourses of language and culture loss are concerns about how younger and older people relate to one another. Lack of Apache language and cultural fluency in the young is taken as a symptom of a crisis in pedagogical relations within extended families. And though language and culture maintenance programs are often posed as remedies, they rarely address the core concern about the breakdown in reciprocal relations among members of extended families.

RECIPROCITY RELOCATED: CULTURAL BROKERAGE

It is obvious that dislocations brought about by the rapidly changing position of Apache families with respect to mainstream society and culture have led to a perceived disharmony in the intents and actions of elder and younger speakers of Apache. It is perhaps ironic that, as traditional storytelling has become disembedded from daily family life, it has become more involved with mainstream society. For an example we once again turn to Mr. Altahah, who at times acts in the capacity of what Silverstein (1998a:15) has termed a "cultural broker"—someone whose actions articulate with culturally different idioms of social discourse and exchange and "mediate the encompassing polity's views of [the] minority language, and the local language community's construction/construal of its own locality." He was willing to work with us—two *ndaa,* or "white," researchers—in part because he was interested in documenting Apache stories, but also because we were willing to pay him a modest fee for the stories. As noted above, Mr. Altahah was also paid a stipend to tell stories in some of the reservation schools. These instances of exchange did not represent for him the commoditization of his stories. Quite the opposite: he explained to us that the money received for the stories was not for "services rendered" but instead was a necessary sign of respect that was ultimately being paid to the ancestors. It should be noted that money payments are similarly worked into the gift exchanges that are part of enlisting the services of *diyiń* to perform ceremonies.

Reservation residents, as is the case for people in many other post-colonial communities, participate in contrasting exchange systems, each with its attendant ideology about the relationship between goods, people, and their transfer (Keane 2007). All families on the reservation participate in a monetary economy that may include employment in tribal government or in businesses, circulation of money from government assistance programs, and its use for purchase of consumer goods and services. Most also participate in a ceremonial exchange economy that for traditionalists includes gifts to ceremonial specialists to put on a variety of ceremonies, elaborate gift and feast exchanges between families related through the Sunrise Ceremony, as well as less formalized gifts between in-laws. For Apache evangelicals a parallel set of ceremonial exchange events applies to the establishment of godparent relationships as well as relations between churches in reciprocal revival visits.

The monetary economy and ceremonial exchange economy operate side by side and often interpenetrate. Objects that are normally part of ceremonial exchange may be alienated from their previous association, commoditized, and sold for cash—as in the case of a traditional burden basket necessary for the Sunrise Dance and sold at the Culture Center gift shop. On the other hand, cash may be appropriated into ceremonial exchanges and as such be interpreted not as an abstract value but as a morally loaded instantiation of the effort, intentions, respect, prayer, and awareness of parties involved. In this way, Mr. Altahah and other *diyiń* successfully appropriate money into ceremonial exchange, including storytelling.

However, it is also true that the stories *diyiń* and other elders tell within schools and to researchers are framed within a set of practices and interpretive frameworks that are integrated with and reinforced by far-ranging institutions of the dominant society. Further, as Samuels (2006) notes for the neighboring San Carlos reservation, schools and museums have become increasingly naturalized as sites of authoritative traditional knowledge, particularly for younger people. So although it is important to recognize that cultural brokers like Mr. Altahah invest their participation in school culture programs with meanings consistent with their ceremonial roles, it is also possible to see this partial overlapping of two different kinds of exchange practices as part of a hegemonic process in which the interpretive practices surrounding storytelling are progressively decentered from intergenerational reciprocity and recentered (Bauman and Briggs 1990; Silverstein and Urban 1996) in terms of the authority structures, discourse genres, and language ideologies of the schools, museums, and academic researchers.

Recontextualizing Apache language and stories in the schools and Culture Center creates new models of what it means to know Apache language and culture, models that exist alongside of, and often contrast with, their counterpart in families and ceremonial contexts. For example, we worked on an Apache language project with an Apache language teacher. She had been a fluent speaker since childhood but took some linguistics classes for Native language instructors through the summer NALDI (Native American Language Development Institute) program. She was often the public face of our project and described herself in several presentations to Apache teacher's aides (many of them older than her and all fluent in Apache) as "not really knowing my own language" until learning how to write it and break it into grammatical elements and explicitly compare its structure with that of English.

Another fluent Apache speaker, a man in his thirties who had grown up in East Fork, spoken Apache since childhood, and described staying up many nights telling and listening to stories with other men in that community, similarly described himself as only "getting to know his culture" when he worked as an intern at the Culture Center.

Claims to cultural knowledge based upon authorization through universities or through training at the tribe's museum do not go uncontested. And those who assert them may also cast their work in a transposed idiom of reciprocity, that is, as a form of giving to the community or the schools.[3] Regardless, such claims form part of what has become a contested discursive terrain in this and other Native American communities. Therefore, it should come as no surprise that, as Kroskrity notes for Tewa and Neely for Kiowa (this volume), and as born out in our own experience with White Mountain Apaches, there is often resistance from sectors of the community to recontextualizing stories within institutional maintenance programs.

STORY TEXTS CIRCULATING ACROSS DIVERGENT CONTEXTS:
RADICAL TRANSLATION

Traditional stories are forms of entextualized discourse, that is, they are marked off from the flow of ongoing speech and have the status of something that can be retold and recontextualized in a new instance of speaking (Bauman and Briggs 1990; Silverstein and Urban 1996). Stories, through linguistic cues and established interpretive practices, are framed in such a way as to prompt people to identify new performances as recurring instances of preexisting stories. In the contemporary reservation community, traditional stories are circulated across familial and ceremonial contexts, on the one hand, and Culture Center and school contexts on the other. The fact that "the same" story may be performed in either set of contexts masks the extent to which the act of performing it serves different purposes, mediates relationships between different sorts of agents, and underwrites different authority relationships in each. We argue that the movement of stories from extended family and ceremonial contexts to school and museum can be viewed as "radical translation," following Keane's (2007) discussion of radical conversion, in the sense that it involves recontextualization across different semiotic regimes in which the purpose of speaking, the status of words, and the location of agency are configured differently. From here we attempt to draw out the contrast further.

The power of traditional Apache stories told in familial and ceremonial contexts is that they provide an opportunity for bringing ancestral agencies and contemporary human participants to bear upon one another, a relation that allows ancestors to speak to people (if the person is "listening") and to play a shaping role in people's awareness and interpretation of ongoing events (Basso 1996; Opler 1996; Toelken and Scott 1981). The delicate task of the storyteller is to evoke the stories but to avoid directly interposing herself or himself between the ancestors and listeners' imaginations of the unfolding story. Accordingly, storytelling style is spare, with maximal gaps between utterances for listeners to fill in with their own imaginations. Common reference points in familiar places and scenes are utilized to orient listeners to the ancestors, the remnants of whose actions are located in those places, and to key listeners to fill in context imaginatively. Some storytellers make extensive use of quotative particles, like *ch'idii,* or "people say," that locate the source of the story outside the storyteller and index prior acts of speaking extending from the present day to the imagined time of the ancestors. The task of the storyteller is to bring listeners into imaginative relation with ancestors so that they can see what the ancestors saw, hear their voices, stand where they stood (Basso 1996). Other conditions on storytelling involve limiting the performance of cosmological stories to the winter months and under appropriate conditions of reciprocity. Observing these constraints orients listeners to ancestors as potential participants who must be approached correctly, and whose awareness waxes and wanes with the seasons. Care must be taken, and respect demonstrated, in careful timing and in careful wording, because one wants to exert control over the extent and manner in which the powers associated with ancestors enter into one's life.

Performances of stories in familial settings like this are informed by a set of ideas about the primary function of language, conventional criteria for evaluating performance, and the efficacy of language in mediating human and nonhuman agencies that are quite different from those that frame the school and museum. In the former the primary function of language is indexical—it mobilizes participants' orientation to and awareness of ancestors anchored in local places, and it mobilizes the awareness and agency of ancestors in the lives of contemporary human beings. A storytelling performance is judged successful to the extent that participants are able to see, hear, and vividly imagine the actions of the ancestors; and to the extent that the story, not the storyteller, exerts a lasting (salutary) effect on the listeners. Here language is not primarily a conduit of referential meaning encoded by the storyteller and decoded by the listeners but an invitation to each listener to imagine, to orient themselves through awareness of place and ancestral actions, and as the story unfolds to come to their own revelatory meaning, to get what Rebeckah Altahah described above as "the joke in it."

Traditional stories told within a school classroom, to a researcher, or in a culture center museum are necessarily recontextualized through orientation to a language ideological regime (Kroskrity 2000b) that differs from that of the familial storytelling context described above. Here the speaker's role is transformed from that of respected elder family member to "cultural expert." The primary function of language, which authorizes the speaker and justifies his or her expert status with respect to "Apache culture," is referential (Keane 1995). Here performance standards are oriented toward criteria of cultural knowledge and authenticity. Expert storytellers tell stories in such a manner, and adhering to conventionalized sequence of actions and characters, so that others credit them with knowing the story. Storytelling in this setting is a demonstration of distinct cultural knowledge. The story is transformed into an item of cultural knowledge to be documented by researchers, transmitted to students in the schools and to laypeople in the culture center. In some cases storytellers alter the style and form of the stories to fulfill genre expectations associated with the new context, such as translating traditional stories into the form of moral fables, fairytales, folklore, or Bible stories. In other cases care is taken to replicate the formal features of traditional storytelling, but in this context their primary function is as markers of traditional authenticity.[4] What Keane notes for recontextualization of ritual speech also applies to much traditionalist narrative:

> Their textual character is in part a function of the perceived challenges of communicating with distant interlocutors, such as the dead, and of obtaining from them recognition and responses. The character of ritual words in turn facilitates their use in new contexts, supplying an emergent folkloric discourse with materials that are interesting primarily for what they denote or as a code awaiting exegesis. It should be no surprise that the speech performances that most lend themselves to entextualization are favored as lasting cultural objects. (2007:262)

In fact, the same poetic devices that serve to mark off stories of ancestors from other kinds of speech form the ethnopoetics (Hymes 1981; Tedlock 1983) through which a story is recontextualized within academic documentation practices as a culturally and linguistically distinctive body of oral literature.

In this sense, traditional storytelling is an example of what Hanks (1987) terms a "threshold genre" in that storytelling performances circulate between two different discursive regimes, with different interpretative consequences within each. Viewed in this light, even a faithfully recorded, transcribed, and linguistically rendered story undergoes a sort of radical translation (accomplished to varying degrees by storyteller and other parties, including researchers) when it moves from performance in family and ceremonial settings to schools, museums, and archives (Keane 1995; Nevins et al., forthcoming). Many, like Jerry Altahah, move smoothly from one authorizing context to another—but that does not mean that Apache culture taught in the schools and museums, although it is often treated as if it stands in for continuity of intergenerational relations, begins to address adequately the problem of "loss" for many in the community.

ORAL LITERATURE AND AMBIGUITIES OF COLLABORATIVE RESEARCH

In a sense, the expectation upon scholars to produce scholarship, and upon museum directors to amass language-themed items in their archives—and the legitimizing orientation of both to the genre expectations of anthropology, oral literature, linguistics, folklore, and the rest—has tended to limit experimentation in forms of discourse that fit ongoing concerns of the community more directly.[5] This limitation on experimentation is reinforced by an apparent collusion of interest between concern in the community to save a heritage language and culture and concern of scholars and other language experts to document items of language and culture. Certain *diyiń* and selected elders serve bridging, or brokering, roles as cultural experts, and their interest in valorizing Apache culture in relation to analogues in the dominant society overlaps that of researchers. However, these efforts at best only indirectly address concerns voiced more broadly in the reservation community concerning breakdown in the terms of intergenerational pedagogy and reciprocity.

Linguistic and oral literature documentation efforts directly answer the concerns of scholarship. They can segue felicitously at times with the concerns of those whose job it is to teach the heritage language and culture, by providing materials useful for developing curricula parallel to English language curricula (e.g., Adley-Santa Maria 1997, 1998; de Reuse 1997). They can also provide materials useful to tribal museum directors and cultural resource directors looking to fill their archives with items of traditional culture (Silverstein 2003a), although ethical conflicts emerge in the movement from whatever social relations characterized the documentation process to those that frame proposed "public" access (Silverstein 2006). Still, there is a strong tendency built into the relation that these schools and culture center museums bear to the local community, and to the larger national polity of which they are a part, to allow these forms of documentation to stand in for local discourses more broadly, and in a way that underscores the authority of linguists and other academic researchers (Silverstein 2003c) while undermining forms of authority constituted in other terms. Put another way, there is a tendency toward erasure of the diversity of local discursive practices (Irvine and Gal 2000; Kuipers 1998:125–48). This includes erasure of competing local discourses that articulate concerns about language and culture loss in different terms and that underwrite the authority of differently delimited sets of social actors (in this case elders more broadly conceived). One of the ironies of language and cultural maintenance programs is that they are often represented as if they stand in for continuity in local linguistic and cultural practices, when in fact they represent a radical transformation of these in terms more recognizable within the discourses and institutions of the dominant society (see also Collins 1998b; Silverstein 1998a:408).

Emerging Contexts for Pedagogical Reciprocity on the White Mountain Apache Reservation

The ambivalent portrait we are painting is not, we believe, without a silver lining. The fact is that storytelling has not disappeared and relationships between generations have not been severed. The pervasive sense of decline is troubling, but the diversity of discourses focusing on problems of intergenerational pedagogy is, we would argue, actually a sign of vitality, to borrow a term from discourses of language endangerment. That decline in forms of intergenerational pedagogy is such an important matter of concern (Latour 2004) for Apache speakers should alert us to the fact that members of the Apache speech community are neither unaware nor mute with regards to problems of loss as they constitute them.

One formal context where pedagogical reciprocity is very much in evidence is the *Na'íees*, or Sunrise Ceremony (Nevins 2005). The *Na'íees* is a quasi-public coming-of-age ceremony for young women and has become increasingly prominent over the past thirty years. The ceremony involves elaborate exchanges between two families as well as occasions of oratory and storytelling, all hinging on an explicitly pedagogical relationship among the young woman undergoing the ceremony and her godmother, the young woman's parents, and members of the grandparental generation who know the proper ways of preparing for and performing the ceremony. It also involves formal exchanges between families and ceremonial specialists. The ceremony itself lasts four days, but preparations take the better part of a year, and follow-up exchanges extend the relationships established

in the ceremony for many years. The ceremonial gift exchanges and feasts
that precede the actual ceremony of the *Na'íees* require families of the
young woman and her godmother to each enlist the help of a *diyiń* and the
diyiń's group of singers to lead processions of gift givers into the opposite
camp. At certain prescribed moments in the buildup to the ceremony, *diyiń*
instruct their singers, the girl, and the godmother in the meaning of the
event as well as in proper comportment and orientation. But much of the
preparation and support for the ceremony must be accomplished by family
members: fixing on an appropriate godmother, constructing camps, feeding participants, obtaining the requisite ritual items to secure the agreement of the godmother and the help of the *diyiń*, assembling suitable gifts
and feasts for the other camp, butchering cattle, gathering herbs for making
traditional beverages, and finding an appropriate person to "speak for you"
at the ceremonies. And for guidance in carrying out all these tasks, the parents, aunts, and uncles of the girl must seek the help of their own parents,
aunts, and uncles. There are many Sunrise dances held every summer at the
several ceremonial grounds around the reservation. Given the complexity
of the ceremony, the experience of the elder generation is necessary to its
successful conduct. So the *Na'íees* acts as a setting that mobilizes people
in their thirties and forties to learn from their parents and grandparents by
way of idioms of reciprocity and shared sustenance.

CONCLUSION

In sum, the problem of storytelling in the present-day Apache speech community should not be viewed exclusively through the lens of academic and
popular discourses of "language and culture endangerment." Instead, if we
hope to make sense of the situation that this community finds itself in, we
must engage it in its own terms. The critical discourses we have discussed
here are part of a complex, sophisticated, and heterogeneous speech community. The term "endangerment" serves as a ready English language index for certain concerns of this community, but we should not conflate
the commonsense popular meaning of this idea with the nuances of meaning attributed to it by Apache speakers. Similarly, we suggest that a focus
on "language" or "stories" as endangered resources obscures the social relationships within which they have meaning. Relocating stories within the
authority structure of institutional language programs needs to be the subject of careful consideration and experimentation in order to avoid (if this

is possible) exacerbating crises in intergenerational social relationships, such as those described in Apache discourses of language and story loss.

NOTES

We gratefully acknowledge financial support for this research provided by two grants from the Wenner Gren Foundation for Anthropological Research as well as grants from the Phillips Fund for Native American Research of the American Philosophical Society and the Jacobs Research Fund of the Whatcom Museum. This chapter has benefited from the critical editorial guidance of Paul Kroskrity. Particular thanks are due to the Apache language teachers who involved us in their work on a number of projects developed in the educational offices of the White Mountain Apache Tribe. There are key parents, grandparents, *diyiń*, and young people who helped us, and while they remain anonymous in this chapter, they know who they are and richly deserve our enduring gratitude. Any shortcomings, of course, are our own.

1. *Nłt'éégo nagoldi'e* is translated as "saga" by Basso (1996:49–50) and stands in contrastive relation to *godighįhgo nagoldi'é*, a story of power presenting the beginning and transformation of the world (deemed appropriate by Mr. Altahah and other *diyiń* of our acquaintance to *diyiń* training to sweat lodge preparations for participation in ceremonies, to winter nights among family, but not for wider circulation). However, whereas Basso describes the temporal placement of *nłt'éégo nagoldi'e* as *diijįigo*, which he translates as "modern times" and in local Apache English idiom is commonly glossed as "nowadays," the corpus we recorded were set at a further temporal remove: *do'áníína*, or "way back."

2. There are many other examples of reciprocity as a prominent idiom in storytelling from other Athapaskan groups (e.g., Cruikshank 1990, 1998; Smith 2002, 2003) and from other Native American groups more generally (e.g., Fienup-Riordan 2005). In fact, it is the focus on transmission of stories over and above consideration for the social relations in which they are embedded, so characteristic of many documentation and education efforts, that stands in dramatic contrast to storytelling practices in Native American communities.

3. The transposition of idioms of reciprocity and the moral stances involved in giving and receiving to the context of the tribe as a whole, or to other extended socialities, strikes us as a topic that deserves more consideration than we can devote in this chapter.

4. In fact, the existence of ancestors as potential overhearers, or potential voices in the contemporary world, is destabilized by recontextualization within

institutional forms underwritten by modernist discourses that limit ongoing expressions of agency to contemporary human actors (see Keane 2007 for a discussion of the role of delimiting attributions of agency in conversions to modernity).

5. A notable exception is a recent work coauthored by Anne Fienup-Riordan titled *Wise Words of the Yup'ik: We Speak to You Because We Love You* (Fienup-Riordan 2005). She describes this work as unique among her other collaborative projects with members of the same Yup'ik community in that it was framed from its inception by her Yup'ik consultants. It is the compilation of speeches given by members of the Calista elders' council at a series of public events to which young people were invited. The meetings directly addressed the problem of intergenerational communication, and elders attempted to remedy what they described as a breakdown in intergenerational pedagogy by imparting the "words of wisdom" that they were given by their own elders to a new generation of young people. The elders in their speeches directly confronted their sense of duty to impart "words of wisdom" and also expressed the reasons for their reticence to speak directly to young people today. What results makes an awkward book by the standards of academic or literary genres; instead, we see an experiment in community-researcher collaboration that is unique in that it is focused on a series of speech events in which elders attempt to speak directly and personally to young people and labor to make the case for the relevance of traditional knowledge to contemporary personal and social issues that young people face.

CHAPTER 8

GROWING WITH STORIES
Ideologies of Storytelling and the Narrative Reproduction of Arizona Tewa Identities

Paul V. Kroskrity

We all tell and hear stories. Though I hear we do have direct experiences of our worlds, it is useful to reflect on just how much of this experience is vicarious, and how much our different narrative worlds can be taken for granted. Personal, historical, official, and traditional narratives fill much of our lives. And if we accept Jarett Zigon's (2008:146) recent definition of narrative as "those stories persons tell one another (or themselves) in order to create and maintain meaning in one's (or a community's) life," we must assume that, especially in the case of traditional narratives, this meaning and order are achieved by orienting to tradition. As Ochs and Capps have argued about narrative-embedded moral stances, they are "rooted in community and tradition [and aim] toward what is good and valuable and how one ought to live in the world" (2001:45). Narratives are clearly critical resources for the mutually dependent projects of constructing selves and maintaining community.

But even though most human groups seem to display a penchant for stories, it is redundantly clear that not all stories are equally valued, supported, or permitted. Aesthetic and moral evaluations of narratives, what I prefer to term "narrative discriminations," are as ubiquitous as the stories themselves. By narrative discriminations I mean the attention to and evaluation of stories and their narrative conventions by tellers and listeners.

Parts of this chapter were presented at the 2005 and 2006 annual meetings of the American Anthropological Association in sessions organized by Pamela Bunte and Susan Needham (2005) and Margaret Field and the author (2006). Portions of this chapter were published in the *Journal of Linguistic Anthropology*.

151

My preference for this notion stems from the fact that its double meaning directs attention to the linkages of the aesthetic and the political. Aesthetic evaluations often merge or interact with the associations of social hierarchy and cultural stratification. As commonsense actors, we find it possible to talk about having a discriminating "taste" in cultural and artistic realms without necessarily exploring the connections between such an appreciation and associated social discriminations that both index and reproduce social hierarchies (Bourdieu 1984). But "narrative discrimination," as a sensitizing concept, attempts to direct scholarly attention precisely to these linkages.

Native American traditional stories and their performances provide sites of ideological struggle both within Native communities and between Native communities and the dominant society (Kroskrity 2009a, c; in this volume, see Neely, Nevins and Nevins, Perley). In this chapter, I look at a struggle over stories, and their capacity to create identities and make communities, that is taking place within a single Native American community—the Village of Tewa, First Mesa, Hopi Reservation (in northeastern Arizona).[1] In a prior treatment of Arizona Tewa traditional narratives (Kroskrity 1985), I focused on a kind of "structural" growth of the narratives themselves as Tewa narrators engaged in text-building practices featuring the layered organization of lines, verses, and stanzas. In this chapter I complement the prior study by emphasizing other types of "growth," some recognized, some misrecognized, by Arizona Tewa people in their own ideologies of storytelling, narrative practices, and the indexical orders (Silverstein 2003b) in which *péé;yu'u,* traditional stories, are embedded.[2] Such local notions associate Tewa storytelling practices with the growth and moral development of children, the fertility and growth of sustaining plants, and the growth and perpetuation of the Arizona Tewa community itself. Here I recognize the kind of authority that Tewa narrators attribute to these traditional narratives and examine attempts at what Bauman (2004:8) has termed "generic regimentation" of these highly esteemed narrative resources. In so doing I attempt to relate local theories of intertextuality to beliefs and practices that both widen and narrow the intertextual gap associated with *péé;yu'u.* Finally, I also examine the intertextual relations between participation in traditional storytelling and the language ideologies associated with the powerful discourse of "kiva speech" (*te'e hiili*), which I have analyzed in greater detail in prior research (Kroskrity 1993, 1998).

Though neither as powerful nor as regulated as kiva speech, the more mundane language of Tewa *péé;yu'u* nevertheless receives considerable attention in some quarters of the Tewa community as a resource requiring regulation. This impacts the present study significantly. Even though my chapter is not centrally about telling or structurally analyzing specific stories, my awareness of debates within the Tewa community suggests considerable internal variation about the representation of Tewa language texts to audiences outside of Tewa homes.[3] As an outsider who has been privileged to study the language over the past three decades and who hopes to continue working with all sectors of the community toward the ends of language documentation and linguistic revitalization, I attempt to minimize the number of Tewa examples and completely refrain from representing entire narratives or even large fragments in deference to those members who deem it inappropriate. Since my goal is more to reveal the cultural matrix and interdiscursivity in which traditional storytelling forms, practices, and ideologies are embedded, deferential restraint in the use of examples does not deter me from making the relevant observations about traditional storytelling that are my objective here.

THE ARIZONA TEWAS: REPRODUCTIONS AND REPRESENTATIONS

Today the Arizona Tewas number around seven hundred individuals who reside on and near the Village of Tewa on First Mesa of the Hopi Reservation. They are the descendents of those Southern Tewas (or *Thanuuge'in T'owa*) who moved, at the request of the Hopis, from pueblos they abandoned in the Rio Grande in the aftermath of the second Pueblo Revolt of 1696 (Dozier 1954, 1966). We know, from both historical documents and their own oral history, that their ancestors played a major role in the revolt and that they refused to resettle their pueblo, preferring instead to fight a guerilla war against the Spanish until the time of the Hopi invitation in 1700.

The contemporary Arizona Tewas have been studied most intensively by Edward Dozier (1954, 1966) and by me (Kroskrity 1993, 1998, 2000a). They are an especially remarkable people for two reasons that are relevant here. One, they are the only group in a Pueblo diaspora of almost one hundred villages and pueblos that managed to relocate yet retain their heritage language. This persistence despite the likely fate of assimilation into the Hopi majority has won for the Arizona Tewas some notoriety in the literature on language endangerment. In works by both Dorian (1989) and Crystal (2000), for example, there is a tendency to depict the Arizona

Tewas as especially persistent and to regard the way they use languages as a clue to the very nature of linguistic persistence.[4]

Although it is gratifying to see my work on the Arizona Tewas be useful to other scholars, particularly those with the noble goal of calling an alarm to imminent and widespread language death or of promoting language revitalization, it is also a source of dismay for which I must take considerable responsibility. Perhaps my own representations of the Arizona Tewas have led others to view them primarily as paragons of persistence. This view, however, fails to appreciate their actual linguistic struggles and the real work they do in managing their linguistic and cultural resources. For the Arizona Tewas, like so many contemporary speech communities surveyed and reviewed by Silverstein (1998a), have undergone great transformation within the past century. Economic incorporation, urban migration, relocation and the reservation-urban orbit (Hodge 1971), the wired and mediated world (Spitulnik 1998), the increasingly diverse ethnoscapes (Appadurai 1996) now available, and many other consequences of globalization have brought greater internal diversity to this community than ever before. A community that once unanimously declared that speaking Tewa was a determining attribute of Tewa identity has now had to confront the fact that the vast majority of its children are growing up with English as the main language of the home and *without* the heritage language the community had successfully maintained post-diaspora for more than three hundred years. A community that once uniformly rejected the possibility of schools as a site for Tewa language socialization, because they viewed this as exclusively the domain of Tewa homes and their associated kin, now debates—with expected generational and interclan variation and contestation—the costs and benefits of tempering its hardline stance on Native literacy programs and on schools as a site for Tewa instruction. I return to this later. Certainly in comparison to many other Native American and other world indigenous languages, it would be inappropriate to view the Arizona Tewa language as severely endangered, but the community itself now does appear to recognize that there is a crisis evidenced by the fact that most young people are not growing up speaking the language. Informal surveys conducted during the early period of my research (1973–85) and my most recent research excursion in 2010 indicate that the perception of a crisis is quite well founded, since the past thirty years have produced a decline in the number of homes in which young people were learning and actively speaking the language from 50 percent to 10 percent.[5]

Traditional stories among the Arizona Tewas have long been culturally valorized as a key means of cultural maintenance and transmission, and it is no wonder that today, at a time of linguistic crisis, many Arizona Tewas plan a return to them as a cultural resource in the community's language renewal efforts. In this chapter I provide relevant historical background on the Arizona Tewa community and explore some key semiotic connections linking the Arizona Tewa language to various ethnic identities. I then analyze Tewa ideologies of storytelling efficacy and aesthetics, exploring the way traditional Tewa narrators have chosen to create "authoritative" voices that "speak the past" while producing performances that are still innovatively designed for their "present" audiences. After examining the ways traditional narrative practices provide developing children with a domestic preadaptation to dominant language ideologies that are inscribed in the key site of *te'e* (kiva) practices, I return to the dilemmas confronted by community members who seem to share ideals of narrative performance but not the linguistic resources necessary to realize them.

THE ARIZONA TEWAS: LANGUAGES AND IDENTITIES

Here I briefly review some of the many important connections between language and identity that provide a relevant background for examining the identity work that traditional stories perform. Since much of this has been presented in greater detail elsewhere (e.g., Kroskrity 1993, 1998, 2000a), an abbreviated treatment shaped to the proportions of this chapter suffices here. Convergent yet distinct perspectives are provided by "objectivist" and more "experience-near" (Geertz 1983) ways of understanding.[6] In addition to historical observations made above, the objectivist perspective confirms a consistent cultural preference for "indigenous purism" resulting in a dispreference for loanwords from other languages and strong preference for extending native vocabulary to fill lexical gaps.

Extremely minimal borrowing from Spanish (seventeen words) and Hopi (two words) despite long periods of former or current multilingualism clearly displays the practice of indigenous purism (Kroskrity 1993).[7] This promotion of indigenous linguistic resources and exclusion of foreign forms has often been regarded as identity fostering, especially in resistance to a politically or socially dominant group (e.g., Henningsen 1989). But the Arizona Tewa practice of indigenous purism, especially in regard to their three centuries of contact with Hopi, is also critically revealing of how purism functions to mask change and erase cultural borrowing. An important example is how changes in Arizona Tewa kinship and social organization—changes necessitated by transitioning from a social system featuring patrilineal moieties (as in other Eastern Pueblos) to one centered on matrilineal clans (Hopis and other Western Pueblos)—were erased by extending Native terms. The Arizona Tewas extended their word for "people" (*t'owa*) to add an additional sense "clan's people." They used Tewa vocabulary to label these clans (e.g., tobacco, bear, sand, or corn) and become compatible with a Hopi system in which clans played such major roles as regulating marriage, allocating land use rights, and exercising ceremonial rights and duties.

This pattern of apparent linguistic purism camouflaging cultural influence and convergence is also especially germane to storytelling. Arizona Tewa traditional stories, like those of the Hopis, display very high rates of using "hearsay" evidential particles—Tewa *ba,* Hopi *yaw*—in their traditional stories (Kroskrity 1993, 1997). Though the Tewas have clearly retained their own evidential particle, they now use it in a manner unlike other Tewa-speaking pueblos in the east who have the same word (Kroskrity 1997). In the Rio Grande Tewa languages, such particles are often used in the beginning of a story and infrequently throughout the narrative. But the Arizona Tewas use their *ba* in frequencies and functions that now closely approximate Hopi discourse conventions. In both languages, the respective evidential has assumed the form of a "genre signature" (Shaul 2002)—the pervasive structural marker that the storyteller is performing a traditional story. Though this example of discursive convergence suggests the powerful influence of Hopi discourse models, use of the indigenous evidential *ba* masks any evidence of that influence to contemporary Tewa speakers who quite expectably have no awareness of any alteration of discourse norms that they brought with them from New Mexico more than three hundred years ago.

Although an objectivist approach may reveal the structural and usage patterns that disclose language ideologies of practice, only a more "experience-near" perspective allows us to view Arizona Tewa "beliefs and feelings" in the expression of their "discursive consciousness." Evidence of this cultural awareness surfaces most prominently in the Tewa expression *Naa-im-bí hiili naa-im-bí woowac'i na-mu* 'Our language is our history.' Most Arizona Tewas know their language is related to languages spoken in such Eastern pueblos as San Juan, Santa Clara, and San Ildefonso. They also know that the comparative lack of Spanish lexical and phonological influence in their Tewa language distinguishes their language from those of other Tewa-speaking pueblos. The Rio Grande Tewa languages, for example, have words like *konfesa* (from Spanish *confesion*) "confession" and *pinsipa* (from Spanish *principales*) "political leaders" and sounds like /x/ and /f/ (Dozier 1964 [1956]:514), all of which are alien to Arizona Tewa and viewed by its Native speakers as evidence of the linguistic impurity and cultural inferiority of the New Mexican Tewa pueblos. Tewa elder Albert Yava (1978:1) denigrates other Tewa languages in accord with the local language ideology of indigenous purism when he says, "In New Mexico the Tewa language has been corrupted by other Pueblo languages and Spanish." Thus the combined ideologies of indigenous purism and language as historical product both contribute to an additional project of constructing the Arizona Tewa language as an icon of ethnic identity.

Another local notion that weaves language, identity, and history together is the "linguistic curse" placed upon the Hopis by the ancestors of the Arizona Tewas. According to the folk history of the Tewas (and verified by some Hopi accounts), the ancestors of the Arizona Tewas responded to Hopi failure to live up to the terms of an agreement in which their military service to the Hopis would be repaid by granting land use rights and other concessions. An obligatory part of tribal initiation ceremonies, Arizona Tewa narratives of the events leading up to the curse depict the cruel and unfeeling treatment of victorious but starving Tewa warriors after they had vanquished Hopi enemies. In Dozier's translation, the clan chiefs of the Tewas respond with this curse: "Because you have behaved in a manner unbecoming to human beings, we have sealed knowledge of our language and our way of life from you. You and your descendents will never learn our language and our ceremonies, but we will learn yours. We will ridicule you in both your language and our own."

Apart from the continuing belief in the efficacy of this curse more than three centuries after it was originally uttered, the curse is especially remarkable for two reasons. One, it represents the Tewas as agents in the production of an asymmetrical bilingualism that would have been the expected outcome of their minority status. Two, it celebrates the maintenance of the Tewa language as a cultural victory, further laminating the language with significance as an enregistered emblem of ethnic identity (Agha 2007:235).

A final point of discussion regarding the intimate association of the Arizona Tewa language and its use as a means of expressing ethnic or tribal identity might be described as "the cultivation of difference." Some members use their agricultural experience as a source of imagery to naturalize their language ideologies and linguistic practice and provide a cultural rationalization for such language ideologies as "compartmentalization," indigenous purism, and even the iconization of specific languages to corresponding social identities. Like the Hopis, the Arizona Tewas plant many small fields consisting of a single color of corn (e.g., blue, red, yellow) in order to eliminate the hybridization and mixing of color that would occur if two colors of corn were planted in the same field. One senior consultant explained: "That's why we have so many fields far from one another. Same way our languages. If you mix them they are no longer as good and useful. The corn is like our languages—we work to keep them separate" (Kroskrity 2000a:330).

Clearly one can see how the Tewas find a common pattern in their agricultural practice and in the dispreference for loanwords mentioned above. But one of the consequences of culturally proscribing mixing is that is keeps the linguistic repertoire of each language as distinct from the other as possible. Within this context of a deliberate cultivation of linguistic difference, and aided by a Tewa language ideology that sees language as a means of creating various social and personal identities (Kroskrity 1993:44–47, 193–212), code switching between the languages of their linguistic repertoire often provides a means for signaling relevant social identities by selecting their iconized and otherwise indexed languages (Tewa, Hopi, and English). Since there is a cultural recognition of a multiplicity of identities and the role of languages as a means of expressing them, the "cultivation of difference" further enhances the consubstantial relationship of Tewa language and identity.

TRADITIONAL NARRATIVES AND TEWA IDENTITIES

The capacity to speak Tewa is both a touchstone of Tewa identity and also a means of participation in the traditional narratives of the community. Those who do not speak Tewa can neither tell nor hear stories belonging to the *péé;yu'u* genre. As in contemporary San Juan Pueblo (Martinez 2004), the Arizona Tewas still tell traditional narratives that can be classified as either sacred or mundane. Sacred narratives are closely associated with historical accounts and with ceremonial contexts. Such tellings are intended only for the ears of initiated kin and religious sodality members. Unlike such esoteric narratives, *péé;yu'u* are viewed as mundane yet firmly tied to the home, to domestic practices, to the socialization of children, and to the maintenance of valued moral and cosmic orders. The *péé;yu'u* genre tends to presuppose children as focal, though not exclusive, audience members. As with other performance genres, *péé;yu'u* presuppose and prescribe sets of roles and role relationships between participants (e.g., Hanks 1996). Thus, a minimal participant structure would include an adult storyteller and one or more children who must periodically vocalize their ongoing attention and ratify the extended turn of the storyteller. In actual practice, most storytelling sessions are embedded in larger kin gatherings, with two or more adults rotating responsibility for storytelling to a collection of siblings, cousins, and occasional neighbors.

Proper performance in this genre is ideally reserved for winter evenings and usually the performers are adults, male or female, who perform for their immediate and extended families. Performances in the genre provide a domestic, "informal learning" style and developmentally early exposure to many of the key language ideologies embodied in the authoritative register known as "kiva speech" (Kroskrity 1998)—one that they will gain greater familiarity with as adolescents and young adults.

Performances in this storytelling genre are exclusively encoded in Arizona Tewa, thus illustrating an ideological conformity to indigenous purism. Illustrating the ideology of "regulation by convention," the genre has a relatively formulaic beginning and ending and almost always contains a brief song associated with the story's protagonists. In addition these stories display the quintessential marker of tradition in that narrators must use at least one evidential particle per clause. I have argued elsewhere that this is the ego-effacing voice that aligns the storyteller with a traditional past, thus using linguistic practice to locate—or, in this case, to erase—the identity of the speaker (a third language ideology). And finally the ideology of compartmentalization—these stories are told in everyday Tewa with strict avoidance of vocabulary indexing other levels such as "kiva talk" or "slang."

Thus Tewa *péé;yu'u* represent important resources for socializing Tewa children to cultural values that emphasize the traditional wisdom of the ancestors and the importance of collective versus individual identities. Even though these narratives are also directed at uninitiated children so young that they have no actual experience with the ceremonial system, it

is nevertheless especially noteworthy that many ideologies of Tewa storytelling converge with those of kiva speech (Kroskrity 1998) and preadapt
the child to appreciate the aesthetics of an indexical order anchored in the
exemplary ritual site (Silverstein 1998b) of Tewa religious and cultural
authority.

LOCAL IDEOLOGIES OF NARRATIVE EFFICACY

Describing the form of the stories does not account for why they are perceived as useful and powerful. Tewa ideologies of narrative efficacy associate them with two distinct kinds of growth. My first awareness of one
of these patterns came as quite a shock. I had been working for more than
five years on Arizona Tewa stories with my key consultant, Dewey Healing. Healing was an amazing man who composed new songs every year
for Tewa social dances, told many traditional stories, and had served in
the highest positions of tribal government both on First Mesa and as tribal
council chairman of the Hopi Tribe. He was certainly a practical man and
one who freely expressed cynical remarks about certain notoriously ultra-
conservative Hopis whom he had confronted while tribal chair.

Once, while we were taking a break after having checked, sentence by
sentence, the transcriptional accuracy of a story we had earlier recorded,
it dawned on me that, despite our deep involvement in analyzing the stories, I had not asked him a very basic question about his appreciation of
them. I spontaneously remarked, "You know, after working on these stories with you for so many years, I think I am beginning to understand why
they are so well liked and popular, but I haven't asked you directly, what
do you like about the stories?" Without missing a beat, Dewey made eye
contact with me, looked off ever so briefly, and returned his gaze to me,
saying, "I like the way they make the crops grow." His facial expression
was very serious—this was not one of his jokes. I was stunned, fumbled
with the controls of my tape recorder, and only hours later managed some
much-needed, follow-up questions. Yes, he really did believe that there
was a causal connection between telling these stories and the success of
his corn crop. Surely some of his beliefs surrounding the connection between storytelling and horticultural success will remain a mystery to me.
But was this an example of the Pueblo penchant for intricate cosmic orders
in which every thing and every action needed to be in its place? Winter
was the prescribed time for telling stories and also for hunting and gaming.

But, no! Storytelling, as I gathered from what Dewey told me, was indexically connected to more than hunting or gaming, and he guided me to see an analogy between telling stories to children and sprouting seeds into seedlings (a winter kiva practice)—"It makes them grow right."

Though space does not permit me to unpack this important cultural indexical connection here, I do want to observe that Healing's view is by no means idiosyncratic. In researching for her *Tewa Tales,* Elsie Clews Parsons (1926:7) noted, "On First Mesa, on concluding a tale, the narrator might stretch his arms out or up and say, 'May my melons grow so large, may my corn so high!'" Of course, Tewa narrators acknowledge the efficacy of storytelling not just on the plant kingdom but also on the socializing impact it has on raising their children. "We grow them," my consultants would say while pointing to either their children or grandchildren, "with stories. Our food makes them strong but our stories make them complete/good (*óyyó-'an*)."

This association with moral development is further revealed in two other ideological manifestations of varying degrees of explication. One was a folk definition of *péé;yu'u* that I elicited as part of a dictionary project. When I asked an accomplished storyteller and song composer how he would define that term, he gave a use-oriented definition that can be translated as "When people tell traditional stories, they are showing something good but also revealing something bad."

These fundamental dualistic morality tales usually break down into positive models provided by the family-oriented, team-player, work-ethic-endowed, and otherwise sociocentric characters like the Ant People, the Deer, and the Birds. These characters are usually depicted as teaching valuable skills to their young or engaging in group-oriented work invariably associated with culturally appropriate work songs, in contrast to the negative characters like Old Man Coyote or Coyote-Woman, who are represented as the antithesis of Tewa values: egocentric, dislocated, arrogant, lacking in decorum, and, of course, impulsive. In other stories, positive models are often aligned with village chiefs, as when they decide to use supernatural means to deal with the moral decay of their communities— the Pueblo counterparts to Sodom and Gomorrah—by using supernatural allies (like the god of the underworld, Maasaw) or an army of mangled Zuni warriors brought back from the dead) in order to "scare" their communities "straight."

A second manifestation of language ideologies that acknowledge the socializing role of stories appears in a culturally sanctioned rebuke of those who misbehave: "Didn't your grandmother ever tell you the stories?" The Arizona Tewa version of this rebuke is not as conventionalized and gender specialized as in other groups indigenous to the American Southwest, and Arizona Tewa speakers may insert other ascending generation kintypes into the grandmother slot. This may reflect a less-gendered practice of storytelling among the Arizona Tewas, where such skills in traditional narrative performance appear to be evenly distributed along gender lines and not disproportionately performed by women. This flexibility is also, no doubt, a by-product of contemporary social change in which more households are nuclear families and the participation of grandparents in the lives of their grandchildren is not as constant as it once was. In sum, traditional stories continue to be viewed by Tewa people as important, even powerful, resources for creating and maintaining both social and cosmic order.

LOCAL IDEOLOGIES OF NARRATIVE PERFORMANCE

As in the acquisition of the non-esoteric registers of Arizona Tewa itself, Arizona Tewa people neither require nor receive any formal training. Storytellers simply "catch on" (*maak'a-'an*) by hearing others tell the stories and gradually incorporating both the textual content and the ideals of narrative performance. Though many people agree on who are especially adept narrators, they rarely complicate this evaluative discourse by abstracting the criteria that motivate these distinctions. My extended discussion with knowledgeable performers embedded within a long-term ethnographic preoccupation with this genre and its performance practices did yield the following criteria:

1. The use of storytelling conventions, *péé;yu'u tú;* 'story words': Foremost among these conventions, and the most important grammatical/discourse resource for creating the voice of the traditional narrator, is the evidential particle *ba* 'so they say,' about which I have written more extensively elsewhere (Kroskrity 1985, 1993). These stories display the quintessential marker of tradition since narrators must use at least one evidential particle per clause. Example (1), from a recorded performance of "(Coyote and) Birds Story," represents a typical sentence.

(1) *Kídí di-da-kelen 'haedi ba*
    And then, after they got quite strong, so

'a:khon-ge-pe'e ba
over to the plain, so
'óóbé-khwóóli-n-di im-bi yiyá-'in-di.
they were flown by their mothers.

In most stories the evidential particle *ba* not only supplies the evidential information—the hearsay, second hand, "so-they-say" information—but also functions as a discourse marker of the storyteller's persona: these particles, for both the Arizona Tewa *ba* and their Hopi neighbors' *yaw,* appear two or three times per clause (Kroskrity 1997; Shaul 2002).[8] Suffice it to say that use of *ba* in these narratives is both the paramount traditionalizing trope (Bauman 1992) and genre signature (Shaul 2002) of Arizona Tewa *péé;yu'u* just as Hopi *yaw* is for Hopi *tutuwutsi.* I have also argued elsewhere that this usage helps narrators construct an ego-effacing voice that aligns the storyteller with a traditional past, thus using linguistic practice to formulate—or in this case erase—the identity of the speaker. Note that this linguistic construction of the authoritative voice of the traditional storyteller also preadapts young story listeners to a language ideology in which positional identities are discursively constructed.

2. Use of archaic words (*héyé tú;*) both in the dialogue of characters and in the narrative itself: Since most narratives in this genre are set in a vaguely distant past, this is a sort of authenticating move that establishes an older time period. The use of archaic expressions in everyday speech is very rare and judged as unusual, but it is not viewed as a violation of register consistency as in the case of uttering words that are indexed to kiva speech. The effect of Old Man Coyote saying *Némáha* 'marvelous,' in (2) below, when he sees a mother bird teaching her baby birds their flying songs is thus analogous to an English speaker using words like "hark" or "forsooth." These archaic words are heard as a discourse that allows us to understand the speaker as occupying an earlier historical time. Audience members do not see this as a style switch between slang, everyday, and ceremonial registers.

(2) Coyote: *Di háwákan 'óbí-'ó? Némáhá! Dii-khehedi-ná hama déh-khwóóle-mí-dí.*
Oh, so that's how you do it! Marvelous! I wonder if I could fly that way?

3. Use of stylized facial expression (*cee-po*) especially in the dramatic imitation of story characters: Narrators differ dramatically in terms of how they use conventional or more innovative facial expressions. In several tellings of a story about how the Ants squeezed Old Man Coyote to death by making him participate in an ordeal involving a rope tied progressively tighter around his waist, most narrators opened their eyes more widely, as if surprised, and more innovative narrators also opened their mouths and produced a feigned cry of pain.

4. Use of prosodic and paralinguistic effects by narrators to imitate the voices (*tú;*) of story characters: Imitating voices of story characters was typical of those narrators judged as more skilled. Old Man Coyote, for example, would often be portrayed in a deeper, gruffer voice than other characters. These distinctive voices permitted dialogue between characters without the need for a full identification of the speaker after each utterance.

5. Use of thematic songs (*khaw'*): For many narrators and audience members, songs are often viewed as important, even criterial attributes of the genre *péé;yu'u*. Audience members were quite explicit about the importance of a narrator having a strong, clear voice and displaying control of the tune. In all three of the stories that have been published to date, these songs are a conspicuous feature (Kroskrity 1985; Kroskrity and Healing 1978, 1981).

6. "Carrying it hither" (*-maadi-ma'a*), which can be paraphrased as situating the narrative for the present audience—the practice of recontextualizing story scripts to the needs and capacities of actual audiences: Bakhtin (1986:63) once observed that "not all genres appear to be equally conducive to reflecting the individuality of the speaker (or writer)," and here it is appropriate to extend this observation by suggesting that not all genres may be equally conducive to the interactive demands of recontextualizing (Bauman and Briggs 1990:72) a story text in performance to a unique audience. Tewa narrators of *péé;yu'u* appear to be torn between the apparent conflict of values that both stipulate highly conventional language, gesture, and song—on the one hand—yet demand that narrators somehow "carry hither" their stories, somehow recipient-design a traditional product. Arizona Tewa narrators must cope with the performer's paradox of working almost equally arduously to recontextualize these stories to the perceived needs and interests of their audiences and to erase any evidence of their innovative work.

SPEAKING THE PAST (AND THE PRESENT): TRADITION AND INNOVATION
IN TEWA NARRATIVES

The criteria above suggest a heavy reliance on conventional norms and an aesthetic cultural preference for stylized and established tropes and not for the innovations and explorations that are often valued in Western verbal art. Bauman (1986:78) has identified the relationship of tradition and innovation as one of the most fundamental questions for scholars of the verbal art of oral traditions: "Perhaps the most basic persistent problem confronted by students of oral literature is gauging the effect of the interplay of tradition and innovation, persistence and change, as manifested in the oral text." Though I suggest that there is an important difference between cultures and cultural actors in the kind of available stances on this interplay of tradition and innovation, I do not claim that Tewa narrators lack the ability to innovate or lack resources that allow them "to speak the present." Alton Becker (1979:212–13) rightfully observes that all forms of speech manifest both tradition and innovation, "speak both the past and the present." But though all language activity may consist of both, it is the proportion of each that distinguishes speech genres and their contextualized performances. In this section I discuss, on the basis of original ethnographic investigation first mentioned in Kroskrity (1993), how Tewa narrators effectively deploy several interconnected devices to achieve these ends. One is episode editing and elaboration. Subplots and tangential stories can be discarded, diminished, or developed as narrators see fit. A second is the use of traditionalization (Bauman 1992) achieved through both the frequent use of the *ba* particle and the disclaimer of novelty that it encodes, along with other performance conventions that project the ego-effacing perspective of the "traditional narrator." In a third device, authors deploy a variety of narrative and personal voices to promote flexibility while maintaining a basic adherence to valued narrative traditions.

One of the preferred ways to address the critical interplay of tradition and innovation is to use multiple versions of the same story (e.g., Bauman 1986; Briggs 1988; Hymes 1981, 2003). Though almost all of my field research on *péé;yu'u* has been based on elicited texts collected during summer research, I did have the opportunity in the winters of 1978 and 1981 to hear a total of nine stories performed by three different storytellers in two distinct domestic settings. Three stories, already familiar to me from prior fieldwork, happened to be performed among the ten to twelve stories that were performed on each of these occasions. I heard "Coyote Woman and the Deer Children" (Kroskrity and Healing 1981) performed by the same narrator on occasions several years apart and once again during the latter winter visit by another storyteller. I also witnessed two different storytellers perform "Ant Story" in the latter visit. Finally, I also had the pleasure of hearing two different raconteurs perform "Coyote and Bullsnake"— once during each of my winter visits.

A key set of resources for contextualizing traditional stories to specific audiences and particular contexts is provided within the "voice of the traditional narrator"—a culturally preferred positional identity associated with the ancestors. Within this ancestral voice, four distinct means of contextualizing are observable. The most salient of these in terms of textual impact is episode editing and development. In the two versions of "Ant Story" told by two different narrators, this was particularly apparent. Both versions featured the same basic plot, but their narrators devoted special attention to details they thought would interest and edify their audiences. The story's main plot concerns how a village of Ants manage to fool their nemesis, Old Man Coyote, into thinking that the delicate shape of Ants' waists is the result of their using a rope on each other to compress their middles. Coyote envies their shape and asks the Ants to perform the procedure on him. The Ants comply and, after making a strong rope, form two massive lines on each side to tug at the rope fastened around his waist. Coyote dies when the Ants use the opportunity to squeeze him to death while pretending to effect their beauty treatment.

In the first version of this story, I observed the performance of a grandmother before a domestic audience consisting of her husband, their two daughters, and three grandchildren (ranging in age from four to nine). Displaying a high involvement with the narrator through eye contact, body orientation, and periodic vocalization, the three grandchildren contrasted markedly with the less embodied adults, who provided appropriate vocalized responses but were often oriented to other activities—like cleaning up after dinner and organizing personal belongings—so that even gaze direction to the narrator was intermittent at best. Playing to her most attentive audience, the grandmother added some clarifying remarks about Ant social organization that did not appear in either the other performed version I heard or the one I had transcribed from elicitation sessions several years before.

Shifting gaze direction from grandchild to grandchild in an alternating sequence, the grandmother elaborated many details about Ant society— their clans, households, kiva groups—which served a double function of both describing a group that was organized much like their own Tewa Village community and in the process fostering identification with that community in the minds of the grandchildren who would use this either as an indirect way of learning about the organization of their own group or as a means of experientially and empathetically connecting with "good" story characters—those to which the children were to align morally. Importantly, this descriptive addition was traditionalized in the voice of the ancestral narrator, using *ba* and other conventions, even though this elaboration was an innovative contextualization designed to reinforce the children's understanding of their own traditional social norms at a time when their families and communities were experiencing unprecedented social change.

The other version of this story amplifies what is usually a minor subplot involving the Ants searching for suitable rope-making material that they will ultimately use on their gullible victim. In this elaborated version the Ants send out an expedition to a distant spring where they find a yucca-like plant that can be processed into a strong rope. This version was provided by a grandfather who knew that his audience included two grandsons who seemed to have a special affinity for learning about Native technologies. He has done similar elaborations in stories involving hunting, farming, and trapping episodes. But in this case the result is especially remarkable because the contextualization involves the expansion of a minor plot detail into a portion of the narrative that is longer than the exposition devoted to the main storyline.

Though episode editing provides a dramatic means of contextualizing performances and masking innovative textual elaborations as the reproduction of tradition, narrators do have other resources at their disposal that involve comparatively minor textual permutations. One of these devices involves the use of personal names associated with audience members; the other utilizes place names that are familiar to the given audience. An example of the former occurred in a version of "Coyote Woman and the Deer Children" told by a grandmother to an audience of family members, including two grandchildren. Similar to other versions I had heard earlier, her version included two minor textual differences that seemed to contribute to a dramatic change in contextualization. All versions displayed the same basic plot, in which a mother Deer advises her children about how to escape from Coyote Woman should the mother fall prey to her. These versions agree in depicting the young Deer siblings as struggling with both their sadness over their mother's death and their attempts to locate Old Man Beaver, who will presumably take them to safety across the river.

In stories told by men in my small sample, the men made the male
sibling the older, wiser one who was able to console his younger sister.
But in the grandmother's version the roles were reversed, with the sister
presented as the older, stronger, and more supportive sibling. It may be
wrong to attribute this performance strategy solely to the gender of the
narrator, since she is also recipient-designing the stories for her two grandchildren, who just happen to be the approximate ages represented in her
"Deer Children" story.

This strategy of promoting identification between the grandchildren
and their same-gender and age-similar story counterparts was further promoted by her use of the grandchildren's (Tewa) names for the Deer. When
I asked the storyteller later about this performance, she told me she was
aware that her (older) granddaughter was somewhat resentful of the extra
responsibilities for her younger brother that were associated with her status
as his *kaakhá* (older sister) and that she was trying to get her granddaughter
to see this as a special, and culturally valorized, relationship. Despite the
novel insertion of names, the storyteller reproduced the voice of the traditional narrator through her use of evidential *ba* and other traditionalizing
conventions including a reliance on dialogue between story characters.

In addition to personal names, the use of place names by storytellers
also contributes to the immediacy of storytelling performances. Similar
strategies involving place have been noted by Tedlock (1983:163, 291) for
Zuni storytellers. In "Bird Story" (Kroskrity 1985), Dewey Healing chose
to situate the narrative in the familiar topography of the First Mesa area.
T'ílí' Khyuge 'Hawk Cliff' is readily visible from Tewa Village, and it is
very experience-near for children who have grown up in the First Mesa
area. Resituating narratives in places that are part of the audience's local
knowledge and sensory experience provides a means of contextualizing
performances that contributes to their felt immediacy and relevance.

Another narrative resource is the use of embodied communication.
During the nine performances I saw, I observed narrators strategically use
such resources as tactility, eye contact, and body orientation while in the
voice of the traditional narrator. In many of these cases, the embodied
communication provided another means of innovating and contextualizing, while the verbal communication was offering the desired traditionalizing effect. In the elaborated version of "Ant Story" mentioned above,
during the digression about rope making the narrator made frequent eye
contact with the grandson whom he knew to have an exceptional interest
in Native technologies. Though it is customary for storytellers to distribute

their gaze evenly across the attentive and listening audience, this episode was marked by long periods of mutual gaze between narrator and grandson, providing an embodied parallel to the recipient-designing of textual elaboration and editing in the verbal channel.

In another example of strategic embodied communication, I observed the storyteller of "Deer Children" engage his oldest grandson in mutual gaze as he introduced the older (and, in his version, male) Deer sibling and then shift his gaze to a younger granddaughter seated next to him. As he touched her shoulder lightly with his outstretched hand, he introduced the younger Deer sibling. Though embodied communication is more difficult to interpret than the addition and deletion of verbal text in regard to interpreting either its intentionality or its intended function, I know that other narrators and audience members, when interviewed by me, were divided in their interpretation of this as a deliberate performance strategy or merely one that emerged "naturally" and "unconsciously" from the practice of an experienced storyteller. Though divided on issues of intentionality and awareness, those consulted were surprisingly unanimous in their interpretation of the meaning of the storyteller's embodied practices. "Of course, he wants the children to see the different persons in the story in a particular way and to know which ones to side with and think about in a certain way," was a representative response.

Though much of a *péé;yu'u* needs to be performed in the authority-conferring voice of the traditional storyteller, other types of voices are available to narrators, including those of story characters (in dialogue), their own personal voice, and even—rarely—voices from story-external sources. I have treated these in greater detail elsewhere (Kroskrity 1993); here I provide two brief examples. The first example is a narrator's choice to deliver a story-ending evaluative coda in his own voice and not from the more positional voice of the traditional narrator. Though Tewa stories are typically delivered without an explicit moral being drawn by the narrator, some narrators choose to provide one "as a teaching moment" and do so in their own personal voice, deliberately and abruptly stopping their use of Tewa *ba*, which had been deployed an average of two or more times in every preceding sentence of the story other than the actual represented speech of story characters.

In this example, the narrator performs the last sentence, as well as all prior sentences, of the narrative in the traditional voice of the narrator and then switches to a personal voice to spell out the moral of the "(Coyote and) Bullsnake Story":

1. Grandfather: *p'o [na-keledi ba*
                    since the water was strong—ba
2. Grandson 1:   *[hoy*
                    yes (m.)
3. Granddaughter: *[úh*
                    yes (f.)
4. Grandfather: 'óó-p'ohon kidi 'óó-p'ohey.
                    he was carried away and drowned.
5. Naéhaé in-nán naéin Naala péé;yu'u na-mu.
   This is the end of the Bullsnake story.
6. Kinán [bayaena-senó 'úú-pódi-yán
   Since *this* happened to Old Man Coyote
   [Grandfather gazes, smiling, in direction of granddaughter,
   seated to his right
7. towi' [wé-dii-su'odaedi
   a person should not imitate others.
8. Granddaughter: [heheha
                    [laughter]
9. Grandmother: mán-mowa
                    He finished.

In this brief strip of a story closing, a storyteller identified as Grandfather is viewed speaking the last narrative sentence and using *ba* as a
marker of his telling the story in accord with ancestral voices. The audience members, two grandchildren, each provide a gender-specific vocalization that is the expected sign of attentive listening behavior. They have
provided such vocalizations about every second or third narrative sentence
and have done so in near simultaneity with no clear pattern about who vo-
calizes first and no apparent attempt to coordinate exactly. But in line 5 the
storyteller announces the end of the story in his own voice and proceeds
to provide a brief moralizing, one-sentence coda. As he delivers the coda
he looks at his granddaughter. She laughs as her grandfather finishes his
moral. The storyteller's wife concludes the episode by explicitly noting
that her husband has finished his performance.

This particular performance contrasts in subtle ways with a published
version of a comparable elicited text (Kroskrity and Healing 1978:168),
since in that performance Dewey Healing provided a nearly identical evaluation but coded it in the voice of the traditional narrator, never stepping
outside of that persona. But the storyteller depicted above does mark the

move to a personal voice both by not using *ba* and by personally engaging with his granddaughter. His broad smile directed at her is a marked embodied departure from the stylized facial expressions and gestures associated with his positional identity as traditional storyteller. A follow-up interview with the storyteller revealed that he had made his daughter the locutionary target in this mild rebuke. His granddaughter had annoyed several family members through her habit of imitating a variety of media personalities she had been exposed to by magazines and television.

As a final example of a narrator using story-external voices, I offer one on the other side of the spectrum of subtlety, since it would be wrong to suggest that narrators are always so considerate of the feelings of their audiences or so nuanced in their performance. Indeed some storytellers have discussed their craft as similar to the activities of Tewa sacred clowns (*k'oyaala*) and claimed the right to critique and ridicule audience members for improper behavior. This is not a commonly held point of view, but it is often stated by older children as one of the reasons they have mixed feelings about attending a storytelling session. "You kind of never know when they might come at you with their stories, it's definitely not all 'fun,'" one teenage boy told me.

Certainly most of my short sample of naturally performed stories does suggest that most storytelling is done in a relaxed, warm, and very congenial atmosphere conducive to the very goals of telling *péé;yu'u*. I introduce an exception to this pattern in part because it serves to illustrate that not all storytellers do strictly conform to accepted canons of performance. During one performance of the "(Old Man Coyote and) Bullsnake Story," I witnessed a storyteller's growing dissatisfaction with the lack of participation by an older grandchild. Whereas other members of the audience were providing periodic vocalizations in accord with their traditional role expectations, an older grandson seemed indifferent to the entire storytelling event. In a performance frame-breaking move, the storyteller interrupted his own narrative with a code switch to English, turning to the offending party and asking, "Are you *present,* Billy? Say 'present,'" while glaring at his grandson before finally resuming his narrative.

This storyteller was invoking the norms of pedagogical discourse associated with the Euro-American educational system. He implicitly questioned his grandson's knowledge of the norms of this Native form of education by invoking the norms of participation that characterize the classroom. This was definitely viewed by all as an intrusive voice—even by those who judged his words to be both potent and, for some, justified.

This innovation may have been rhetorically effective, but it was ultimately regarded as improper—for though such intrusive voices may help carry the story to the listeners, it does not accomplish this in a manner that preserves tradition, in a manner that "speaks the past."

TRADITIONAL NARRATIVES AND "THE AUTHORITATIVE WORD"

Since Tewa traditional stories are presented as "authoritative" based on their connection to tradition, they invite comparison to Bakhtin's notion of "the authoritative word." Though a humble genre of domestic storytelling may seem a far cry from the religious dogma and scientific truths Bakhtin presented as his prototypes, I can conclude by reflecting on the appropriateness of his multifaceted notion of the authoritative word as a means of better understanding the Tewa genre and its performance goals. Bakhtin writes: "The authoritative word demands that we acknowledge it, that we make it our own; it binds us quite independent of any power it might have to persuade us internally; we encounter it with its authority already fused to it. The authoritative word is located in a distanced zone, organically connected with a past that is felt to be hierarchically higher. It is, so to speak, the word of the fathers. Its authority was already acknowledged in the past. It is a prior discourse" (1981:342).

This aspect of the authoritative word strongly suggests its value for us in understanding Arizona Tewa narrators and the manner in which they derive a special authority by connecting to the prior discourses of their valorized ancestors. So fused with authority are these mere folktales that even the most worldly and cynical Tewa villagers still find their explanations for landmarks, biological givens, and cultural practices more than "partially true." But Bakhtin also further develops his notion when he says, "It is not a free appropriation and assimilation of the word itself that authoritative discourse seeks to elicit from us; rather it demands our unconditional allegiance. Therefore authoritative discourse permits no play with the context framing it, no play with its borders, no gradual and flexible transitions, no spontaneously creative stylizing variants of it" (1981:343). Thinking omnivorously about authoritative discourse, Bakhtin attempts to locate and to understand the authority that underlies such diverse speech forms as ritual prayers and scientific formulae. But here is precisely where the applicability to Tewa storytellers breaks down. Though they recognize the need for authority-conferring connections, they know their stories are not the fixed-text prayers of ritual performance. They know that speaking the past into the present requires the agility to connect both with ancestral discourses and with the needs and interests of their children and grandchildren. They need to "carry" their stories "here."

Tewa storytelling ideologies thus prescribe a narrow but significant generic intertextual gap by recognizing the emergent aspects of storytelling performance and the need for recontextualizing story scripts in accord with the particulars (e.g., setting, participants, ends) of actual performance. Though these ideologies make a concession to the emergent properties of performance, they otherwise do valorize a particular regime of calibration that demands that individual performances closely conform to the genre's dominant emphasis on speaking the past—for, although ideologies of generic performance and intertextuality are widely recognized throughout the community, they are more selectively interpreted and enforced. As Bauman has observed concerning the politics of generic regimentation, "Prescriptive insistence on strict generic regimentation works conservatively in the service of established authority and order, while the impulse toward the widening of intertextual gaps and generic innovation is more conducive to the exercise of creativity, resistance to a hegemonic order, and openness to change" (2004:8).

Though Bauman is discussing a more general pattern, his remarks can be readily and profitably applied to the Arizona Tewa community. Those who speak against widening the intertextual gap, who voice opposition to the use of Tewa stories in schools, and who oppose the making of written Tewa texts are indeed mostly those who are closely tied to the established authority and order of ceremonial leaders.[9] Not surprisingly, those most associated with the upper echelon of the ceremonial hierarchies are most vocal about narrowing the intertextual gap and imposing the usual canons of kiva speech in attempts to authorize some performances and delegitimate others. Though they rationalize their actions not as acts of suppression but as a means of maintaining traditional standards, some community members can only interpret the stance of these "made people" (*paa t'owa*) as intolerant and unsympathetic to the needs of those who struggle to maintain contact with tradition.[10] This latter group includes many college-age young adults as well as the vast majority of younger children, who have had few opportunities to learn their heritage language let alone its esoteric registers. Also included in this tradition-marginal group are a significant number of middle-age adults and their families who have spent considerable time away from their First Mesa "homes" due to the need to gain

higher or specialized education or the need to find off-reservation employment. Their removal from the community often means a disruption in
their kinship and social networks that denies them access to those cultural
domains in which the Tewa oral tradition still prevails.

Though youngsters can experience tribal initiation even if their heritage
language fluency is weak, entry into all other valued ceremonial associations is still denied them through gatekeeping practices that require greater
fluency in Tewa. Even for those who have no ambition to attain higher ceremonial stations, there is often a desire to know Tewa as a heritage language.
Though most are aware that older members of the community regard Tewa
fluency as a marker of legitimate membership, almost all nonspeakers, or
those of severely limited fluency, say their desire to know their heritage
language has personal meaning to them as a means of understanding and
affirming their cultural identity. As one young man put it, "If I cannot speak
Tewa, how can I think like my folks, and their folks—like our ancestors."
A young woman said, "How do you fit in here if you cannot speak Tewa. It
is very limiting like I am in a corral or something. Without Tewa, I cannot
even connect to some members of my own family and clan."

Clearly this linguistically disenfranchised group has an opposing view
to that of the traditional elite regarding Tewa. The disenfranchised strongly
favor bringing the heritage language into the schools and adult education
classes, preparing Tewa story textbooks, and creating bilingual texts and
performances in Tewa and English. But such innovation, creativity, and
hybridity directed at unifying the Tewa community—no matter how useful or necessary it might appear to be—is overtly rejected by some elders
who see this sort of concession as "watering down" the heritage language
and culture. They say, "We have been doing it this way for hundreds, even
thousands of years. Why should we change things for this generation?
They need to change themselves and their ways." Though such words can
be interpreted as a harsh, Native version of "blaming the victim," the apparent intent of traditional leaders is not punitive as much as it is the rigorous maintenance of community values.

STORYTELLING FOR THOSE WHO CANNOT TELL THEM IN TEWA

Today the Arizona Tewas face a serious dilemma. The intracultural diversity of their communities, especially along generational lines, has produced
a basic division between those who "have" the Tewa narrative tradition

and those who do not. Caught in the middle are those who attempt to mediate by telling the stories in English. Example (3) below is transcribed from a recording of a narrator who must tell his story in English; neither he nor his family members are sufficiently fluent in Tewa to permit him to use the heritage language exclusively. But despite his obvious disjuncture of telling "traditional" narratives in a nontraditional language, note the attempts to traditionalize the introduction to this narrative.

> (3) Narrator: Oh, yeah, it's time now so . . .
> Once upon a time, so they say
> A chief, what the Hopis call a *kikmongwi*, . . .
> He, they say, was living there
> At a place, so they say, they call Walpi.
> We Tewas call it *Walabi*.
> And they say that at this time,
> He was not very happy.
> He was not very happy, they say,
> About how his people were choosing
> To live their lives. . . .

Though this narrator tells the story of "How the Walpi Chief and Maasaw Saved His Village" in English, he clearly has some idea that the performance should include a formulaic introduction ("once upon a time" on the model of Tewa *'owaeheeyámba*) and some translation equivalent for the evidential particle *ba*. This is certainly a performance by a narrator who is able to reproduce some Tewa discursive traditions in an English language narrative. But such performances are especially controversial. Though they are clearly informed by an awareness of Tewa narrative tradition, many Tewas reject such narratives as utterly inauthentic and even inappropriate because, in their English form, they violate such ideological tenets as indigenous purism and strict compartmentalization.

CONCLUSIONS

An attempt to produce an experience-near understanding of the Arizona Tewa genre of *péé;yu'u* has lead inevitably to local ideologies of the genre and its performance. Such ideologies lead in turn to the linkage of poetics and politics in the form of generic regimentation. In other intertextual explorations, I have attempted to suggest what might be termed a dual influence of kiva speech on *péé;yu'u* text-building and performance practices. Since the storytellers of *péé;yu'u* are adults who have become conversant with the norms of kiva speech through their own tribal initiations and ceremonial participation, they are guided by the traditional ways of speaking that are indexed to ceremonial efficacy, political (and moral) authority, and the tangible construction of Tewa tribal identity (Kroskrity 2000a). Under this influence, the intertextual convergence of storytelling on the model of kiva speech is quite pervasive even though many narrators and audience members acknowledge that traditional stories are not examples of the "authoritative word" and must instead be shaped by the needs and interests of a human novice audience rather than in accord with the dictates of supernatural or cosmic forces.

In addition to contestation regarding appropriate and authentic languages for traditional narratives, there is also the debate about appropriate and authentic sites for performing these stories. Perhaps expectedly, the two sides in this debate correspond to those who tell traditional stories in Tewa and those who do not. Those who do tell them still contend that Tewa homes are the only sites where Tewa narratives should be spoken or heard. This group has consistently opposed the use of Tewa stories in school settings. But those who do not enjoy narrative access in their homes—usually the younger, the less rooted—are more likely to voice the suggestion, and occasionally the demand, that schools be used as a means of continuing this tradition and as a place where the Tewa language and its storytelling traditions are taught. In a statement about performance variation that is useful here, Bauman observes:

> Taking responsibility for correct doing may impel a performer to close replication of past performance in an enactment of traditional authority, while distancing of a performance from established precedent may foreground the distinctiveness of present exigencies. Indeed, ideologies of performance—and of genre—characteristically foreground and valorize particular regimens of calibration, that is, expectations and values bearing on the degree to which individual performances should conform with or depart from what is taken to be normative for the genre. (2004:10)

Though Bauman is noting general patterns, his remarks allow us to better understand diverse perspectives as applied to the Arizona Tewa case where a conflict exists between those traditional leaders who represent "correctness" and "authority," on the one hand, and community members, as victims of massive language shift, who have unprecedented linguistic and discursive exigencies.

This is an ongoing struggle within the community, and it is an extremely consequential one. There is indeed little consolation in seeing the community unified regarding the potency of traditional stories when it appears hopelessly divided on legitimating or delegitimating nontraditional sites and languages of transmission. Given the valorized linkage for the Arizona Tewas of cultural reproduction and narrative performance, it is no wonder that traditional storytelling has emerged as a site of ideological contestation. In this struggle, clan elders can readily turn to the discourse of kiva speech for a culturally prescribed means of narrowing the generic intertextual gap associated with traditional stories and thereby limit the creativity and flexibility that would be necessary to be more inclusive. Such a metadiscursive move has the potential to deny access to storytelling to the vast majority of younger members of the speech community. Though few elders want to be responsible for the death of the Arizona Tewa language or the destruction of Arizona Tewa culture, they rationalize their stance as a nonnegotiable demand that those who have "failed" to acquire the language and its oral tradition conform better to cultural ideals. Though such words can be interpreted as a harsh, Native version of "blaming the victim," the apparent intent of traditional leaders is not punitive as much as it is the rigorous maintenance of community values. What is neglected in such a metadiscursive stance is the role of parenting generations in not actively promoting Tewa as a language of the home; the in-progress language shift is misrecognized not as a failure of parents and community but rather as a failure of the children (see also Kulick 1992, Reynolds 2009).

Though cultural reproduction and transformation are typically linked in theoretical discussions of sociocultural change (e.g., Giddens 1984:170; Kulick 1992), the relationship of these processes has become further intensified in actual Tewa language ideological struggles. It is possible to argue that the community cannot reproduce itself without considerable transformation aimed at inclusion of those now outside the inner discursive circle.

Two discourses, each with its own distinct intertextual basis in speech practices, have emerged as competing moral stances. In one, anchored in the unassailable logic of kiva speech, there is no flexibility—stories need to be told in home settings exclusively in the Tewa language. No schools, books, nonkin as teachers. But the other model, based on storytelling itself, provides a measure of flexibility. Can the ideal of "bringing it here" accommodate such novel textual practices as Native literacy, bilingual texts, school and other nondomestic settings? The morality plays of story content are thus paralleled by morality debates in which each side seeks to define relevant context and within them "responsibility." For those who situate their stance in the discourse of kiva speech, the relevant context is extremely local—Tewa families, clans, community. Responsibilities are all associated with maintaining ancestral traditions. But for the younger and less ceremonially connected, the relevant context is the intercultural complexity of their hybridized and transforming worlds, worlds in which considerable time must be spent away from "home" for economic and educational purposes, worlds in which more English is spoken than Tewa. For them responsibility is balancing these demands, and they are likely to find "irresponsibility" in their parents' generation for not speaking more Tewa to them as they were growing up.

As a linguistic anthropologist attempting to work with the community in its announced effort to engage in language revitalization, I am perhaps at the eye of the moral storm about stories. Although I appreciate the demand for adherence to traditional values by the "old guard" as an expression of the very strength that has permitted the Tewas to endure as a group, I can only wonder about the potential consequences of an intolerant stand that may silence the language they cherish. My only influence so far at the planning stages of a community-based language revitalization project has been to foster this same haunting wonder on the elders as we engage in acts of what I have elsewhere called "ideological clarification" (Kroskrity 2009b). Kiva speech so values tradition and indigenous purism that its norms demand replication of past ceremonial forms. Those guided by this model may opt to abandon the Tewa language and its discursive traditions in much the same way ceremonialists have abandoned actual ceremonies where there was insufficient knowledge transmitted to ensure their faithful reproduction.[11] Those guided by storytelling ideals—especially the need to "carry it here"—enjoy a more flexible and adaptive model. Within this stance inclusion could be more easily rationalized as the necessary steps dutiful performers must take to reach their audiences. But though storytelling is highly regarded by virtually all in the community, there are now certainly fewer accomplished storytellers than there are experienced ceremonial practitioners.[12]

It is useful to conclude this chapter by making two related points about storytelling. Both are tied to the capacity of stories and storytelling performances to construct and shape the identities of their participants. The first concerns what I would call the "moral force" of stories. These traditional narratives are saturated with moral significance. It is commonplace for both folk accounts and functionalist academic ones to view the propositional content of traditional stories, especially those designed for young listeners, as morally instructive, but moral stance taking also pervades their practice and the storytelling ideologies that inform those performances. Though the Tewa metadiscourse for this is comparatively more explicit than that of many groups, speakers in each of these languages recognize certain speech practices, especially those associated with traditionalization, as linked to their construction of moral authority. And though many storytelling ideologies are emblazoned in discursive consciousness, some performance practices evade explicit ideologization despite their apparent linkages to moral regimes. I am thinking here, for example, of the required audience vocalizations that are so necessary in Hopi and Tewa storytelling that Western Pueblo storytellers stop their stories in midstream when the audience fails to collaborate and cooperate respectfully in story production that is, for groups like the Tewas, at least, construed as a team performance. Yet, despite its obvious significance to outside observers and insider performers, this collaborative and interactive aspect of storytelling receives no local metalinguistic or metapragmatic attention. This morally saturated nature of storytelling at all levels probably accounts for why these genres are so valorized from within and so often viewed as a key, or even *the* key, cultural resource in responding to cultural crises like language endangerment.

My second observation concerns the narrative discriminations associated with narrative inequality (Hymes 1996). As part of a hegemonic project of the state, narrative discriminations associated with educational regimes that proscribed Native language and discourse further contributed to assimilationist national policies that aimed to erase linguistic and cultural differences. But within the Village of Tewa, the discriminations of narrative inequality are decidedly much more local. Because they are members of the same cultural group, there is more shared knowledge about storytelling practices and structures and none of the marginalization and trivialization (as mere children's stories; e.g., Perley, this volume) that one finds in the dominant society's view of traditional narratives. As evidence for their moral authority, the narrowing of a more shared generic gap thus represents an ideologically motivated deauthentication of those who would write Tewa, make bilingual textbooks, introduce Tewa language stories into classrooms, or tell "Tewa" stories in English. Of course, neither regime is enforced within what Goffman (1961) might call a "total institution." Suppression of indigenous languages may have produced the language shift to English but it also has, in the long run, fueled counter-hegemonic efforts to revitalize heritage languages and deploy indigenous narrative performance toward that end. The political power of Tewa elders in their home community is significant, but though they may determine the kinds of linguistic practices that go on in schools, it is doubtful that they can or even want to control linguistic practices in Tewa homes.

So what can we ultimately make of this ideological struggle over traditional stories? One can either hail this as a forceful expression of Tewa language ideologies, involving the need for cultural and linguistic purity and the need for making boundaries to external cultural influences, or deride it as a bitter moral and political struggle over inclusion and exclusion within an increasingly diverse Tewa community. Like the traditional narratives themselves, these contending views may thus be interpreted as illustrating something "good" and something "bad" in this story of how stories should be told.

NOTES

All transcription of Arizona Tewa follows the largely Americanist orthographic norms described in Kroskrity (1993) with three exceptions: (1) Vowel length is written here as a double vowel previously indicated by [V:]. (2) Nasal vowels are indicated by a following semicolon [V;]. (3) The front, low mid vowel previously written as [ɛ] is written here as [ae]. These changes are based on current discussions with Tewa villagers about an official writing system for the Village of Tewa although, as of this writing, no official orthography has been selected by the community.

   1. "Village of Tewa" is a relatively new, self-designated, official place name for the village on First Mesa, Hopi Reservation, in northern Arizona, occupied primarily by a group—distinct from the Hopis—who have been variously known as the Hanos, the Hopi-Tewas, or the Arizona Tewas.
   2. The description of *péé;yu'u* as "traditional stories" is primarily my translation of this indigenous genre label. My understanding of this word, based on

previous research, is that its primary denotational sense is a narrative genre characterized by familiar cultural content and practices of entextualization and recontextualization that are highly conventionalized. Tewa people identify this genre as consisting of fables and folktales that have been told countless times. These narratives are considered community property, and storytelling rights to such narratives—in contrast to clan histories or personal narratives—are not restrictively owned by specific clans, ceremonial societies, kiva groups, or individual authorities. In addition to content, Tewa members identify the genre with the established canons of performance and with conventionalized narrative practices of the type that can be analytically termed as "traditionalizing" (Bauman 1992). In a secondary sense the term *péé;yu'u* can denote any narrative.

3. For readers who are not familiar with contemporary Pueblo societies and their language ideologies and discursive practices, it is important to at least briefly note that many forms of heritage language use are closely regulated via practices that have been identified as external and internal secrecy (Brandt 1980, 1981). In many other Pueblo communities, including other Tewa-speaking pueblos like San Juan and Nambe, many forms of heritage language use are regulated. Native literacy materials are often strictly controlled, their availability limited not only to outsiders but to insiders as well. In the Arizona Tewa community, attempts to regulate the heritage language were once strictly limited to the esoteric registers of kiva speech. Recording or writing down the texts of ceremonial speech would potentially make these discourses available to those who were in the local view "unworthy" to receive this knowledge. But in recent years intracommunity debates have surfaced in which proponents of the older view are now challenged by those who seem to be informed about the regulatory norms of other Pueblo groups. Thus for some members, although not the majority, any written heritage language story may be viewed as esoteric knowledge that should not be made widely available. This is an especially controversial position because it would seem to undermine the collective and collaborative efforts of a prospective, community-wide language renewal program that is now in the planning stages and viewed as necessary by all factions (Kroskrity 2009b).

4. Most often this persistence is attributed to the need for using the Tewa language as a means for participating in the highly valued ceremonial system of the community (Crystal 2000; Dorian 1998) and as a consequence of local language ideologies being shaped by those surrounding the practices of kiva speech (Kroskrity 1998). Secondarily, the authors have also regarded Hopi tolerance of Tewa as a factor in Tewa language maintenance. Though the second point warrants more discussion than I can here afford it, it is important to acknowledge Hopi tolerance in a manner that contexts Hopi belief and practices of "tolerance"

in the larger pattern of Tewa bilingual accommodation to the Hopi majority. Except for Tewa homes, Hopis are spoken to by Tewas in Hopi.

5. Though there are hundreds of speakers in both the older (forty to fifty years) and elder (fifty-one to ninety years) generations, younger speakers typically demonstrate greater English dominance and less fluency in Tewa. Since the population is skewed to youth, the current comparative abundance of knowledgeable elders hardly ensures the viability of the language. In fact, the local recognition of a "sociolinguistic tip" (Dorian 1989) in progress is what led several members of the community to reach out for advice and assistance from professional linguists like myself in 2006.

6. By "objectivist" I mean the strictly analytical perspective that does not concern itself with the local categories involved in a perspective that attempts a more phenomenological or, in Geertz's parlance, "experience-near" point of view. In my attempt to unpack the manifold ways that language and identity are intertwined for the Arizona Tewas and their Tano ancestors, both of these complementary strategies for understanding produce convergent results. Thus some of the evidence for the connection of language and identity can be read directly from the "facts" of historical linguistics whereas others require ample contextualization of actual linguistic practices, like code switching, and a more interpretive approach toward local meanings of the Tewas themselves.

7. For more details about these loanwords and how they were identified, see Kroskrity (1993:67–77).

8. In both Hopi and Arizona Tewa text samples, the number of evidential particles is between two and three per clause, clearly in excess of what would be grammatically necessary. For more precise numbers based on actual text counts, consult Kroskrity (1997). For a comparative discussion of this usage placed against a larger typological context of the role of evidentials in discourse, see Aikhenvald (2004:312–13).

9. Their pragmatic and metapragmatic calibration is primarily of a type identified by Silverstein (1993:53) as "nomic," where "such forms constitute mechanisms for *authorization* of a particular event, grounding its event-status in the authority of some non-experienced realm" such as mythic, sacred, and ceremonial orders. "Nomic calibration" is part of a typology of metapragmatic calibration first suggested by Silverstein (1993).

10. Note that this kind of marginalization and "erasure" of a group judged by the powerful to be discursively defective is somewhat similar to the pattern of hegemonic marginalization imposed by the Indonesian state on various forms of Sumbanese genres of "ritual speech" (Kuipers 1998). The difference here, of course, is that the discursive regimentation and marginalization are being

exercised not by a nation-state on a minority cultural group but rather within a relatively small community.

11. Ceremonial elites and other important ceremonialists are depicted in Tewa stories and the scholarship on Western Pueblos like the Hopis as having a special responsibility for the moral well-being of their communities. Sometimes this sense of responsibility leads to the conclusion that the group is beyond repair and can be saved only by destroying the social order, as in some local accounts of the destruction of the Hopi village of Old Oraibi (e.g., Whiteley 1988).

12. Greg Sarris's (1993) representation of his Pomo community and Deborah House's (2002) discussion of Navajo factionalism in regard to the evaluation of the heritage language and its associated ceremonial and other verbal culture provide useful reminders that Native communities are not unanimously in favor of promoting traditional oral culture, whether in situations of formal (e.g., schools) or informal (e.g., homes) education.

CHAPTER 9

SILENCE BEFORE THE VOID
Language Extinction, Maliseet Storytelling, and the Semiotics of Survival

Bernard C. Perley

The third-grade students in the classroom were agitated with excitement because the Native language teacher was going to tell them a story. After everyone in the classroom had settled down to listen, the teacher began telling the students that they were going to hear a Kloskap story. The teacher then asked, "Does anyone know who Koluskap is?"[1] One student straightened up and said, "Yeah, that's what my mom calls my dad!" The teacher and I both smiled as we suppressed our laughter; the name "Koluskap" has been translated into English as "liar."[2] The teacher proceeded to explain to the students that Kloskap was the Great Chief of the Maliseets. He was responsible for transforming the landscape and the animals so that the Maliseets could live happy lives. After that brief introduction, the teacher began to read "The Coming of Gluskabi" from Michael J. Caduto and Joseph Bruchac's 1998 text *Keepers of the Earth*. After the reading of the story she instructed students to draw and color their favorite part of the story.

The above ethnographic vignette is typical of the storytelling portion of the Native language class at Mah-Sos Elementary School on Tobique First Nation in New Brunswick, Canada.[3] The vignette is an example of significant changes in Maliseet language use and Maliseet storytelling practice. Not only was the story presented in English, the story was *read* to the students. The absence of the Maliseet language in the Maliseet language classroom during a story reading is indicative of a dangerous juncture for Maliseet language use and Maliseet storytelling practice. That juncture is *the silence before the void.*

What do I mean by "silence"? It is rare to hear the traditional Maliseet stories told in the Maliseet language. Maliseet communities are witnessing the silencing of the Maliseet language in most cultural domains—

particularly storytelling. What do I mean by "the void"? Language scholars and advocates have argued that the loss of a language is a loss of "diversity" of distinct cultures (Crystal 2000; Grenoble and Whaley 1998; Hinton and Hale 2001; Mithun 2004; Nettle and Romaine 2000), "human knowledge" (Crystal 2000; Harrison 2007; Wilson 2005), and "identity" (Crystal 2000; Wilson 2005). The Maliseet void, then, is the loss of distinct culture, distinct knowledge, and distinct identity. The gradual loss of the Maliseet language in Maliseet storytelling, the retelling of Maliseet stories by non-Maliseet storytellers and scholars, and the predominant use of English while *reading* Maliseet stories are key transformations in Maliseet storytelling that present several linguistic and cultural dangers for Maliseet communities. The greatest of these dangers are the extinction of the Maliseet language as well as the collateral extinctions of distinct Maliseet culture, knowledge, and identity. The precarious state of the Maliseet language and Maliseet storytelling practice is the result of a long process of transformation.

I had returned to my birthplace to do my anthropological fieldwork in the mid-1990s. My primary focus was on language politics in Canada and the causes of Maliseet language endangerment. I have learned that there is no simple explanation for how or why the Maliseet language and Maliseet storytelling practice have reached states of endangerment. However, an exploration of Maliseet storytelling transformation over the past one hundred years can provide some insights into the kinds of changes that lead to Maliseet stories now being read in English and the Maliseet language now in danger of becoming extinct.

The focus of this chapter is Maliseet storytelling that has been variously categorized as legends, tales, texts, and stories by scholars over the past century. The common characteristic in the collections discussed here is their respective representations of Maliseet oral poetics.[4] These categories and representations often reflect the ideologies of their particular times (Bauman and Briggs 2003; Briggs and Bauman 1992). When viewed in isolation they do not reveal the trajectory toward language death and storytelling silence, but by comparing representations across texts the trajectory toward silence can be summarized as a series of representational shifts. The first indicates a shift from the oral performance to textual representation, or from interdiscursivity (face-to-face conversations and storytelling) to entextualization (writing down face-to-face exchanges into textual form) (Silverstein 2005). The second representational shift is from early collections of texts to varieties of contemporaneous representations.

This shift may be analyzed as a move from entextualization to generic intertextuality (creative rewriting of stories from previously written texts) (Briggs and Bauman 1992). The third shift is from popular representations to oral poetic practice. I describe this phase as a shift from intertextuality (creative rewriting of stories from previously written texts) back to inter-discursivity.

These three shifts also reflect changes in salvage ideologies. The first period, late nineteenth- and early twentieth-century salvage anthropology, was "salvage work as documentation." The second period of salvage work, the early 1960s, was "salvage work as preservation." The third (and current) mode of salvage work is "salvage work as revitalization." These shifts in representation and salvage work can be summarized as *entextualization as documentation*, *intertexuality as preservation*, and *interdiscursivity as revitalization*. To facilitate the analysis, I compare different representations of a Maliseet story describing the origin of the Tobique Rock. The story is of particular importance to Tobique First Nation because the "rock" is located at Neswakik on Tobique First Nation. The changes in representing the story in the three periods identified above reflect the changes in Maliseet language use in Maliseet stories.

The Maliseet story of the Tobique Rock is shared by many First Nations communities, including the Passamaquoddy people (who speak a "mutually intelligible" dialect of an Eastern Algonquian language (Goddard 1978:70; LeSourd 2007:viii), Penobscots, Abenakis, and Micmacs. Including the Maliseets, these five nations constitute the Wabanaki Confederacy, and today members of the Confederacy refer to themselves collectively as "the people of the dawn." The Wabanakis are also "Algonquin" because they speak (or spoke) varieties of Eastern Algonquin languages. The geographic center for the ethnographic examples and discussion in this chapter is the Maliseet community of Tobique First Nation, New Brunswick, Canada. However, the examples also come from neighboring areas of northeastern North America along the national border where the other Wabanaki nations are located. The spelling and nomenclatural variations reflect the representations used by the storyteller or collector.

THE POETICS OF EXTINCTION

The Maliseet language has been diagnosed as "on the verge of extinction."[5] There are many factors contributing to Maliseet language death. Most of them are similar to those identified by Schmidt (1990) as the loci of language death and attrition: assimilatory pressures from educational institutions, the hegemonic role of the mass media in further promoting English and other state languages, and missionization—a process that further bolsters the state-endorsed religion and language. Additional factors that contribute to the endangerment of Maliseet include massive social change and the metamorphosis of speech communities through social transformations such as mixed marriages, emigration, relocation, and, most important, cessation of Native language use in particular speech genres in particular speech events and domains.

Maliseet storytelling is just one of many Maliseet speech genres that have undergone radical transformation. This chapter focuses on scholars and storytellers who have *represented* Maliseet texts at three different times over that the past 120 years. I use the term "representation" instead of "translation" to foreground the initial separation of Maliseet stories from Maliseet voices and Maliseet people through the process of writing down what Maliseet speakers and storytellers had said into a textual form that can be reinterpreted at a later time.[6] This process of rendering discourse into text is also informed by the methods and practices of each period of time. Each "scholar" (translator) renders cohesiveness and coherence to texts as conditioned by his or her milieu. A close examination of the early representations of Maliseet texts by Charles G. Leland at the turn of the nineteenth to twentieth century illustrates "salvage work as documentation" through entextualization.

Leland stated, in 1884, that his collection of Algonquin legends was his attempt "simply to collect and preserve valuable material." His reason: "I believe that when the Indian shall have passed away there will come far better ethnologists than I am, who will be more obliged to me for collecting raw material than for cooking it." Leland's modesty seems disingenuous when one sees how he "cooked" the corpus of Algonquin stories by compiling them into a form that supported his argument that the collected stories were the equal of any Norse saga (Leland 1992) and that the mythology was "far grander" than Schoolcraft's Chippewa corpus (Leland 1992:iii; Parkhill 1997). In his introduction, Leland makes his argument for the merit of the Algonquin legends, but he erases Algonquin interpretations of the stories by privileging his own interpretations: "When it is born in mind that the most ancient and mythic of these legends have been taken down from the trembling memories of old squaws who never understood their inner meaning, or from ordinary *senaps* who had not thought of them since boyhood, it will be seen that the preservation of a mass of prose poems, equal in bulk to the Kalevala or Heldenbuch, is indeed almost miraculous" (Leland 1992:13).

Leland's representation of the Tobique Rock story is in prose and in English only.

> Up on the Tobiac are two salt-water rocks (that is, rocks by the ocean-side, near a freshwater stream). The Great Beaver, standing there one day, was seen by Glooskap miles away, who had forbidden him that place. Then picking up a large rock where he stood by the shore, he threw it all that distance at the Beaver, who indeed dodged it; but when another came, the beast ran into a mountain, and has never come forth to this day. But the rocks which the master threw are yet to be seen. (Leland 1992:21)

Though this excerpt seems unremarkable by itself, a comparison with his 1902 version reveals a change in Leland's philosophy regarding representing Algonquin "legends":

> Yet another tradition tells
> That after cutting the dam
> The Master sat and watched,
> And yet no Beaver came forth,
> For Kwabit had escaped by a hole
> Which led back to the other side;
> Kulóskap then tore up
> A rock and he threw it
> Very far indeed,
> One hundred and fifty miles,
> To frighten the Beaver back;
> But over the Grand Falls
> Kwabit had gone in haste
> And so for the time escaped;
> Yet the stone remaineth there
> As a wonder to this day. (Leland and Prince 1902:115–16)

This second representation of the Tobique Rock story was a collaborative project with John D. Prince in their 1902 publication *Kulóscap the Master*. This is a significant departure for Leland because he has rendered his collected stories in "English metre" and enlisted the assistance of Prince to "revise, correct, and compare [his] metrical version with the original text" (Leland and Prince 1902:13). He recalls that he had heard the stories were originally sung in verse and wanted to produce an authentic version by reinterpreting them in verse. He rationalizes this new representation: "A few of the poems contained in this volume have already appeared in prose form in the 'Algonquin Legends of New England.' As these were in fact poetry, or chanted in rude measure, I had at first the intention to give them in English in their original form and to group all those referring to the divinity in an epic, as Lonnrot made the Finnish Kalevala, or Homer his own great works. This I have to a degree accomplished in the present volume" (Leland and Prince 1902:15–16).

This statement reveals Leland's preoccupation not only with polite literary sensibilities but also with his projected audience. In short, Leland was intent on preserving the "poetry" but not the "rude measure" of Algonquin poetry and chants. He is clearly conflicted about his new representation: "I with great care put the Mitchell Anglo-Algonkin into English metre, having been impressed, while at work, with the exquisitely naïve and fresh character of the original, which, while it often reminded me of Norse Poetry, in many passages had strictly a life and beauty of its own" (Leland and Prince 1902:12).

There is no question that Leland had high regard for Algonquin epic poetry, but his representation was rendered into polite literary forms rather than Algonquin "rude measure." Leland's "poetics" effectively erased Indian voices from their own stories, and Leland's and Prince's authorial license could be justified by their anticipation that the audience for their representations were people of European descent with modern literary sensibilities. It seemed, by the end of the nineteenth century, that the erasure of Indian voices was a regrettable inevitability. As Leland notes, "I venture to say from the deepest conviction that it will be no small occasion of astonishment and chagrin, a hundred years hence, when the last Algonkin Indian of the *Wabano* shall have passed away, that so few among our literary or cultured folk cared enough to collect this connected aboriginal literature" (Leland and Prince 1902:15).

Leland's collaborator in the epic poem, John Dyneley Prince, shared Leland's sentiment about the vanishing race: "Let then our labor in this work suffice merely to present to the English-speaking public a few interesting and characteristic specimens of the traditions of a rapidly perishing race—a race which fifty years from now will have hardly a single living representative" (Leland and Prince 1902:40). Leland's estimate of the projected extinction of the Wabanaki peoples was one hundred years and Prince's estimate was fifty years. Both men were convinced that the Indians would disappear but that their own important salvage work of writing down the "poetic" speech (entextualizing) and documenting the stories would live on.

Prince continued to work on his own Algonquin legends project and in 1921 published his *Passamaquoddy Texts*. What had changed in the intervening years? Prince distinguishes his collection from the others as a reproduction from memory of original documents that were destroyed in a fire in 1911. He states that "other matter" has appeared in other publications in "imperfect form." Specifically, "poetical and inexact English renderings of some of the Kuloskap material . . . have appeared in Leland and Prince 'Kuloskap the Master'" (Prince 1921:3). In Prince's revisiting of the previous representations, he clearly is uncomfortable with the "imperfect" forms the 1902 representations took. His key points of contention are the poetic forms and the English forms of the earlier representations. His 1921 Passamaquoddy collection represents his solution to achieving representational accuracy (or perfection, as Prince insinuates).

Some important differences between Leland's representation and Prince's begin with Prince's introductory notes. Prince explicitly mentions the Maliseet as part of the Algonquin family, whereas Leland never mentions the Maliseet at all. Prince makes no mention of Indians vanishing or becoming extinct. Instead, he presents a couple of pages devoted to a phonological explanation of his Passamaquoddy transcription. Despite representing the "tales" in prose, a key additional difference is in the fact that he also represents them in the aboriginal language, Passamaquoddy. His representation of the Tobique Rock story (Prince 1921:38–39) provides a marked contrast to Leland's "imperfect" representations:

> *Kuloskap potmat nidcans'l; etudi-wikweta'kw sopek-apskw naka w'telakan kwilotanhan; pekw's en nil'muk Ne(k)wutkok. Nit-te metc-teke etek epastuk Wulastukuk.*
>
> Kuloskap drives away the young one; he picks up a salt water rock and throws it, seeking to hit him; it sticks fast by Ne(k)wut-kook. It is still there right in the middle of the St. John's River.

The most significant difference between Prince's and Leland's versions is the inclusion of Passamaquoddy text on the preceding page opposite the English text. Prince has moved away from Leland's preoccupation with polite literary forms, scholarly obsession with world-class epics, and the uncritical representation of Maliseet (Passamaquoddy) voices. Instead, Prince's use of Passamaquoddy and his word-for-word translation is his attempt to minimize the distance between face-to-face storytelling by aboriginal storytellers (the interdiscursive breach) and nonaboriginal readers.

These three different versions of representing the Tobique Rock story, and their authors' statements regarding the imminent disappearance of the Maliseet people, reveal the prevailing attitude toward collecting and writing down Maliseet texts as "salvage work as documentation." Each text draws from a prior discursive practice (storytelling event) that required breaking the discursive continuity in order to create bounded texts that could be taken out of aboriginal communities (decontextualized) and repackaged and retold (recontextualized) for audiences with literary sensibilities. This was the beginning of the uncoupling of the Maliseet stories from the Maliseet language. Equally important, it anticipated the uncoupling of the Maliseet language from the Maliseet people. In less than five decades, a new round of representations of Maliseet stories would coincide with a new phase of salvage work that perpetuated the "vanishing Indian" sentiment as well as the continued transformation of aboriginal stories into literary representations. It was also the time when the Maliseet language "tipped" toward the void.

INTERTEXTUALITY AND TIPPING TOWARD THE VOID: "REWRITING THE STORIES"

The Leland and Prince representations of Maliseet stories were produced in a period of "salvage work as documentation." Documentation by writing down purported face-to-face storytelling events initiated the uncoupling of the Maliseet language from Maliseet stories. Fifty years later, a second phase of salvage work continued the uncoupling of the Maliseet language from Maliseet stories, but it also initiated the uncoupling of the Maliseet language from the Maliseet community. But first, the process of "writing it down" uncoupled the stories from their aboriginal contexts. This was accomplished through entextualization because the process rendered the oral poetic event as an object, which, in turn, "serves to render the text extractable from the context of production" (Bauman 2004:4). This is significant because the act of "writing it down" allows the scholar or reader to place the "text" into new settings and toward new purposes.[7] In the Maliseet case, the processes of taking the stories away from Maliseet contexts (decontextualization) and redirecting them to non-Maliseet audiences (recontextualization) indicates a shift from *performance* to *reading*, as evidenced by the opening vignette. This shift is accomplished through processes of rewriting the stories (intertextuality) that also unwittingly initiates "salvage work as preservation" processes.

In 1962, three weekend folklorists were collecting folktales to fulfill a Saturday extension course requirement.[8] One of the trio submitted two seven-inch reels of tape and "about twenty pages" of text to the instructor.[9] The editor (and instructor), Edward Ives, recounts his own surprise that stories are still being told by Maliseet storytellers to Maliseet audiences. In his introductory comments regarding the provenience, contextualization, and editing of the collection, Ives shares thoughts regarding the displacement of aboriginal antiquity with civilizing modernity:

> Now the birchbark canoes are in the museums, what wigwams there are are in the tourist business, and the Indians are in the reservations. They wear the white man's clothes, practice his religion, go to his schools, and eat his food. Acculturation has gone a long way here in the Northeast, and it will go even farther, we can be sure, perhaps even to a time when the old ways will not even be what they are today: a tale, a legend, a bright place in the forest dark at the back of the mind, something told in the old tongue by a mother to her daughter of a long winter evening. (Ives 1964:6)

Ives's sentiments are the perpetuation of discourses of "vanishing" inherited from fifty years earlier. According to him, the Indians may not be vanishing but their aboriginal way of life certainly is. Ives's phrase "something told in the old tongue by a mother to her daughter" suggests that despite the success of acculturation he has been privy to unexpected primordial continuity of aboriginal interdiscusive practice.[10] Significantly, Ives notes that the storyteller "preferred to tell her tales in Malecite rather than English," but this did not prevent him from editing out the original discursive representation in Maliseet. His "writing down" of aboriginal face-to-face storytelling was intended "to make the stories easier to read." Ives accomplished this by omitting "meaningless" phrases, providing titles for the stories, standardizing spelling, and making omissions but not

noting all of them, among others. Just as Leland had done fifty years earlier, Ives was representing aboriginal stories in an intertextually (an alien
"literary" form) suitable form for a literate audience. Just how was this
accomplished, and what are the results of this "readability" editing?

> [Kluskap] picked up a rock and tried to hit him, but this beaver
> was too smart, too fast for him. He went up the St. John River,
> and the first hiding place he came to was going up on that Pokiok
> Falls. That's where he struck the first rock landed. So this beaver
> thought that was too much for him. So he went further up the St.
> John River, and right now you can see them rocks. I mean you
> can't now; since they built the dam [i.e. at Beechwood] they're
> all under water. There's two big rocks. [[Speaking to her daugh-
> ter, Mrs. Black]]: You've seen them, huhh? [Mrs. Black:Uhmhm].
> They call [them] "Tobique Rocks." There's one about three miles
> below Perth and one right here at the mouth of the Tobique. Well,
> a little below. [[Aside:]] Oh, right here! I thought I was over in the
> point! [i.e. at the reservation]. And one at the Grand Falls. That's
> what made the falls. (Ives 1964:17)

Ives indicates that the story was transcribed from a tape recording.
His editorial contributions were marked with brackets and underlined
words. Stage directions, gestures, and false starts were omitted. Ives's entextualization does reflect more colloquial speech forms than do the representations of the Tobique Rock stories described earlier. Through his
editing process, Ives did attempt to preserve the immediacy of the interdiscursive exchange; but, in the end, it is still a text artifact designed to
have greater "readability." Ives consciously shifts from discursive forms
to literate forms. He does so in English despite having a recording of the
Maliseet available for transcription. The decision to render Maliseet stories into readable and literate forms would be echoed by a contemporary
non-Maliseet "storyteller" who made no attempt to evoke the immediacy
of aboriginal (Maliseet) interdiscursivity.

 While Ives was writing down a storytelling event, Kay Hill, another
storyteller in the Canadian Maritimes, promoted her own representations
of Wabanaki stories. Hill's work is an example of stories rewritten from
previous publications and texts (entextualization as intertexuality). Her
goal was to retell the stories for public consumption. The venue for public
consumption was television. In the short, two-plus pages of the foreword

to *Glooskap and His Magic: Legends of the Wabanaki Indians* (1963), Hill describes her involvement in representing Wabanaki stories as a part of a larger production:

> These stories, so far as we know, were first told in the wigwams of the Wabanaki Indians, long before the White Man came to North America. Later, white men learned them from the Indian, translating and preserving them in book form. In August, 1960, I was invited to adapt the published Legends to a new art form, that of television, for a program called "Indian Legends," conceived and produced by Mr. Sandy Lumsden of CBHT, Halifax, Nova Scotia. Miss Kathleen Currie, Chief Librarian of the Children's Department of the Halifax Memorial Library, dressed in Indian costume, appeared before the cameras and related the stories, with graphics and background music and sound. (Hill 1963:7)

I quote at length to include Hill's summary history of "Indian Legends" and the role she played in the television production. Although it is not explicitly stated, the White Man learning the stories and preserving them in book form evokes the idea of vanishing cultures expressed by Ives and Leland. Curiously, Hill goes on to describe the chief librarian "dressed in Indian costume" relating the stories accompanied by the "graphics and background music and sound" that only television can make possible. These comments and activities indicate the growing distance between Maliseet language and Maliseet stories. The separation of Maliseet voices from Maliseet people (decontextualization) and the repackaging and rewriting for non-Maliseet audiences (recontextualization) underscore the shift toward collateral uncoupling of the stories from Maliseet language, landscape, and experience. Hill's "literary" retelling of Wabanaki stories does not include the Wabanaki people. The irony in her participation in the television program is that not only are white men and women telling Indian stories, they are "playing Indian" too.

Kay Hill was not the one "playing Indian," but she was the one invited to entextualize the "Indian Legends." Her involvement in the television program led to her subsequent project of "preserving" her representations of Wabanaki stories in book form. The television show became entextualized as a children's book, thereby relegating the Wabanaki stories to the status of children's stories. But the prior representations from original discursive events did not conform to literary standards, and Hill was compelled to render them suitable for children:

> Much of the original material meticulously recorded by Rand and Leland was found to be unsuitable for an audience of children. Although generally moral in tone, the Legends contained a great deal of religious symbolism, meaningful only to the Indian, as well as some savage and erotic elements. They were inclined to wander down byways in the course of which the characters changed disconcertingly not only from good to evil, but from human to animal. Children today are accustomed to the Aristotelian concept of a unified story with a beginning, middle, and end. It therefore seemed necessary to tighten plots, develop characterization, and invent incidents to explain motivation. In doing this, I merely followed the example of the Indian storytellers themselves who, in passing on the songs and poems of the Old Time, departed in a large degree from the original poetry, omitting some incidents and adding others as memory served. (Hill 1963:8–9)

It is unclear whether Hill means children of European descent or a universal "all children." What is certain is her self-assuredness in assuming authorial discretion in the editing of Wabanaki stories. Her justification that she is "merely following the example of the Indian storytellers themselves" does little to acknowledge the absence of Wabanaki voices. Her intertextual representation (rewriting from Rand and Leland) of the stories in an "Aristotelian concept" of children's stories is a decontextualization of Wabanaki stories that are subsequently stripped of their linguistic and cultural contexts.

Unfortunately, Hill did not entextualize the Tobique Rock story. It would have been interesting to compare her version to Ives's. In any case, both authors/editors anticipated a reading public who are not Maliseet (or Wabanaki). Their literary presumptions in rewriting Maliseet stories into English furthered the uncoupling of the stories from the Maliseet language and Maliseet contexts. Despite the presence of contemporary Maliseet and Wabanaki peoples, the authors/editors overlooked the face-to-face storytelling practices that were occurring while their respective texts were being published. In the 1960s, then, the Maliseets had already vanished from their stories. It seemed that all that was left to do was salvage what was left of Indian stories by "preserving" the stories in book form. Ives's representation of Maliseet stories is the 1960s break with interdiscusivity, and Hill's representations illustrate intertextuality in practice. Taken together, Ives and Hill display key differences in rewriting Maliseet stories. Ives attempts to bring some fidelity to the storytelling genre, whereas Hill takes basic elements from Wabanaki stories to render them appropriate for television and popular children's books. Both, however, direct their (inter) texts to nonaboriginal audiences.

These two approaches to rewriting Maliseet stories coincide with active processes of assimilation and enculturation in Canada in the 1950s and 1960s. While non-Indian storytellers were publishing repackaged and rewritten story collections, other agents working in and near Indian communities were working to dis-integrate Indian people from Indian language, culture, and identity through programs of "enfranchisement" by amending the Indian Act (Clatworthy 2003). The assimilatory forces that continued to dis-integrate the Maliseet language from Maliseet people and Maliseet worlds would find their greatest expression in Canada's White Paper of 1969, the policy to abolish the "Indian Act" (Royal Commission on Aboriginal Peoples 1996:17) and thereby eliminate the category "Indian" from government programs and services. The assault on aboriginal worlds contributed to the loss of the Maliseet language in Maliseet storytelling, forced restriction of Maliseet language use in Maliseet communities, and tipped the Maliseet community of Tobique First Nation toward the void of language death.

Awareness of these collateral extinctions made the "preservation" of Maliseet stories by nonaboriginal story collectors a worthy endeavor. However, what was being preserved had less to do with the Maliseet and more to do with the preservation of the nonaboriginal imagination. The reinterpretation of Maliseet stories as literary products indicates how great the gap between Maliseet stories and Maliseet worlds had become.[11] Not only are the stories written in English, but they are also directed at non-Maliseet audiences. Nevertheless, this did not preclude the possible reintegration of Maliseet stories with the Maliseet language and landscape and into Maliseet lives. The collective aboriginal resistance to the White Paper and the growing solidarity of First Nations activism in the 1970s had resulted in a growing movement for aboriginal self-determination. The aforementioned gap may have served the nonaboriginal story collectors, but Canada's First Nations would take advantage of it for their own purposes. Significantly, for Tobique First Nation this gap is serving as the catalyst for creative rewriting of Maliseet stories by Maliseet people for the Maliseet community.

FROM INTERTEXTUALITY BACK TO INTERDISCURSIVITY: "WRITING IT DOWN TO SPEAK MALISEET"

When the teacher read the Kloskap story to the children in the classroom, she was participating in what was once a Maliseet face-to-face storytelling event that transformed into the literate practice of reading Maliseet stories. The story had been entextualized and rewritten for general audiences. Over one hundred years have passed since Leland "wrote down" the stories from the "trembling memories of old squaws." We cannot ignore the ideologies that compelled the story collectors (Leland, Prince, Ives, Hill, and others not mentioned in this chapter) to "document" and "preserve" the stories or how those ideologies influenced their representations of the stories. The ideologies as well as the representations echo across the decades.[12] All representations are reflections of the collector/performer/ethnographer. As a Native ethnographer, I exploit the "gaps" between the texts over the past one hundred years to reconfigure, repurpose, and redirect the stories.

Each representation in isolation cannot reveal the "larger sociohistorical frameworks" of discourse. Furthermore, discourse is only one aspect of representation. Each discursive event is embedded in a broader semiotic field. "Attempts to study discourse are, in effect, attempts to study the co-deployment of linguistic and nonlinguistic signs in social interaction" (Agha 2005:1). A performer's (or ethnographer's) choice of reconfiguring, repurposing, and redirection across the gap, as well as the question of whether the performer's attempts are ratified by audiences, must be analyzed across semiotic encounters. Not only must reconfiguration, repurposing, and redirection across the gap be analyzed, but attention must be paid to intertextual variations and hybridity.

Briggs and Bauman suggest that generic hybridity is the mixing of discursive genres within a given event (Briggs and Bauman 1992:7). I agree with their characterization of generic hybridity, but I conceive Maliseet forms of generic hybridity to encompass a broader semiotic field that includes nonlinguistic signs such as landscape, images, and clothing. Furthermore, by positing a broader semiotic form of generic/creative hybridity,

I argue that doing so can widen the gap. By widening the gap, I can reconfigure across "texts" to promote a return to Maliseet interdiscursivity—in other words, initiate Maliseet storytelling in the Maliseet language.

One hundred years ago Leland and Prince entextualized Algonquin discursive events. Today, I am entextualizing Maliseet intertextual artifacts. This chapter's opening vignette presents tangible evidence of the silencing of the Maliseet language from Maliseet stories. Furthermore, it also depicts the *reading* of the stories—not the *telling* of the stories—in the Native language classroom. Whereas the two earlier phases of salvage work were "salvage work as documentation" and "salvage work as preservation," my entextualization projects represent "salvage work as revitalization." As Agha (2005) notes, any analysis of discourse must consider nonlinguistic as well as linguistic signs. More important, the recognition of the codependence of linguistic and nonlinguistic signs is fundamental to understanding social interactions. The previous phases of salvage work marked differing dis-integrations of the Maliseet language from Maliseet stories. My work is intended to reintegrate nonlinguistic signs with linguistic signs for the sole purpose of encouraging the retelling of Maliseet stories in the Maliseet language.

One such project, my graphic novel, has drawings of specific places on and near Tobique First Nation. The graphic novel incorporates mythic time and the present in the retelling of the Tobique Rock story. The illustrations also differentiate conceptions of time through the size of the frames and the rendering techniques (e.g., larger frames for larger time periods, and gestural drawings for mythic time versus more precise drawings for the present time). The scope of generic/creative hybridity is expanded to include representations of Maliseet landscapes, Maliseet people, and Maliseet mythic time. Generic/creative hybridity is not limited to discursive genres. In the graphic novel, generic hybridity includes texts. In the category of texts I include graphic images, framing devices, and type fonts. In short, it is not just the language that I am attempting to salvage; it is also the landscape, the stories, and the Maliseet peoples' experience.

At a UNESCO conference in 2002, I argued that sharing the story was about the reenchantment of the landscape (Perley 2003). In 2007, when I shared the Tobique Rock story (Perley 2007), it was not just a children's story; rather, it was a story for all of us, and it is relevant to issues of today. The graphic novel is my latest sharing of the Tobique Rock story. I am currently working on the Maliseet translation so the text will be in English as well as Maliseet. The Maliseet version is intended to serve as a catalyst for telling the story in Maliseet, not in English, and not read in English or Maliseet. My graphic novel is "salvage work as revitalization" in practice.

CONCLUSION: SEMIOTICS OF SURVIVAL

Intertextuality (rewriting texts) is a heuristic concept that is valuable for tracing the reconfiguration, repurposing, and redirection between texts from different periods and scholars/performers. Equally important, it is also useful for discerning the political and ideological implications behind the choices made by scholars/performers in the degree of widening of interpretive gaps. Bauman's use of intertextuality is notable for his insistence on the discourse of the performer and his recognition that the performer may initiate the mediation of the process of textually representing (entextualization) the discursive event between the performer and the ethnographer (2004:161–62). Nonetheless, Bauman's analysis is still just one more example of separating face-to-face interactions from the moment of storytelling (decontextualization) and repackaging the storytelling moment (recontextualized) as a textual artifact (entextualization) of "Other's words" into one more ethnographic representation of dialogue (Bauman 2004; Clifford 1988). More important, Bauman's goal is to trace the reconfigured, repurposed, and redirected texts to discern creative rewriting and to understand the implications for widening interpretive gaps in the performance of dialogue.

My examples above do not have the benefit of firsthand observation of oral poetic performance. The Maliseet representations of the Tobique Rock story are intertextual in the broader sense of the term. I agree with Bauman when he explicitly states that intertexuality is the "relational orientation of a text to other texts" (2004:4). But I also agree with Allen that "the text becomes the intertext" (2000:1). By incorporating both formulations of intertexuality I purposefully incorporate broad semiotic fields across disparate discursive (intertextual) events so they may be deployed in varieties of social interactions and domains. My approach echoes Agha's characterization of semiosis and social relations whereby he states, "The social relevance of inter-event semiosis, its capacity to formulate and maintain social formations, depends on a complex interplay between language and nonlanguage" (2005:4). By introducing the local landscape through drawings of recognizable places, sketching representations of contemporary Maliseet-ness, and invoking Maliseet oral poetic literatures, I take advantage

In anger, Apotamkon began fighting Klohskap. The two of them fought furiously!

Apotamkon realized he couldn't win so he escaped from Klohskap in the muddy water.

forty

Klohskap couldn't catch the monster so he scooped out a huge rock from the riverbed.

In doing so, he created the falls at Grand Falls and that rock is known today as The Tobique Rock.

Klohskap then tossed the rock

Maliseet story as graphic novel. Bernard Perley.

So, Klohskap transformed himself into a giant beaver and swam after Apotamkon.

Apotamkon.

he missed

But

downriver.

kilometers

He caught the monster farther down the river and there they continued fighting.

The two of them fought for days! Finally, they were both too exhausted to fight any more. So they went their separate ways, knowing they would continue their fight another time.

of the gap to create a new text that I deploy in the service of promoting interdiscursivity. I do not want members of the community merely to read the text. I want them to "experience the text," because place is critical as a meaningful part of the reading. Most important, the text is intended to encourage face-to-face interdiscursivity. The graphic novel is not supposed to sit on a shelf and collect dust. It is designed to defy the silence before the void. It is designed to provoke Maliseet community members to *tell* the story to one another in Maliseet.

NOTES

1. The spelling used by the Maliseet language teacher when I was conducting fieldwork in 1997 was "Koluskap." There are numerous spellings as well as variations in the name of the Wabanaki hero figure among the Wabanaki nations, such as Gluskabi (Abenaki), Glooskap (Passamaquoddy and Penobscot), and Glooscap (Micmac). The spelling variation in the illustration from my graphic novel, "Klohskap," is based on my memory of an earlier recommendation for proper spelling and proper pronunciation from a community elder. After a recent consultation with the elder, I was corrected and advised that the proper spelling should be "Kloskap." The text follows that recommendation. It should be noted that the elder is also my mother, who is a fluent speaker of Maliseet and English. See also note 2.

2. In the recently published Passamaquoddy-Maliseet dictionary (Francis and Leavitt 2008:196), "Koluskap" is the "name of first man, according to Wabanaki oral tradition," whereas the word for "liar" is "koluskapiyiw." Nevertheless, "koluskap" is commonly used to denote "liar" as well as the culture hero in the Tobique community. See also Ives (1964:17).

3. I have been granted permission by the chief of Tobique First Nation to use the actual name of the community in my professional publications.

4. James Clifford (1988:43) had argued that ethnographic accounts "remain *representations* of dialogue" between the ethnographer and the informant. Bauman (2004:161), however, places the emphasis on the performer as the source of the representation process in anticipation of the ethnographer's mediational relay.

5. "On the verge of extinction" is the assessment made in a comparative study of the respective state of language vitality for aboriginal languages in Canada ranging from "viable" to "extinct" (Perley 2011). Other recent assessments categorized the Maliseet language as "severely endangered" (UNESCO, n.d.,

interactive atlas, accessed 2010) and as "viable small" (Statistics Canada; see Norris and MacCon 2003:176).

6. This is also the ethnographic interdiscursive break (Silverstein 2005) from oral-discursive Maliseet storytelling events through the entextualization by non-Maliseet (and, later, Maliseet) storytellers and scholars. Bauman and Briggs define entextualization as "the process of rendering discourse extractable, of making a stretch of linguistic production into a unit—a *text*—that can be lifted out of its interactional setting" (Bauman and Briggs 1990:73). Bauman elaborates by stating that entextualization accomplishes the important task of producing a "text" that can be "bounded off to a degree from its discursive surround (its co-text), internally cohesive (tied together by various formal devices), and coherent (semantically intelligible)" (Bauman 2004:4). Silverstein describes interdiscursivity as "a structural relationship of two or more situations, and an indexical one at that. Within any situation in which we participate, we can experience the relationship by a semiotic act of 'point-to,' which of course implies point-to from someplace (the arrow or pointing finger starts somewhere and ends somewhere else). It is situational locatability, interdiscursivity can be seen to be a strategic positioning of participants in a semiotic event such that an inter(co(n)textual structure emerges" (2005:9).

7. Bauman states that "entextualization potentiates decontextualization" but points out that the process does not end there: "But decontextualization from one context must involve recontextualization in another, which is to recognize the potential for texts to circulate, to be spoken again in another context" (2004:4). Briggs and Bauman focus on performance in their analysis of entextualization.

8. Delores Daigle, Marilyn Daigle, and Geraldine Hegeman were the three women collecting folktales.

9. Ives attributes this work to Geraldine Hegeman.

10. The "mother" (and storyteller) is identified as Mrs. Viola Soloman (my grandmother), and her "daughter" is Mrs. Henrietta Black (my mother).

11. The intertextual practices of Ives and Hill were practices of decontextualization. An important product of decontextualization of texts through entextualization and their subsequent circulation through recontextualization is what Briggs and Bauman have called the intertextual gap (Bauman 2004, 2005; Briggs and Bauman 1992). In the Maliseet case, intertextual gaps can enable both the loss of the Maliseet language in Maliseet storytelling and the revitalization of the Maliseet language through generic intertextuality. It should be noted that Bauman has stated that "interdiscursivity" is a "better general term . . . reserving *intertextuality* for matters having to do with texts" (2005:146).

12. Bauman states that "each act of textual production presupposes antecedent texts and anticipates prospective ones." Furthermore, as Bauman paraphrases

Bakhtin, "the orientation of the now-said to the already-said and the to-be-said, is ubiquitous and foundational, comprehending all of the ways that utterances can resonate with other utterances and constitutive of consciousness, society, and culture." Each representation of a particular speech event, therefore, is indexical of "prior situational contexts" as well as "emergent elements" that forge "links to the adjacent discourse, the ongoing social interaction, instrumental or strategic agendas, and other situational and extrasituational factors that interact with generic orienting frameworks in shaping the production and reception of the utterance." More important, "these in turn will influence the ways in which the constituent features of the generic framework are variably mobilized, opening the way to generic reconfiguration and change. Thus, generic intertextuality inevitably involves the production of what Charles Briggs and I have called the "intertextual gap." Bauman recognizes that the "alignment" and "calibration" of texts across the gap can have serious political and ideological implications depending on how closely the calibration across the gap conforms to perceived orthodoxy or how widening the gap can be viewed as adaptive strategies to "emergent circumstances and agendas" (Bauman 2004:4–7). Each representation, then, reflects the ideological and political situatedness of the performer/ethnographer.

CHAPTER 10

To Give an Imagination to the Listener
Replicating Proper Ways of Speaking in and through Contemporary Navajo Poetry

Anthony K. Webster

This chapter concerns the relationship between the oral tradition of story-telling among Navajos and contemporary written Navajo poetry that can be and is performed orally. When Navajos talk of contemporary poetry in Navajo, they often speak of poetry as *hane'* 'narrative, story.' In fact, many Navajo poets directly link their poetry with the oral tradition (here understood as encompassing narratives, chants, and song). As Navajo poet Laura Tohe once pointed out about her poetry, "This is not just my voice, but the voice of my ancestors." Here we need to remember that for many Navajos contemporary poetry is not considered to be the sole invention of a creative individual. Although the individual voice, the individual poet, is important, this importance is mitigated by acknowledgment of the words of those who have come before. Contemporary Navajo poetry is often intentionally "traditionalized" (Bauman 2004), that is, explicitly linked with poetic features of the oral tradition. Navajo poetry is often, though not always, narrative in structure. In this chapter I suggest some of the ways that contemporary Navajo poetry aids in the circulation of language ideologies about proper language use among Navajos. In using language ideologies, I follow Kroskrity (2004:498) and understand them as "beliefs, or feelings, about languages as used in their social world." I also suggest something of the tension in the ways that Navajo, as a language, is represented by Navajo poets and the ways that tension aids in creating an imagined Navajo language community.

The Navajo Nation, covering parts of Arizona, New Mexico, and Utah, is roughly the size of West Virginia. According to the 2000 U.S.

Census, there are nearly 300,000 people who identify as Navajo. Further-more, 178,014 people identified themselves as speakers of Navajo, with roughly 120,000 of them also identifying themselves as residents of the Navajo Nation. Rough numbers, then, give an impression that the Navajo language is widely spoken (in fact, it is spoken in every state) by a signifi-cant number of people. However, as Navajo scholars such as Tiffany Lee (2007) and Ancita Benally (Benally and Viri 2005) point out, the Navajo language is a threatened language. It is threatened in the sense that young Navajos are not learning the language at a rate that ensures the continued use of the language. Also, despite several efforts over the years, literacy in Navajo is still rather limited (McLaughlin 1992; Spicer 1962:456–457; Spolsky 2002). Still, Navajo is used in much contemporary poetry, and poets such as Rex Lee Jim, Laura Tohe, and Nia Francisco have all written poetry in Navajo only. The use of Navajo can now also be found in the hip-hop lyrics of Navajo musical artists such as Mistic and Shade. Verbal and artistic domains in which Navajo can be found have expanded as Navajos have become interested in such expressive genres.

For many Navajos there is an oppositional language ideology that sees *Bilagáana bizaad* 'English (Whiteman's language)' and *Diné bizaad* 'Navajo' as wholly distinct codes that reveal telling attributes about their respective speakers (see also Peterson 2006). Here Navajos seem to con-cur with Raymond Williams (1977: 21) that "a definition of language is always, implicitly or explicitly, a definition of human beings in the world." Navajos have explained to me that "Navajo is verb based and English is noun based" (i.e., Navajos are concerned with process, and Anglos with things); "Navajo is more powerful spiritually, English is more powerful in the secular world" (i.e., Navajo is the language of ritual, English is the lan-guage of external power); "Navajo pronouns are connected like Navajos, English pronouns are isolated like Anglos" (i.e., since Navajo pronouns are bound morphemes, this is similar to the ways Navajos are connected via clan relations; English has free morphemes and reflects the relative disconnectedness of Anglos); "Navajo is like a companion, English is a stranger" (i.e., Navajo is the language of comfort and social intimacy, English is distant); and "Navajo is more poetic than English" (i.e., Navajos are born poets, English is a "flat" language). In each case, Navajo is posi-tively valorized and contrasted with a negatively viewed English. Here it is important to add that this "English" is often the "standard" English associated with outside regimes of knowledge and not the local ways of speaking and writing (often stigmatized) called by some of my consultants "Navajo English" (Webster 2010).

Many Navajos see the ability to speak Navajo as essentially linked to being Navajo (House 2002; Webster 2009a). The speaking of Navajo indexes Navajo-ness but is also iconic of being Navajo. Language—or discursive choices of semiotically salient forms—becomes an icon of being Navajo (Irvine and Gal 2000)—that is, speaking Navajo becomes naturalized as "what Navajos do." Such a belief, however, is now in tension with the linguistic practices of some younger Navajos who do not speak Navajo or who speak bilingual Navajo (a mixed English/Navajo code). This tension can be seen in contemporary Navajo poetry as well.[1]

NAVAJO POETRY: A VERY BRIEF HISTORY

In 1933 a short eight-line poem was published in *Indians at Work,* a U.S. government publication (Hirschfelder and Singer 1992). The poem was composed by a collection of Navajo students at Tohatchi School, New Mexico. This poem, "If I Were a Pony," is one of the first published poems by Navajos. It was written in English, with no use of bilingual Navajo. Other poetry in English would follow. In the late 1960s and early 1970s, Blackhorse Mitchell (1968, 1969, 1972a, b, c), among others, published poems in English about things Navajo, about the future, about the past, about grandparents, and about herding sheep. Gloria Emerson (1971, 1972) published politically engaged poetry in *The Indian Historian*. During the 1970s more and more Navajos began to write poetry. In 1977, Nia Francisco published a poem in Navajo in the journal *College English*. In the 1980s and 1990s even more poetry was published by Navajos, appearing in major literary journals as well as university press publications. By the mid-1980s individually authored books of Navajo poetry were appearing. Poetry was published in Navajo and English and combinations of the two as distinct codes. However, poetry that intermixed Navajo grammatical forms with English forms—that is, code-mixed forms—are almost nonexistent. More recently, some Navajo poets have begun to eschew large regional university presses in favor of smaller presses or to self-publish chapbooks that provide those poets more control over what it means to be a Navajo poet.

As the 1933 example suggests, much of the early Navajo poetry was supported by the U.S. government. The BIA promoted the teaching of creative writing and poetry at BIA schools in the late 1960s and 1970s. A crucial feature in the poetry of Navajo poets of the period was their ability to display a command of English. A suggestion of the importance of the use of poetry as a display of English language proficiency can be found in a brief editor's note in the *Navajo Times,* from a short-lived 1962 feature titled "Poet's Corner": "The following short poems were written by Eugene Claw, a Navajo Junior at Manuelito Hall and display a fine grasp of the English language as well as imagination and good poetic syntax."

As an example of "a fine grasp" of English, there were no examples of bilingual Navajo in Claw's poetry. Other examples could be cited from government publications, but one should suffice to give a sense of the importance of poetry as an exemplar of English language command. More recently, Diné College has published collections of poetry written in Navajo by students in its Navajo creative writing courses (Begay 1998; Casaus 1996). Likewise, during the short-lived run of the "Navajo Page" in the *Navajo Times,* poems were published in Navajo to highlight Navajo language literacy. In both cases, however, poetry was seen as an exemplar of language command (notably reckoned in terms of literacy).

Navajo poets, however, write poetry not (just) as an exemplar of language command or literacy but for a multitude of personal, aesthetic, and social reasons—as, I might add, I believe Eugene Claw did. We need to understand to what uses Navajo poetry in any code may or may not be put. Indeed, some poets who write in Navajo do so to create a corpus of literary materials in Navajo. Others write in Navajo for purely—or at least primarily—aesthetic reasons. They simply believe certain things sound better in Navajo. Concerning this distinction, Rex Lee Jim writes this: "I write to make sense out of who's Navajo and who's Diné. I write to make sense out of this writing I think—am I feeling it?—the bottom line is that I write to communicate with myself. That's why I write mostly in Navajo. I only wish I could have written this in Navajo" (2000:243).

Again, because literacy in Navajo is still relatively uncommon, many Navajos write in English because they cannot write in Navajo. Laura Tohe, for example, was taking courses in Navajo literacy while I was doing fieldwork in 2000/01. Although she was fluent in Navajo, she did not write Navajo as well as she wanted. Most of her poems in her 1999 book of poetry were in English, with some code switching into Navajo. Her more recent 2005 book of poetry is in both Navajo and English, with some poems written entirely in Navajo.

Luci Tapahonso had this to say in a 1995 interview: "I think because I learned how to write in English I um couldn't associate written poetry with Navajo although I think the process of writing poetry begins in Navajo for me because it seems to me my basic thought processes and basic um expression occurs in Navajo but because I learned how to write in English then my writing of poetry almost has to be in English, I don't associate written Navajo or I can't write written I have a real hard time writing in Navajo the written process has to be in English."[2] We need to take seriously what Tapahonso says about her poetry being influenced by Navajo. Many of the poets I have interviewed stated that their written poetry was influenced by the Navajo language and by the "oral tradition."

Much of contemporary Navajo poetry is in English and Navajo English (a local way of speaking and writing), and it is often through these versions of English that Navajo poets assert a Navajo identity (Webster 2010). By writing in this way, they make these poems more accessible to the larger non-Navajo English-speaking society, but—and this is in no way trivial—they are also more accessible to many young Navajo readers who are not literate in Navajo. Indeed, for many Navajos who are not literate in Navajo, poetry composed in Navajo is still largely accessed as an oral phenomenon. Navajo poets who write in Navajo can occasionally be heard performing their poems on KTNN, the Navajo radio station. They also perform at public venues before largely Navajo audiences (at fairs, concerts, individual homes, Diné College, the Navajo Nation Museum, coffee shops, and the like). Such performances are routinely announced on KTNN and reported in the *Navajo Times*. Navajo poets also perform at local coffee shops and bookstores off the reservation as well as at various colleges and universities (in the Southwest and across the United States). Some Navajo poets also perform internationally (Webster 2009a).

MODELING PROPER SPEECH

In this section, I briefly look at one way Navajo poetry performances often model proper ways of speaking. This modeling occurs prior to the actual performance of poems, at the beginning of the performance. Navajos are matrilineal and a have a set of complex clan relations. When Navajo poets perform before audiences—in venues as diverse as LineBreak, a program about poetry produced on National Public Radio in Buffalo, New York, or poetry readings at a persons' house or at the Native American Music Festival—many invariably introduce themselves via their clan relations in Navajo. Even Navajos who are not fluent in Navajo perform this greeting and introduction in Navajo (Webster 2008b). It is a formula many Navajos learn, and it is appreciated as a formula. For example, at the Diné Language Fair in 2001 at Diné College in Tsaile, Arizona, elementary and middle school students were judged on the ease by which they were able to introduce themselves in Navajo. To some Navajo people this locates a person within an existing clan structure, stating what relationship may or may not exist with particular audience members. It is a specific kind of assertion or reckoning of Navajo-ness and resonates in a specific way for many Navajos. Yet some Navajo poets worry that young Navajos are not learning their clans or that they treat clan names as superficial "brands" (without an understanding of the responsibilities that adhere to clan relations). Laura Tohe introduces herself at every performance I have documented by her clan relations:

> Yá'át'ééh
> Shí éí Laura Tohe
> Shí éí Tsénabahiłnii
> Tódích'íinii éí bá shíshchíín

Tohe tells the audience, in Navajo, that her mother's clan is Tsé Nahabiłnii 'Sleepy Rock People' and her father's clan is Tó Dich'íi'nii 'Bitter Water People.' Such introductions matter in making her locatable within Navajo clan reckoning and in calling attention to clan relations. They also model proper ways of speaking. They aid in reinforcing a language ideology based on "regulation by convention" (Kroskrity 1998:105–107). But this formula is not invariant; it can be played with. Esther Belin, for example, sometimes includes as her fourth clan hólahéi 'I don't know.' Gloria Emerson sometimes includes, for playful reasons, the fictitious clan tsé'áwózí 'pebble' in her introductions. Such playful expressions of the formula are done before both Navajo and non-Navajo audiences. When done before a Navajo audience, the audience is often let in on the joke. They recognize that neither hólahéi nor tsé'áwózí are actual clans; the first suggests that Belin is unsure of her fourth clan, and the second reasserts a mischievous identity that Emerson enjoys. When done before non-Navajo speaking audiences, as Belin did in Carbondale in November 2008, it is often misrecognized by most of the audience as a regular display of identity.

Some Navajos have explained to me that clan names, kinship terms, and place names cannot be translated into English. They are the words of the ancestors, and the ancestors spoke in Navajo. The felt attachment to the Navajo language form cannot, then, for these Navajos, be transferred from Navajo into English; there is a language ideology of incommensurability between Navajo and English (Webster 2008a). Such introductions also reinforce views about the importance of clan relations and the expression of those relations in Navajo. Identity and language are here interwoven.

PLACE NAMES IN NAVAJO *HANE'*

Harry Hoijer told Keith Basso in 1973 that "even the most minute occurrences are described by Navajos in close conjunction with their physical settings, suggesting that unless narrated events are spatially anchored their significance is somehow reduced and cannot be properly assessed" (Basso 1996:45). The use of place names by Navajo narrators continues in contemporary *hane'*. Stories about the "trotting Coyote," *Mą'ii jooldloshi hane'*, for example, often begin at named and knowable locations (Toelken and Scott 1981). They localize these narratives, providing a sense of Navajo ethnogeography and allowing Navajos to imagine the location of events described in a narrative.

Contemporary Navajo poetry also uses Navajo place names. Some poets write the place names in Navajo and then give their English equivalent (often not a translation, but the English name for the place). Other poets write them in Navajo and do not give an English equivalent. Some give the place names only in English. Navajos differ in their view of how best to represent place names in contemporary poetry. Nevertheless, the localizing of much contemporary Navajo poetry—that is, the grounding of narratives in specific named and knowable locations—is a feature of much contemporary Navajo poetry and thus reinforces ideals about proper ways of speaking.

As I note above, Navajos sometimes say that Navajo place names cannot be translated into English. Many English language place names that superficially refer to the "same" place as a Navajo name are not translations but rather based on English-language naming traditions. For example, one of the Navajo sacred mountains is known in Navajo as *Tsoodził* 'tongue mountain,' but in English it is named Mount Taylor. Mount Taylor is not a translation of the Navajo form and, contrary to Navajo place-naming practices, is named after a deceased person. As Navajo Nation council speaker Lawrence Morgan stated, "Most of those are names [English place names] given by the early settlers, and then they moved away. . . . The Navajo names have always been there" (Whitehurst 2007). In replicating and reinforcing this language ideology, we find that some Navajo poets do not translate Navajo place names into English language–dominant poems. Here is an example from Laura Tohe's (2002:100) "In Dinétah." Note that the title also contains the Navajo term for the traditional Navajo homeland:

> Sis naajiní rising to the east,
> Tsoodził rising to the south,
> Dook'o'osłííd rising to the west,
> Dibé Nítsaa rising to the north

There is no attempt to "translate" the Navajo place names into English in this poem. The representation of sacred mountains in an east-to-north trajectory also reproduces ideals of proper speech and is a recurrent feature in much Navajo poetry. The use of Navajo place names in English language poetry is, again, a recurrent feature of Navajo poetry. It aids in a metasemiotic stereotype (an idealized representation of how, by whom, and in what form the Navajo language is used; Agha 1998; Webster 2009a) articulated explicitly by Tohe when she told an audience in Illinois, "We'll always use our own names for the places on our homeland." At the same time, in everyday practice and in Navajo poetry, Navajos do use English language place names for places within the traditional Navajo homeland. For example, *Tséyi'* 'between the rock' is a large canyon complex that sits in the middle of the Navajo Nation—known in English as Canyon de Chelly, an important place in Navajo beliefs, and the only National Park with Navajo families living permanently within the park boundary—was sometimes called *Disney* by my Navajo neighbor in Chinle, Arizona. The pleasure that my neighbor had in using *Disney* was from the "phonological iconicity" between *Tséyi'* and *Disney* (Samuels 2001). According to my neighbor, they "sound alike." Another Navajo I knew said that rather than *Tséyi'* being *Disney*, it was instead *Tsé Ná'áz'élí* 'the rock that water flows around.' This place is also in *Tséyi'*.

That Canyon de Chelly National Park—which is not controlled by the Navajo Nation—is now a tourist stop for both American and international tourists brings a relevance to the verbal play by Navajos of *Tséyi'* or *Tsé Ná'áz'élí* as *Disney*. For some Navajos these places have become like

Disney(land) in that they attract Anglo-American and international tourists. In such ways, we can see the ways that linguistic play calls attention to social realities such as the influx of tourists onto the Navajo Nation and the lack of control of such places by the Navajo Nation. Tohe has published a collection of poetry titled *Tséyi': Deep in the Rock* (2005). Note that the English place name is not included in the title.

OPENING FRAMING

Several Navajo poets use some version of the phrase *'ałk'idą́ą́' jiní* 'long ago, they say' in the openings of their poetry. In traditional narratives, this form is a genre-framing device that indexes that a certain kind of *hane'* 'narrative' is about to take place. In discussing *'ałk'idą́ą́' jiní*, Navajo historian Jennifer Nez Denetdale (2007:43) notes, "This way of beginning a story gives an indication of how old the story is, for it has passed through many generations since time immemorial. The phrase reflects an important measure of responsibility that the listener takes on to see that the story continues to be relayed." Here are two examples: the first, from "In Dinétah" by Tohe (2002:100), recounts a Navajo-centric history of the Navajo; the second, from "The Dark World" by Hershman John (2007:47), recounts certain events from the origin of the Navajos:

(1) *Ałk'idą́ą́' adajiní nít'ęę'*
   They say long ago in time immemorial:
   the stories say we emerged . . .

(2) *Ałk'idídą́ą́' jiní*
   Listen and remember . . .

When I asked Hershman John about the use of the Navajo form, he told me it was "necessary." It was necessary in the sense that this is how Navajo stories of long ago need to begin. It was also how his grandmother always began such stories. Such uses indexically link the Navajo poem with Navajo narrative traditions and here with a specific narrator, creating an intertextual linkage between poetry and oral genres. They also reinforce ideas about proper ways of speaking, creating a metapragmatic example of the proper way to begin stories of long ago: Navajo stories of long ago begin with *'ałk'idą́ą́' jiní*. This again reinforces a language ideology of regulation by convention. For example, here is the opening of a narrative in Sapir and Hoijer (1942:18). In this example, the significant character— *yé'iitso* 'giant'—is also included in the opening.

(3) *'ałk'idą́ą́' yé'iitso jiní*
    Long ago, a giant, they say

Contemporary conversations in Navajo also use *'ałk'idą́ą́'* to index traditional genres of "long ago" in an ironic way (Field 2007:641–42).

USE OF THE QUOTATIVE *JINÍ*

Another device related to the above example, used to varying degrees by different narrators, is the quotative *jiní* 'they say, one says'. This form is the combination of the fourth-person pronominal *ji-* 'one' and the verb of speaking *–ní* 'to say' (in speech and in some poetry this form is often reduced to *jn* or *jiin*). The fourth person is used mainly for people who are considered socially distant (e.g., the dead) (Uyechi 1990). The form acts as an epistemic distancing device that indicates that the speaker does not have firsthand knowledge of the events being described. Its use is a way of mitigating the individual voice to a broader "voice of tradition." In many traditional Navajo narratives *jiní* appears at the conclusion of every clause outside of quoted speech. It is not normally within quoted speech. Barre Toelken and Tacheeni Scott (1981) and I (Webster 2004) argue that the form is a crucial ethnopoetic organizing device for Navajo Coyote narratives. Navajo poet Blackhorse Mitchell has suggested to me that *jiní* should be used only at the beginning and ending of Coyote narratives. In those instances, it acts as an opening and closing framing device. In William Morgan's (1949) collection of Coyote narratives, *jiní* is used sparingly at the beginnings of those narratives. The use of *jiní* in written poetry resembles the more restricted use of the form in oral narratives. Here are two examples from written poetry, from Jim (1998:69) and Tapahonso (1987:31), respectively:

(4) *Na'ízhdíłkidgo t'éí hoł ééhózin*
    Áko łą́ą́, háádóó ma'ii haaldloozh jiní
    Shį́įgo doo baa hane' da

Ask and you will know,
And so, surely, from where does coyote start trotting, it is
    said?
During summertime those stories are not told.

(5) *'índa mą'ii nachxǫǫgo tłóódi naghá jiin'*
    (they said the coyote walked around outside that night
    pouting.)

It should also be noted that there is native speaker awareness of the form *jiní*. For example, Mitchell explicitly explained to me when, where, and how often the form should be used at the beginning of Coyote narratives. Tohe has written about the form *jiní*. Here is how she describes and exemplifies its use. Note that she begins the citations of stories with the use of a place name in Navajo: "Jiní, *they say*. We accept jiní as part of our stories on simple faith. It's not important who said it, but that it was said. The stories become part of our collective memory. Our stories begin and end with jiní. At Ya'dziilzihii is the place named after a contest where young men shot flocks of arrows toward the clouds to see who could shoot the farthest, jiní. At Séí Delehí, lover's tryst took place on the wide sandy bed near the tamarisks, jiní" (Tohe 2005:11).

It is important to note that *jiní* is still a salient feature for many Navajos, now used in both storytelling and contemporary poetry (also a kind of narrative). Its use in contemporary poetry is a form of traditionalization that places the voice of the poet within a larger voice of tradition and intertextually links with those narrative traditions.

IDEOPHONY AND LOCALITY

An important poetic device found in Navajo chants, songs, place names, narratives, and contemporary poetry is ideophony. By ideophony, I mean sound symbolic forms that "communicate not by referring but by *simulating* the most salient perceptual qualities of an action, event, process or activity" (Nuckolls 2000:235). One component of ideophony is onomatopoeia. In Navajo, onomatopoeia is often described as *hodiits'a'* 'there is a sound.' This is also the form Navajos use when talking about echoes. It appears that echoes and onomatopoeia are linked in Navajo expression.

Among many Navajos there is a general sentiment that language use can create realities (e.g., Reichard 1944; Witherspoon 1977). Thus, speaking, and proper speaking, is valued because such uses of language can cause things in the world to happen; language is here efficacious and creative. According to Gladys Reichard (1950) the use of onomatopoeia and sound symbolism aid in making chants more aesthetically pleasing and hence more efficacious. David McAllester (1980:20) notes, "The imitation of sounds and actions in the Shootingway myth recreate [*sic*] the powers they are associated with here and now in the performance of the ceremony." According to one Navajo consultant, the use of ideophony is a way for a narrator to "give an imagination to the listener." I take this to mean an attempt to give an image or sensation of the world as it might be to the listener. Ideophones are a poetic and aesthetic device that involves the listener in the narrative, what Janis Nuckolls (1992) has termed "sound symbolic involvement." The ability for narratives or poetry to evoke an "image" was one feature that Navajos often gave in their aesthetic evaluation of a story or poem.

I turn now to two examples of ideophones in contemporary Navajo written poetry. The first example is from a poem by Navajo poet Rex Lee Jim (1995:37). Other examples from Jim on the use of onomatopoeia could be given (Webster 2004), but this poem illustrates several devices utilized in oral genres and thus suggests something of the continuity of poetic forms across mediums. I present the poem in Navajo and then an English glossing done in consultation with Rex Lee Jim (Webster 2006b:39). The ideophones are in boldface.

na'asts'ǫǫsí
ts'ǫǫs, ts'ǫǫs
yiits'a'go
ííts'ǫ́ǫ́z
mouse
suck, suck
sounding
kiss

The word for "mouse" in Navajo can be morphologically analyzed as something akin to 'the one who goes about sucking'. It is built up of an onomatopoeia that has productively become the verb *ts'ǫǫs* 'to suck' and has then been nominalized by the use of a nominalizing enclitic *-í* 'the one'. Jim then uses that play-on-ideophone-turned-noun in line two where the onomatopoetic word *ts'ǫǫs* in a reduplicated form. *Ts'ǫǫs* has at least two interlinking evocations: the sound of sucking through a straw and the sound of a kiss. This is particularly interesting because several Navajos I discussed this poem with stated that *na'asts'ǫǫsí* could not be analyzed into its constituent morphology. For them *na'asts'ǫǫsí* meant only 'mouse' and not 'the one who goes about sucking' (Webster 2006b). The third line is the standard way to "quote" that what has just been said is onomatopoetic. In Navajo, after an ideophone one finds the form *yits'a'go* 'it sounds/sounded' (see also Young and Morgan 1987:359). This device functions much as a verb of sounding, indicating that what has preceded it was an ideophone. The third line is also implicated in the alliteration—the consonance—that tumbles through the poem /ts'/. One gloss for this line suggested was "that's how it sounds," but Rex Lee Jim suggested "sounding." I follow his suggestion.

The fourth line means something akin to "it kissed," "it sucked," or "to perform a sucking rite." There is a certain amount of semantic ambiguity here that Jim is attempting to evoke. Ambiguity is often important, because it does not force an interpretation but rather opens the poem up to reflection. This desire to avoid forcing an interpretation, imposing one's will on another, can be found in several other Navajo ways of speaking. For example, Navajos often engage in indirect requests, often allowing the addressee the ability to ignore the request (Field 1998). In traditional narratives, quoted thought is rarely used. Instead, quoted speech is often used. The use of quoted speech instead of quoted thought is another example of not imposing one's interpretation on another person.

At a performance of this poem by Rex Lee Jim to an audience of primarily Navajos, July 18, 2001, in Window Rock, several Navajos in attendance smiled and laughed during the poem. One Navajo woman told me that it evoked the image of a little mouse going about kissing. When I asked another Navajo what she enjoyed about the poem, she told me she enjoyed the "way the sounds go together." Here we see the delight that comes from the use of ideophones.

Here is another example of an ideophone in Navajo poetry. The poem is by Gloria Emerson (2003:33) and is titled "Table Mesa, NM." Here is the relevant excerpt from the poem, again with the ideophone in boldface:

> of songprints
> of **w'u, w'u,**

déłi biyiin,
of first things, first

In a footnote after the poem, Emerson (2003:35) describes the sound
as "approximated sound of an approaching deity." The next line glosses as
déłi' 'crane' biyiin 'its song' or 'songs of cranes.' As Emerson explained
to me, this poem is meant to "deify gravity," and the w'u w'u links both
to deities and to the flapping of the crane's wings taking off over water.
The use of the ideophone w'u, w'u to link with a deity recalls a discussion
by Charlotte Frisbie (1980) concerning one of the functions of Navajo
sound symbols (where deities are associated with various sounds or calls).
This example is related to the use of ideophones in Navajo ceremonialism.
We also again see a continuity of use between oral genres and contemporary written poetry; especially in the use of intertextuality (Webster 2004,
2006a). Emerson's use of w'u, w'u intertextually links beyond the internal
coherence of the poem to a broader set of Navajo aesthetic practices (i.e.,
ceremonialism, songs, narratives, and place name usage).

Ideophones are not restricted to any single genre in Navajo verbal art.
They are integrated into a variety of aesthetic genres. Following G. Tucker
Childs (2001:70), I would argue that Navajo ideophones "are quintessen-
tially social, the mark of local identity" and, I would add, intimacy. In
other words, the use of ideophony becomes an "affective register" (Irvine
1990). At the same time, ideophony is often negatively evaluated by a
Western language ideology that finds such uses "childish" or "primitive"
(Nuckolls 2006; Sapir 1921). The use of Navajo ideophones, because they
can be negatively evaluated by non-Navajos and, indeed, some Navajo
educators, can be seen as an index of intimacy. Ideophones, because of the
negative evaluations and because they often index intimacy and locality,
are often considered "fragile" in language contact situations (Childs 1996;
Nuckolls 2006:47). Yet their use intertextually reverberates throughout
Navajo verbal genres and challenges a Western language ideology overly
fixated on reference (Silverstein 1996).

BILINGUAL NAVAJO AND LINGUISTIC PURISM

From Sapir (1921:196) to more recent work by Robert Young (1989), it
has long been argued that Athabaskan languages and the Navajo language
in particular are "highly resistant" to linguistic borrowing (though the

Northern Athabaskan language Dena'ina seems to provide a counterexample to this claim; see Rice 2004:325). As Young (1989:304) notes, "Spanish and English loanwords integrated into the language [Navajo] historically aggregate little more than fifty terms, all of them nouns." Many Navajos I have spoken with are aware of the lack of lexical borrowing from English or Spanish into Navajo and consider this a point of linguistic pride. As it was explained to me on numerous occasions, Navajos can make their own words and such Navajo words will be more "descriptive" than, in most cases now, English. More recently, however, one Navajo performer has begun to incorporate a comedic skit into his performances highlighting "all the Spanish words" in Navajo. He singles out, for example, *'alóós* (Sp. *arroz*) 'rice,' *siláo* (Sp. *soldado*) 'policeman', and *bééso* (Sp. *peso*) 'money.' He does not, however, include a discussion of the possible influence of English on the emergence of the grammaticization of tense in Navajo using the temporal adverb *ńt'éé* 'then' (Chee et al. 2004) or of the use of the Navajo distributive *-da* as a plural marker (Field 2009). Lexical items are salient markers of language influence; grammaticization of tense or the use of the distributive as a plural marker to more align with English tense and plurality are less salient (for more, see Kroskrity 1998).

It is, however, still the case that many Navajos often valorize the Navajo language for its lack of lexical borrowing (Field 2009). This is also the case when some Navajos have explained to me that clan names, kinship terms, and place names cannot be translated into English. This, I might add, fits a trend on the Navajo Nation in which Navajo chapters (regional political units) are changing their names from English to "traditional" Navajo names. For example, the chapter formerly named Hogback has legally changed its name to the Navajo place name Tse' Daa' Kaan (*Tsétaak'á* 'rock that slants into the water'). There is, then, currently a strong language ideology of linguistic purism among some Navajos (see Kroskrity 1998 on linguistic purism as a language ideology). This purism is often replicated in Navajo poetry as well.

We can get a sense of this linguistic purism by comparing, however briefly, the sociolinguistic complexity on the Navajo Nation with the ways that the Navajo language is represented in contemporary poetry. In particular, we can ask: What does *not* get represented in contemporary Navajo poetry? Since at least the turn of the past century, Navajos have been combining the morphology of the Navajo language with content words of English (Webster 2010). This is a code-mixed form. My consultants have referred to this style as *Navlish* (sometimes *Navglish* or *Navalish*) or

Road sign on Navajo Nation with language mixing. Photo by Anthony K. Webster

"bilingual talk" (see also Field 2009; Scheangold 2003). Charlotte Schaengold (2003) calls it "bilingual Navajo." One finds *shiheart* 'my heart/love'
(*shi-* 'my') used in the comedic routines of Navajo entertainer Vincent
Craig, or *Learning Centerdi* 'at Learning Center' (*-di* 'at') used on signs
around Diné College, or *Jesusgo* 'with Jesus' (*-go* 'with') in Navajo Christian hymns (Webster 2008a). During both my initial fieldwork and more
recent fieldwork in the summers of 2007–10, I commonly heard bilingual
Navajo on the Navajo Nation, where Navajo clitics and affixes were often
attached to English language nouns, and examples of bilingual Navajo on
billboards and signs were also common. I heard bilingual Navajo at Navajo fairs, in conversations at restaurants, at the mutton stands on the side
of the road, at the trading post in Lukachukai, Arizona, at the tire shop in
Chinle, Arizona, in schools in Tohatchi, New Mexico, as well as on long
drives listening to KTNN. Because it involved both Navajo and English, it
was some of the first "Navajo" I was able to comprehend.

Bilingual Navajo, or *Navlish,* is exceedingly rare in contemporary Navajo poetry. In fact, surveying contemporary Navajo poetry I could find
only five examples. Esther Belin (2002:8), for example, writes this:

> With big teeth and smile Coyote asks, háágóóshą'?
> Plaza'góó and before he can respond First Woman adds,
> Shí k'ad dooleeł, hágoónee'

Belin presents the English noun "plaza" with the Navajo enclitic *–góó*
'toward.' The Navajo and bilingual Navajo forms appear to be the quoted
dialogue of Coyote and First Woman. Coyote, an important trickster figure
in Navajo narrative tradition, asks First Woman where she is going. It is in-
triguing that First Woman—important in Navajo sacred narratives—uses
the bilingual code-mixed Navajo form in her response (toward the plaza).
Belin does not gloss the Navajo forms in the poem, nor does she provide
footnotes concerning the Navajo forms. There is no attempt to explain the
Navajo forms in English. Either one understands the Navajo forms or one
does not. In fact, Belin is unsure how many non-Navajos would even recognize that *plaza'góó* is a code-mixed form. Her use of bilingual Navajo
puts Navajo and English into dialogue, through the code-mixed form. The
use of the bilingual Navajo form *plaza'góó* presents an image of the Navajo language and the English language as not exclusive of each other but
rather as potentially intertwined.

Belin's example comes from an edited volume. One of the editors, Laura Tohe, is also a Navajo poet and does not use bilingual Navajo in any of her poems, though she does code-switch into Navajo and write poems in Navajo (Tohe 1999, 2005). In Belin's own book there are no examples of bilingual Navajo, though one could argue that the poem titled "On Telly Biliizh" (Belin 1999:61) is also an example. This is, however, a well-known pun on the English word "television" (Wilson and Dennison 1970:44). According to the joke, older Navajos misheard "television" as *télii alizhgo* 'donkey is urinating.' Indeed, one Navajo consultant read this poem and the attendant pun as a critique of contemporary television. Belin points out that *télii bilizh* is the term her mother used for 'beer,' and indeed she had seen the poem as a critique of things done while drinking. The use of *télii bilizh* 'donkey urine' was a metaphorical description of beer. Belin was certainly intrigued by the pun that my Navajo consultant had suggested. Such punning also opens up "television"—or *Tséyi'* as *Disney* (as we saw above)—to multiple interpretations, highlighting something of the ambiguity of any word, no matter the language.

CONCLUSION: ON LANGUAGE IDEOLOGY AND NAVAJO POETRY

Poems by Esther Belin, Rex Lee Jim, Luci Tapahonso, Laura Tohe, and other Navajos are not just read by outsiders, they are also performed by the poets on the Navajo Nation before largely Navajo audiences. Here they are very much like *hane'*, performed before an audience and meant to be shared. In such performances, Navajo poets circulate attitudes about form, function, and use of the Navajo language to Navajo audiences. Encoded within many of these poems, then, are ideas about the importance of place names in Navajo, the inability of English to express certain ideas and emotions, and metapragmatic commentary on the contexts in which Navajo is not just appropriate but required. Such performances are often displays of proper ways of speaking.

Navajo poetry and the Navajo linguistic forms used thus become both forms of traditionalization (Bauman 2004) and an affective register (Irvine 1990). By "traditionalization," I follow Richard Bauman (2004:27) and see this as the "active construction of connections that link the present with a meaningful past." Such forms of traditionalization are both indexical (pointing to previous utterances) and iconic (resembling such previous utterances). Through the use of genre-signaling devices such as *'atk'idą́ą́'*, contemporary poetry connects with a larger "traditional" stock of knowledge, both pointing to and evoking links with *hane'* 'narratives.' Such forms, then, through a kind of feelingful iconicity (i.e., a felt resemblance to prior utterances; see Samuels 2004; Webster 2009a), "echo" the voices of others (elders here) and are emotionally salient (Irvine 1990:152); they remind some Navajos of the ways grandmother, for example, used to tell traditional Navajo stories. Through displays of the feelingful evocation of linguistic forms such as ideophony, Navajo can act as an affective register (patterned ways of speaking and writing that are emotionally salient), linking the use of Navajo with emotionally salient expressivity. This is the positive valorization of an image of the Navajo language, a language that indexically links with and iconically evokes tradition. The use of Navajo and the use of ideophony challenge a Western language ideology that seeks linguistic homogeneity and monolingualism and is overly focused on reference.

Navajo poets' use of Navajo language also creates specific views of the Navajo language from a particular vantage point. It creates an "imagined" Navajo language. As Mikhail Bakhtin (1981:295) noted, "The actively literary linguistic consciousness at all times and everywhere (that is, in all epochs of literature historically available to us) comes upon "language," and not language. Consciousness finds itself inevitably facing the necessity of *having to choose a language*. With each literary-verbal performance, consciousness must actively orient itself amidst heteroglossia, it must move in and occupy a position for itself within it, it chooses, in other words, a 'language.'" Navajo poets, through their use of certain kinds of Navajo, aid in circulating a certain presentation of "the Navajo language." Far from being, merely, the use of Navajo in English language–dominant poetry, such forms are implicated in the sociolinguistic dynamics of Navajo linguistic practices.

Navajo poets' use of Navajo also replicates a metasemiotic stereotype of "the Navajo language" (Agha 1998). This image of "the Navajo language" is often contrasted with "the English language." As one Navajo once explained to me, "To say one word like in English language has a word for everything, but in *Diné bizaad* [Navajo language], that is why it's been said that Navajo language is very descriptive." The Navajo consultant was trying to explain to me the difference between English (which has a word for everything) and Navajo (which uses descriptive phrases that are often created on the spot to describe things). Or, in a more extended example by Laura Tohe when she was asked a question at a poetry performance

in Illinois to a non-Navajo audience on the process of writing poetry and
the differences between English and Navajo, we hear this:[3]

> the Navajo language is very poetic
> when I first started writing
> I used to think about poems in Navajo
> and then write
> turn them into English
> and I guess maybe in some ways I still do that
> because like I said the language is very poetic
> the way it looks at the world
> the world in terms of dualities
> and even that
> there's this line in that poem about female rain
> about how the luminescence is all around
> it took a long time to try
> to find an equivalent in English
> because the word itself a=h
>
> there's that one word
> I love that word in Navajo
> *nihik'inizdidláád* which
> it's an action
> you know in Navajo it's verb based
> and so *nihik'inizdidláád* means you know
> this light
> just
> poured over us
> or among us
> and there's this relationship you have with the light
> but in the English it seems a little flat
> when you say luminescence all around
> it's just like a reporting about what happened
> and there's none of that
> personal connection
> to light

Tohe also makes a feelingful connection to the Navajo language in
the above example. She explains how she "love[s] that word in Navajo."

She highlights *nihik'inizdidládd* with a slight rise in pitch when she produces the Navajo form. The word *nihik'inizdidládd* can be morphologically analyzed as *nihi-* (cessative or termative prefix); *-k'i-* 'straight'; *-niz-* 'faraway'; *-di-* 'extending along a line'; *-dládd* 'shine a light.' Tohe poetically glosses this as "luminescence is all around." But she considers this glossing to be incomplete. It misses something. It "seems a little flat." Rather than evoking the moment, it is rather merely a report of what has happened. The pragmatic relationship between language use and language form is missing in the English gloss. This relationship, as Tohe notes, is a "personal connection to light" that is evoked by *nihik'inizdidládd*. Part of that personal connection may arise from the homonymy between *nihi-*, the cessative (indicating the ceasing of an event) or termative (indicating the termination of an event) prefix, and the first-person possessive plural prefix *nihi-* 'our' (e.g., *nihizaad* 'our language'). Structurally the termative *nihi-* and *nihi-* 'our' do not align (the termative prefix is attached to verbs, the possessive prefix attaches to nouns). However, as potentially evocative, the homonymy here adds another layer of resonance. Navajo and English are incommensurate because English lacks the feelingful attachment between linguistic form and speaker. Language ideologies are also about the feelings speakers bring to bear about their languages and affective expressivity of those languages. These are the "feeling-tones" of words (Sapir 1921), what I have elsewhere termed "intimate grammars" (Webster 2010).

I have argued that we should not expect Navajo poets to document the complex dynamics of Navajo sociolinguistics "accurately." Rather, we should—as researchers interested in linguistic practices—be concerned with the ways that Navajos represent the Navajo language and the English language and the relations between such codes. As Bakhtin (1981) noted years ago, the representations of languages are never neutral or value free; they are, instead, fully implicated in the beliefs and values—the language ideologies—about dialects, registers, codes, and styles, the very social pragmatics in which language use is always embedded. "Standard Navajo" becomes legitimized through the uses of Navajo in much contemporary written Navajo poetry, while bilingual Navajo or *Navlish* is largely erased (Irvine and Gal 2000). The ideological work done here, following Michael Silverstein (2000:121), is to create an "imagined (language) community." This, as Silverstein notes, reviewing Benedict Anderson (1991), is a part of the nationalist project of "imagined communities." This imagined language community, then, is a part of the larger process of Navajo nationalism (Lee 2007). Thus contemporary Navajo poetry is linked with Navajo nationalism. One central feature of that Navajo nationalism, as Navajo scholar Lloyd Lee (2007:66) argues, is "the Diné language." Lee does not discuss what he means by "the Diné language." Is it a Diné language that will include bilingual Navajo? This is a question for Navajos to answer.

In this chapter, I tried to connect contemporary Navajo poetry to a wider horizon of linguistic practices and language ideologies among Navajos. I suggested some of the ways that Navajo poetry is explicitly linked by Navajo poets with the oral tradition and especially with *hane'*. I suggested something of the intertextual work that such poetic devices do, linking it with forms of traditionalization, affective registers, the replication of language ideologies about proper ways of speaking, and the ways that such displays place the individual poet within a broader voice of tradition. I also suggested the ways that ambiguity is often highlighted in verbal practices more generally and in contemporary poetry more specifically, replicating ways of avoiding the imposition of one's interpretation on another.

Navajo poetry is, however, not unitary, and Navajo poets do disagree on the uses of Navajo in their poetry. There are tensions, tensions between an idealized view of Navajo in the world and the sociolinguistic realities of the Navajo Nation, tensions concerning the role of Navajo in contemporary Navajo life and its relation to English and Navajo English, and tensions between idealized views of the relationships between language and identity as well. It is also important to remember that Navajo poetry is not simply read by outsiders; Navajo poets do perform their poetry before Navajo audiences on the Navajo Nation. As Laura Tohe once explained to me about Navajo poetry, "Poetry is performance." It is in such performances that we can begin to understand contemporary Navajo poetry as fully entangled in Navajo language ideologies about the form, function, and proper uses of—the proper ways of speaking—"the Navajo language" and its relationship to and of Navajo identity. Contemporary Navajo poetry, as a form of a *hane'*, gives an image of Navajo and Navajo identity, but it does not, as of yet, impose an interpretation on a singular image.

NOTES

I thank Paul Kroskrity, Leighton C. Peterson, Aimee Hosemann, and Pauline Turner Strong for comments on various versions of this paper. I also thank the many Navajo poets who have taken the time to talk with me about their poetry and their narrative tradition. Research on the Navajo Nation was done under permits from the Navajo Historic Preservation Office, for which I am grateful. Funding for this research was made possible by Wenner-Gren, the Phillips Fund of the American Philosophical Society, the Jacobs Fund from the Whatcom Museum, the University of Texas at Austin, and Southern Illinois University at Carbondale. I thank them all.

1. On identity, I follow Edward Spicer (1975) and see it as the ways people tell and retell, imagine and reimagine their histories from a particular perspective. As Spicer (1975:46) notes, "Identity is a conception of and feelings about the events which a people have lived through in the course of their history. . . . it is in the telling and retelling of the events from a particular people's point of view" that identity is expressed and, I would add, circulated and made recognizable. Language and language use, and the language ideologies that adhere to such uses, aid in the tellings and retellings, imaginings and reimaginings. Identity is here both indexical—pointing to particular sociocultural positionalities—and iconic—such indexical displays become understandable as feelingfully evocative of identity (Samuels 2004; Webster 2009a). On complementary perspectives to Navajo language ideologies, see Field (2009) and Peterson (2006).

2. Interview from LineBreak, October 12, 1995. Transcription by Webster.

3. These comments were made at Southern Illinois University in Carbondale for Indigenous People's Day, October 9, 2006. I describe this event in Webster 2009.

REFERENCES CITED

Adley-Santa Maria, Bernadette
1997   White Mountain Apache language shift: A perspective on causes, ef-
          fects, and avenues for change. M.A. thesis, American Indian Studies,
          University of Arizona, Tucson.
1998   White Mountain Apache language: Issues in language shift, textbook
          development, and native speaker–university collaboration. Paper pre-
          sented at the annual meeting of the American Indian Language Devel-
          opment Institute. University of Arizona, Tucson.

Agha, Asif
1998   Stereotypes and registers of honorific language. *Language in Society*
          27:151–93.
2005   Introduction: Semiosis across encounters. *Journal of Linguistic An-
          thropology* 15(1): 1–5.
2007   *Language and Social Relations*. New York: Cambridge University
          Press.

Aikhenvald, Alexandra Y.
2004   *Evidentiality*. Oxford: Oxford University Press.

Aitchison, Jean
1991   *Language Change*. Cambridge: Cambridge University Press.

Allen, Graham
2000   *Intertextuality*. New York: Routledge.

Anderson, Benedict
1991   *Imagined Communities*. rev. ed. London: Verso.

Appadurai, Arjun
1996   *Modernity at Large: Cultural Dimensions of Globalization.* Minneapolis: University of Minnesota Press.

Bakhtin, Mikhail
1981   *The Dialogic Imagination: Four Essays.* Ed. and trans. Michael Holquist and Caryl Emerson. Austin: University of Texas Press.
1986   *Speech Genres and Other Late Essays.* Trans. Vern McGee. Austin: University of Texas Press.

Balibar, Etienne
1991   Racism and nationalism. In *Race, Nation, Class: Ambiguous Identities.* Etienne Balibar and Immanuel Wallerstein, eds. Pp. 37–67. London: Verso.

Barth, Fredrik
1969   *Ethnic Groups and Boundaries: The Social Organization of Cultural Difference.* Boston: Little Brown.

Basso, Keith H.
1976   "Wise words" of the Western Apache: Metaphor and semantic theory. In *Meaning in Anthropology.* Keith H. Basso and Henry A. Selby, eds. Pp. 93–122. Albuquerque: University of New Mexico Press.
1979   *Portraits of "the Whiteman": Linguistic Play and Cultural Symbols among the Western Apache.* New York: Cambridge University Press.
1984   "Stalking with stories": Names, places, and moral narratives among the Western Apache. In *Text, Play, and Story: The Construction and Reconstruction of Self and Society.* Edward M. Bruner, ed. Pp. 19–55. Washington, D.C.: American Anthropological Society.
1988   "Speaking with names": Language and landscape among the Western Apache. *Cultural Anthropology* 3(2): 99–130.
1990   *Western Apache Language and Culture: Essays in Linguistic Anthropology.* Tucson: University of Arizona Press.
1996   *Wisdom Sits in Places: Landscape and Language among the Western Apache.* Albuquerque: University of New Mexico Press.
2004   *Don't Let the Sun Step over You: A White Mountain Apache Family Life, 1860–1975.* Tucson: University of Arizona Press.

Bauman, Richard
1977   *Verbal Art as Performance.* Prospect Heights, Ill.: Waveland.
1986   *Story, Performance, Event: Contextual Studies of Oral Narrative.* Cambridge: Cambridge University Press.

1992   Contextualization, tradition, and the dialogue of genres: Icelandic legends of the *Kraftaskald*. In *Rethinking Context: Language as an Interactive Phenomenon*. Alessandro Duranti and Charles Goodwin, eds. Pp. 125–45. Cambridge: Cambridge University Press.

1993   The nationalization and internationalization of folklore: The case of Schoolcraft's "Gitshee Gauzinee." *Journal of Western Folklore* 52:247–69.

2004   *A World of Others' Words: Cross-cultural Perspectives on Intertextuality*. Malden, Mass.: Blackwell.

2005   Commentary: Indirect indexicality, identity, performance: Dialogic observations. *Journal of Linguistic Anthropology* 15(1):145–50.

Bauman, Richard, and Donald Braid

1998   The ethnography of performance in the study of oral traditions. In *Teaching Oral Traditions*. J. M. Foley, ed. Pp.106–22. New York: Modern Language Association.

Bauman, Richard, and Charles L. Briggs

1990   Poetics and performance as critical perspectives on language and social life. *Annual Review of Anthropology* 19:59–88.

2003   *Voices of Modernity: Language Ideologies and the Politics of Inequality*. Cambridge: Cambridge University Press.

Beck, Peggy V., Anna Lee Walters, and Nia Francisco

1977   *The Sacred: Ways of Knowledge, Sources of Life*. Tsaile, Ariz.: Navajo Community College Press.

Becker, A. L.

1979   Text-building, epistemology, and aesthetics in Javanese shadow theatre. In *The Imagination of Reality*. A. L. Becker and A. A. Yengoyan, eds. Pp. 211–243. Norwood, N.J.: Ablex.

Begay, Lydia Fasthorse (ed.)

1998   *Hane' Naach'ąąh*. Tsaile, Ariz.: Diné Teacher Education, Diné College.

Belin, Esther

1999   *From the Belly of My Beauty*. Tucson: University of Arizona Press.

2002   First woman. In *Sister Nations, Native American Women Writers on Community*. Heid E. Erdrich, and Laura Tohe, eds. Pp. 8–9. St. Paul: Minnesota Historical Society Press.

Benally, Ancita, and Denis Viri

2005   *Diné bizaad* [Navajo language] at a crossroads: Extinction or renewal. *Bilingual Research Journal* 29(1): 85–108.

Berman, Judith
1992   Oolachan-Woman's robe: Fish, blankets, masks, and meaning in
            Boas's Kwakw'ala texts. In *On the Translation of Native American
            Literatures*. Brian Swann, ed. Pp. 125–62. Washington, D.C.: Smith-
            sonian Press.

Biolsi, Thomas
2001   *Deadliest Enemies: Law and the Making of Race Relations on and off
            the Rosebud Reservation.* Berkeley: University of California Press.

Boas, Franz
1966   *Introduction to Handbook of American Indian Languages.* Ed. Pres-
[1911]   ton Hodder. Lincoln: University of Nebraska Press.

Bourdieu, Pierre.
1982   *Language and Symbolic Power.* Ed. John B. Thompson, trans. Gino
            Raymond and Matthew Adamson. Cambridge, Mass.: Harvard Uni-
            versity Press.
1984   *Distinction: A Social Critique of the Judgment of Taste.* Cambridge,
            Mass.: Harvard University Press.

Brandt, Elizabeth A.
1980   On secrecy and control of knowledge. In *Secrecy: A Cross-Cultural Per-
            spective.* S. Teft, ed. Pp. 123–46. New York: Human Sciences Press.
1981   Native American attitudes toward literacy and recording in the south-
            west. *Journal of the Linguistic Association of the Southwest* 4:185–95.

Briggs, Charles L.
1988   *Competence in Performance: The Creativity of Tradition in Mexicano
            Verbal Art.* Philadelphia: University of Pennsylvania Press.

Briggs, Charles L., and Richard Bauman
1992   Genre, intertextuality, and social power. *Journal of Linguistic Anthro-
            pology* 2:131–72.

Bright, Jane Orstan, and William Bright
1965   Semantic structures in northwestern California and the Sapir-Whorf
            hypothesis. *American Anthropologist* 67:249–58.

Bright, William
1957   *The Karok Language.* University of California Publications in Lin-
            guistics 13. Berkeley: University of California Press.
1984   *American Indian Linguistics and Literature.* Berlin: Mouton de Gruyter.

Bucholtz, Mary, and Kira Hall
2005   Identity and interaction: A sociocultural linguistic approach. *Discourse Studies* 7(4–5): 585–614.

Buckley, Thomas
2002   *Standing Ground: Yurok Indian Spirituality, 1850–1990.* Berkeley: University of California Press.

Bunte, Pamela A.
2009   You keep not listening with your ears: Language ideologies, language socialization and Paiute identity. In *Native American Language Ideologies: Beliefs, Practices, and Struggles in Indian Country.* Paul V. Kroskrity and Margaret C. Field, eds. Pp. 172–89. Tucson: University of Arizona Press.

Bunte, Pamela A., and Robert J. Franklin
1987   *From the Sands to the Mountain: Change and Persistence in a Southern Paiute Community.* Lincoln: University of Nebraska Press.
2001   Translating a Southern Paiute constitution: A case study of language maintenance. In *The Green Book: Case Studies of Language Maintenance and Revitalization.* Leanne Hinton and Ken Hale, eds. Pp. 255–64. New York: Academic Press.

Caduto, Michael J., and Joseph Bruchac
1988   *Keepers of the Earth: Native American Stories and Environmental Activities for Children.* Golden, Colo.: Fulcrum.

Cameron, Deborah
2007   Language endangerment and verbal hygiene. In *Discourses of Endangerment.* Alexandre Duchene and Monica Heller, eds. Pp. 268–85. London: Continuum.

Casaus, Bernice
1996   Nihizaad, t'áá Diné bizaad. *Journal of Navajo Education* 13(3): 3–10.

Cattelino, Jessica R.
2008   *High Stakes: Florida Seminole Gaming and Sovereignty.* Durham, N.C.: Duke University Press.

Chee, Melvatha, Evan Ashworth, Susan Buescher, and Brittany Kubacki
2004   Grammaticization of tense in Navajo: The evolution of nt'éé. *Santa Barbara Papers in Linguistics* 15:76–90.

Childs, G. Tucker
1996   Where have all the ideophones gone? The death of a word category in Zulu. *Toronto Working Papers in Linguistics* 15:81–103.
2001   Research on ideophones, whither hence? The need for a social theory of ideophones. In *Ideophones*. F. K. Erhard Voeltz and Christa Kilian-Hatz, eds. Pp 63–73. Philadelphia: John Benjamins.

Clatworthy, Stewart
2003   Impact of the 1985 amendments to the Indian Act on First Nations populations. In *Aboriginal Conditions: Research as a Foundation for Public Policy*. Jerry P. White, Paul S. Maxim, and Dan Beavon, eds. Vancouver: University of British Columbia Press.

Clifford, James
1988   On ethnographic authority. In *The Predicament of Culture: Twentieth-Century Ethnography, Literature, and Art*. Ed. James Clifford. Cambridge, Mass.: Harvard University Press.

Collins, James
1998a   Our ideologies and theirs. In *Language Ideologies: Practice and Theory*. Bambi B. Schieffelin, Kathryn A. Woolard, and Paul V. Kroskrity, eds. Pp. 256–70. New York: Oxford University Press.
1998b   *Understanding Tolowa Histories: Western Hegemonies and Native American Responses*. New York: Routledge.

Collins, James, and Richard K. Blot
2003   *Literacy and Literacies: Texts, Power, and Identity*. Cambridge: Cambridge University Press.

Conathan, Lisa
2004   Linguistic ecology of northwestern California: Contact, functional convergence, and dialectology. Ph.D. dissertation, Department of Linguistics, University of California, Berkeley.

Cruikshank, Julie
1990   *Life Lived Like a Story: Life Stories of Three Yukon Native Elders*. Lincoln: University of Nebraska Press.
1998   *The Social Life of Stories: Narrative and Knowledge in the Yukon Territory*. Lincoln: University of Nebraska Press.

Crystal, David
2000   *Language Death*. Cambridge: Cambridge University Press.

Dauenhauer, Nora Marks, and Richard Dauenhauer
1998   Technical, emotional, and ideological issues in reversing language shift: Examples from Southeast Alaska. In *Endangered Languages: Current Issues and Future Prospects*. Lenore A. Grenoble and Lindsay J Whaley. Pp. 57–98. Cambridge: Cambridge University Press.

DeMallie, Raymond
1993   These have no ears: Narratives and the ethnohistorical method. *Ethnohistory* 40:515–38.

Denetdale, Jennifer Nez
2007   *Reclaiming Diné History: The Legacies of Navajo Chief Manuelito and Juanita.* Tucson: University of Arizona Press.

de Reuse, Willem J.
1997   Issues in language textbook development: The case of Western Apache. In *Teaching Indigenous Languages*. Jon Reyhner, ed. Pp. 116–128. Flagstaff: Northern Arizona University.

Dorian, Nancy C.
1989   *Investigating Obsolescence: Studies in Language Contraction and Death.* Cambridge: Cambridge University Press.
1998   Western language ideologies and small-language prospects. In *Endangered Languages: Current Issues and Future Prospects*. L. A. Grenoble and L. J. Whaley, eds. Pp. 3–21. Cambridge: Cambridge University Press.

Dozier, Edward P.
1954   The Hopi-Tewa of Arizona. *University of California Publications in American Archaeology and Ethnology* 44(3): 257–376.
1964   Two examples of linguistic acculturation: The Yaqui of Sonora and
[1956]   Arizona and the Tewa of New Mexico. In *Language in Culture and Society*. D. H. Hymes, ed. Pp. 509–17. New York: Harper and Row. Reprinted from *Language* 32:146–157.
1966   *Hano, a Tewa Indian Community in Arizona.* New York: Holt, Rinehart, and Winston.

Eggan, Fred
1979   Foreword. In *Zuni: Selected Writings of Frank Hamilton Cushing*. Jesse Green, ed. Pp. xi–xiv. Lincoln: University of Nebraska Press.

Eisenlohr, Patrick
2004   Language revitalization and new technologies: Cultures of electronic
            Mediation and the refiguring of communities. *Annual Review of An-
            thropology* 33:21–45.

Emerson, Gloria
1971   The poetry of Gloria Emerson. *Indian Historian* 4(2): 8–9.
1972   Slayers of the children. *Indian Historian* 5(1): 18–19.
2003   *At the Hems of the Lowest Clouds.* Santa Fe, N.Mex.: School of
            American Research.

Evans, Nick
2001   The last speaker is dead—long live the last speaker! In *Linguistic
            Field Work.* Paul Newman and Martha Ratliff, eds. Pp. 250–81. Cam-
            bridge: Cambridge University Press.

Evers, Larry, and Barre Toelken
2001   Collaboration in the translation and interpretation of Native American
            oral traditions. In *Native American Oral Traditions: Collaboration
            and Interpretation.* L. Evers and B. Toelken, eds. Pp. 1–14. Logan:
            Utah State University Press.

Farnell, Brenda M.
1993   *Wiyuta: Assiniboine Storytelling with Signs.* (CD-ROM) Austin: Uni-
            versity of Texas Press.
1995   *Do You See What I Mean? Plains Indian Sign Talk and the Embodi-
            ment of Action.* Austin: University of Texas Press.

Field, Margaret
1998   Politeness and indirection in Navajo directives. *Southwest Journal of
            Linguistics* 17(2): 23–33.
2007   Increments in Navajo conversation. *Pragmatics* 17(4): 637–46.
2009   Changing Navajo language ideologies and changing language use.
            In *Native American Language Ideologies: Beliefs, Practices, and
            Struggles in Indian Country.* Paul Kroskrity and Margaret Field, eds.
            Pp. 31-47. Tucson: University of Arizona Press.

Fienup-Riordan, Anne
2005   *Wise Words of the Yup'ik People: We Talk to You Because We Love
            You.* With translations from the Yup'ik by Alice Rearden. Lincoln:
            University of Nebraska Press.

Finnegan, Ruth
1977   *Oral Poetry: Its Nature, Significance, and Social Context.* Cambridge: Cambridge University Press.

Fishman, Joshua
1991   *Reversing Language Shift.* Clevedon, U.K.: Multilingual Matters.

Fixico, Donald
1998   *The Invasion of Indian Country in the Twentieth Century: American Capitalism and Tribal Natural Resources.* Boulder: University Press of Colorado.

Foley, John M. (ed.)
1986   *Oral Traditions in Literature: Interpretation in Context.* Columbia: University of Missouri Press.

Foley, William A.
1997   *Anthropological Linguistics: An Introduction.* Malden, Mass.: Blackwell.

Francis, David A., and Robert M. Leavitt
2008   *Passamaquoddy-Maliseet Dictionary: Peskotomuhkati Wolastoqewi Latuwewakon.* Orono: University of Maine Press.

Franklin, Robert J., and Pamela A. Bunte
1997   Animals and humans, sex and death: Towards a symbolic analysis of four southern Numic rituals. *Journal of California and Great Basin Anthropology* 18(2): 178–203.

Frisbie, Charlotte
1980   Vocables in Navajo ceremonial music. *Ethnomusicology* 24(3): 347–92.

Geertz, Clifford
1983   From the native's point of view: On the nature of anthropological understanding. In *Local Knowledge: Further Essays in Interpretive Anthropology.* Pp. 55–70. New York: Basic Books.

Giddens, Anthony
1984   *The Constitution of Society.* Berkeley: University of California Press.

Glassie, Henry
1995   Tradition. *Journal of American Folklore* 108(430): 395–412.

Goddard, Ives
1978   Eastern Algonquian languages. In *Handbook of North American Indi-*
          ans 15. Bruce Trigger, ed. Pp. 70–77. Washington, D.C.: Smithsonian
          Institution Press.

Goddard, Pliny Earle
1903   Life and culture of the Hupa. *University of California Publications in*
          American Archaeology and Ethnology 1(1): 1–88.
1904   Hupa texts. *University of California Publications in American Ar-*
          chaeology and Ethnology 1(2): 89–368.
1919   Myths and tales from the White Mountain Apache. *Anthropological*
          Papers of the American Museum of Natural History 24, pt. 2.

Goffman, Erving
1961   *Asylums: Essays on the Social Situation of Mental Patients and Other*
          Inmates. Garden City, N.Y.: Anchor.
1974   *Frame Analysis.* New York: Harper and Row.
1981   *Forms of Talk.* Philadelphia: University of Pennsylvania Press.

Goldberg, Carole, and Duane Champagne
2002   Ramona redeemed? The rise of tribal political power in California.
          Wicazo Sa Review 17:43–64.

Golla, Victor
2000   Language histories and communicative strategies in aboriginal Cali-
          fornia and Oregon. In *Languages of the North Pacific Rim*, Vol. 5. O.
          Miyaoka, ed. Osaka Gakuin University, Japan.

Gómez de García, Jule, Melissa Axelrod, and Jordan Lachler
2009   English is the dead language: Native perspectives on bilingualism.
          In *Native American Language Ideologies: Language Beliefs, Prac-*
          tices, and Struggles in Indian Country. M. Field and P. Kroskrity, eds.
          Pp. 99–122. Tucson: University of Arizona Press.

Gonzales, Alecia
2000   *Thaum Khoiye Tdoen Gyah.* Chickasha, Okla.: USAO Press.
2005a   *Grandma's Spider Song.* Chickasha, Okla.: USAO Press.
2005b   *The Prairie Dog Song.* Chickasha, Okla.: USAO Press.

Goodwin, Grenville
1994 [1939] *Myths and Tales of the White Mountain Apache.* University of Ari-
          zona Press.

Gramsci, Antonio
1971   *Selections from the Prison Notebooks*. New York: International Press.

Grenoble, Lenore A., and Lindsay J. Whaley (eds.)
1998   *Endangered Languages: Current Issues and Future Prospects*. Cambridge: Cambridge University Press.

Greymorning, Stephen
2004   Culture and language: Political realities to keep Trickster at bay. In *A Will to Survive: Indigenous Essays on the Politics of Culture, Language, and Identity*. Stephen Greymorning, ed. Pp. 3–17. Boston: McGraw Hill.

Gumperz, John J.
1992   Contextualization and understanding. In *Rethinking Context: Language as an Interactive Phenomenon*. A. Duranti and C. Goodwin, eds. Pp. 229–52. Cambridge: Cambridge University Press.

Gumperz, John J., and Dell H. Hymes
1964   The ethnography of communication. *American Anthropologist* 66:6 (part II).
1972   *Directions in Sociolinguistics: The Ethnography of Communication*. New York: Holt, Rinehart, and Winston.

Gunn Allen, Paula (ed.)
1989   *Spider Woman's Granddaughters: Traditional Tales and Contemporary Writing by Native American Women*. New York: Fawcett.

Haas, Mary R.
1967   Language and taxonomy in northwestern California. *American Anthropologist* 69:358–62.

Hale, Kenneth
2001   Strict locality in local language media: An Australian example. In *The Green Book of Language Revitalization in Practice*. L. Hinton and K. Hale, eds. Pp. 277–83. San Diego: Academic Press.

Hanks, William F.
1987   Discourse Genres in a theory of practice. *American Ethnologist* 14(4): 668–92.
1996   Exorcism and the description of participant roles. In *Natural Histories of Discourse*. M. Silverstein and G. Urban, eds. Pp. 160–200. Chicago: University of Chicago Press.

Harrington, John P.
1928   *Vocabulary of the Kiowa Indian Language.* Bureau of American Eth-
          nology Bulletin 84. Washington, D.C.: Smithsonian Institution.

Harrison, K. David
2007   *When Languages Die: The Extinction of the World's Languages and
          the Erosion of Human Knowledge.* Oxford: Oxford University Press.

Havelock, Eric A.
1963   *Preface to Plato.* Cambridge, Mass.: Harvard University Press.

Henningsen, Manfred
1989   The politics of purity and exclusion. In *The Politics of Language Pur-
          ism.* B. H. Jernudd and M. J. Shapiro, eds. Pp. 31–52. Berlin: Mouton
          de Gruyter.

Hill, Jane H.
1978   Language contact systems and human adaptations. *Journal of Anthro-
          pological Research* 34(1): 1–26.
1983   Language death in Uto-Aztecan. *International Journal of American
          Linguistics* 49:258–76.
1985   The grammar of consciousness and the consciousness of grammar.
          American Ethnologist 12:725–37.
1995   The voices of Don Gabriel: Responsibility and self in a modern
          Mexicano narrative. In *The Dialogical Emergence of Culture.* Dennis
          Tedlock and Bruce Mannheim, eds. Pp. 97–147. Urbana: University
          of Illinois Press.
2001   Languages on the land. In *Archeology, Language, and History.* J.
          Terrell, ed. Pp. 257–82. Westport, Conn.: Bergin and Garvey.
2002a   "Expert rhetorics" in advocacy for endangered languages: Who is lis-
          tening and what do they hear? *Journal of Linguistic Anthropology*
          12:119–33.
2002b   Two styles for language and social identity among the Tohono
          O'odham. In *Identity, Feasting, and the Archaeology of the Greater
          Southwest.* Barbara J. Mills, ed. Pp. 121–38. Boulder: University of
          Colorado Press.

Hill, Jane H., and Kenneth C. Hill
1986   *Speaking Mexicano: Dynamics of Syncretic Language in Central
          Mexico.* Tucson: University of Arizona Press.

Hill, Kay
1963   *Glooscap and His Magic: Legends of the Wabanaki Indians.* Toronto: McClelland and Stewart.

Hinton, Leanne
1994   *Flutes of Fire.* Berkeley, Calif.: Heyday Books.
2002a   *How to Keep Your Language Alive.* Berkeley, Calif.: Heyday Books.
2002b   Internal and external language advocacy (Commentary). *Journal of Linguistic Anthropology* 12:150–56.

Hinton, Leanne, and Kenneth Hale (eds.)
2001   *The Green Book of Language Revitalization in Practice.* San Diego, Calif.: Academic Press.

Hirschfelder, Arlene, and Beverly Singer
1992   *Rising Voices: Writings of Young Native Americans.* New York: Ivy Books.

Hodge, William H.
1971   Navajo urban migration: An analysis from the perspective of the family. In *The American Indian in Urban Society.* J. O. Waddell and O. M. Watson, eds. Pp. 346–91. Boston: Houghton-Mifflin.

Hohenthal, William
2001   *Tipai Ethnographic Notes: A Baja California Indian Community at Mid-century.* Ed. Thomas Blackburn, et al. Menlo Park, Calif.: Ballena Press and the Institute for Regional Studies of the Californias.

Hornberger, Nancy (ed.)
1996   *Indigenous Literacies in the Americas: Language Planning from the Bottom Up.* Berlin: Mouton de Gruyter.

House, Deborah
2002   *Language Shift among the Navajos.* Tucson: University of Arizona Press.

Hymes, Dell H.
1966   On communicative competence. Paper presented at the Research Planning Conference on Language Development among Disadvantaged Children, Yeshiva University, New York.
1972   The contribution of folklore to sociolinguistic research. In *Toward New Perspectives in Folklore.* Américo Paredes and Richard Bauman, eds. Pp. 42–50. Austin: University of Texas Press.

1974   *Foundations in Sociolinguistics: An Ethnographic Approach.* Phila-
          delphia: University of Pennsylvania Press.
1981   *"In Vain I Tried to Tell You": Essays in Native American Ethnopoet-
          ics.* Philadelphia: University of Pennsylvania Press.
1996   *Ethnography, Linguistics, Narrative Inequality: Toward an Under-
          standing of Voice.* London: Taylor and Francis.
2003   *Now I Only Know So Far: Essays in Ethnopoetics.* Lincoln: Univer-
          sity of Nebraska Press.

Irvine, Judith
1990   Registering affect: Heteroglossia in the linguistic expression of emo-
          tion. In *Language and the Politics of Emotion.* Lila Abu-Lughod and
          Catherine Lutz, eds. Pp. 126–61. Cambridge: Cambridge University
          Press.

Irvine, Judith, and Susan Gal
2000   Language ideology and linguistic differentiation. In *Regimes of Lan-
          guage: Ideologies, Polities, Identities.* Paul V. Kroskrity, ed. Pp. 35–83.
          Santa Fe, N.Mex.: School of American Research Press.

Ives, Edward D. (ed.)
1964   *Malecite and Passamaquoddy Tales.* Northeast Folklore 6. Orono:
          Northeast Folklore Society, Department of English, University of
          Maine.

Jackson, Jason Baird
2003   *Yuchi Ceremonial Life: Performance, Meaning, and Tradition in a
          Contemporary American Indian Community.* Lincoln: University of
          Nebraska Press.

Jahner, Elaine
1999   Traditional narrative: Contemporary uses, historical perspectives.
          Studies in American Indian Literatures 11(2): 1–28.

Jim, Rex Lee
1995   *Saad.* Princeton: Princeton Collections of Western Americana.
1998   *Dúchas Táá Kóó Diné.* Beal Feirste, Ireland: Au Clochan.
2000   A moment in my life. In *Here First.* Arnold Krupat and Brian Swann,
          eds., Pp. 229–46. New York: Modern Library.

John, Hershman
2007   *I Swallow Turquoise for Courage.* Tucson: University Arizona Press.

Keane, Webb
1995 The spoken house: Text, act and object in eastern Indonesia. *American Ethnologist* 22(1): 102–24.
2007 *Christian Moderns: Freedom and Fetish in the Mission Encounter.* Berkeley: University of California Press.

Keeling, Richard
1992 *Cry for Luck: Sacred Song and Speech among the Yurok, Hupa, and Karok Indians of Northwestern California.* Berkeley: University of California Press.

King, Thomas
2005 *The Truth about Stories: A Native Narrative.* Minneapolis: University of Minnesota Press.

Kotay, Ralph
2004 Kiowa Hymns (2 CDs and Booklet). Lincoln: University of Nebraska Press.

Kozak, David, ed.
Forth-   *Inside Dazzling Mountains: Native American Oral Literature of the*
coming   *Southwest.* Lincoln: University of Nebraska Press.

Krauss, Michael
1997 Status of Native American language endangerment. *In Stabilizing Indigenous Languages.* Gina Cantoni, ed. Pp. 15–20. Flagstaff: Northern Arizona University.

Kroeber, A. L.
1925 *Handbook of the Indians of California.* Bureau of American Ethnology 78. Washington, D.C.: Smithsonian Institution.
1976 *Yurok Myths.* Berkeley: University of California Press.

Kroeber, A. L., and E. W. Gifford
1980 *Karok Myths.* Ed. Grace Buzaljko. Berkeley: University of California Press.

Kroeber, Karl
1998 *Artistry in Native American Myths.* Lincoln: University of Nebraska Press.

Kroskrity, Paul V.
1985 Growing with stories: Line, verse, and genre in an Arizona Tewa text. *Journal of Anthropological Research* 41:183–99.

244 REFERENCES CITED

1993   *Language, History, and Identity: Ethnolinguistic Studies of the Arizona Tewa*. Tucson: University of Arizona Press.

1997   Discursive convergence with an evidential particle. In *The Life of Language: Papers in Honor of William Bright*. J. H. Hill, P. J. Mistry, and L. Campbell, eds. Pp. 25–34. Berlin: Mouton de Gruyter.

1998   Arizona Tewa kiva speech as a manifestation of a dominant language ideology. In *Language Ideologies, Practice and Theory*. B. B. Shieffelin, K. A. Woolard, and P. V. Kroskrity, eds. Pp. 103–22. New York: Oxford University Press.

2000a   Language ideologies in the expression and representation of Arizona Tewa ethnic identity. In *Regimes of Language: Ideologies, Polities, and Identities*. Paul V. Kroskrity, ed. Pp. 329–59. Santa Fe, N.Mex.: School of American Research.

2000b   Regimenting languages: Language ideological perspectives. In *Regimes of Language: Ideologies, Polities, and Identities*. Paul V. Kroskrity, ed. Pp. 1–34. Santa Fe, N.Mex.: School of American Research.

2000c   *Regimes of Language: Ideologies, Polities, Identities*. Edited by Paul V. Kroskrity. Santa Fe, N.Mex.: School of American Research.

2002   Language renewal and the technologies of literacy and post-literacy. In *Making Dictionaries: Preserving Indigenous Languages of the Americas*. William Frawley, Kenneth C. Hill, and Pamela Munro, eds. Pp. 171–92. Berkeley: University of California Press.

2004   Language ideologies. In *A Companion to Linguistic Anthropology*. Alessandro Duranti, ed. Pp. 496–517. Malden: Blackwell.

2007   "Doing justice to the stories": Overcoming narrative inequality in the representation of Western Mono traditional narratives. Paper presented at the Annual Meeting of the American Anthropological Association, Philadelphia.

2009a   Embodying the reversal of language shift: Agency, incorporation, and language ideological change in the Western Mono community of central California. In *Native American Language Ideologies: Beliefs, Practices, and Struggles in Indian Country*. Paul V. Kroskrity and Margaret C. Field, eds. Pp. 190–210. Tucson: University of Arizona Press.

2009b   Language renewal as sites of language ideological struggle: The need for "ideological clarification." In *Indigenous Language Revitalization: Encouragement, Guidance and Lessons Learned*. Jon Reyhner and Louise Lockard, eds. Pp. 71–83. Flagstaff: Northern Arizona University.

2009c   Narrative reproductions: Ideologies of storytelling, authoritative words, and generic regimentation in the village of Tewa. *Journal of Linguistic Anthropology* 19:40–56.

Kroskrity, Paul V., Rosalie Bethel, and Jennifer F. Reynolds
2002   *Taitaduhaan: Western Mono Ways of Speaking.* (CD-ROM). Norman: University of Oklahoma Press.

Kroskrity, Paul V., and Margaret C. Field (eds.)
2009   *Native American Language Ideologies: Beliefs, Practices, and Struggles in Indian Country.* Tucson: University of Arizona Press.

Kroskrity, Paul V., and Dewey Healing
1978   Coyote and Bullsnake. In *Coyote Stories.* International Journal of American Linguistics, Native American Texts Series 1. W. Bright, ed. Pp. 162–71. Chicago: International Journal of American Linguistics.
1981   Coyote-Woman and the Deer Children. In *Coyote Stories II.* International Journal of American Linguistics, Native American Texts Series 6. M. B. Kendall, ed. Pp. 119–28. Chicago: International Journal of American Linguistics.

Kuipers, Joel C.
1998   *Language, Identity and Marginality in Indonesia: The Changing Nature of Ritual Speech on the Island of Sumba.* Cambridge: Cambridge University Press.

Kulick, Don
1992   *Language Shift and Cultural Reproduction: Socialization, Self, and Syncretism in a Papua New Guinea Village.* Cambridge: Cambridge University Press.

Langdon, Margaret
1991   Diegueno: How many languages? *Occasional Papers on Linguistics 15.* Proceedings of the 1990 Hokan-Penutian Languages Workshop. Department of Linguistics, Southern Illinois University at Carbondale.

Lassiter, Eric L.
1998   *The Power of Kiowa Song.* Tucson: University of Arizona Press.

Lassiter, Eric L, Clyde Ellis, and Ralph Kotay
2002   *The Jesus Road: Kiowas, Christianity, and Indian Hymns.* Lincoln: University of Nebraska Press.

Latour, Bruno
2004   *The Politics of Nature: How to Bring the Sciences into Democracy.*
         Cambridge, Mass.: Harvard University Press.

Lee, Lloyd
2007   The future of Navajo nationalism. *Wicazo Sa Review* 22(1): 53–68.

Lee, Tiffany
2007   "If they want Navajo to be learned, then they should require it in all
         schools": Navajo teenagers' experiences, choices, and demands re-
         garding Navajo language. *Wicazo Sa Review* 22(1): 7–33.

Leland, Charles G.
1992   *Algonquin Legends.* Mineola, N.Y.: Dover. Originally published as
         *The Algonquin Legends of New England; or, Myths and Folk Lore of
         the Micmac, Passamaquoddy, and Penobscot Tribes* by Houghton,
         Mifflin and Company, Boston, in 1884.

Leland, Charles Godfrey. and John Dyneley Prince
1902   *Kulóskap the Master and Other Algonkin Poems.* New York: Funk
         and Wagnalls.

LeSourd, Philip S.
2007   *Tales from Maliseet Country: The Maliseet Texts of Karl Teeter.* Lin-
         coln: University of Nebraska Press.

Littlefield, Alice
1991   Native American labor and public policy in the United States. In *Marx-
         ist Approaches in Economic Anthropology.* Alice Littlefield and Hill
         Gates, eds. Pp. 219–32. Lanham, Md.: University Press of America.

Loether, Christopher P.
2009   Language revitalization and the manipulation of language ideologies:
         A Shoshoni case study. In *Native American Language Ideologies: Be-
         liefs, Practices, and Struggles in Indian Country.* Paul V. Kroskrity
         and Margaret C. Field, eds. Pp. 238–54. Tucson: University of Ari-
         zona Press.

Lomawaima, K. Tsianina
1994   *They Called It Prairie Light: The Story of Chilocco Indian School.*
         Lincoln: University of Nebraska Press.

Lord, Albert B.
1960   *The Singer of Tales.* Harvard Studies in Comparative Literature 24.
         Cambridge, Mass.: Harvard University Press.

Martinez, Esther
2004   *My Life in San Juan Pueblo: Stories of Esther Martinez.* Urbana: University of Illinois Press.

McAllester, David
1980   The First Snake song. In *Theory and Practice: Essays Presented to Gene Weltfish.* Stanley Diamond, ed., Pp. 1–27. New York: Mouton.

McCarty, Teresa L., Mary Eunice Romero, and Ofelia Zepeda
2006   Reclaiming the gift: Indigenous youth counter-narratives on native language loss and revitalization. *American Indian Quarterly* 30:28–48.

McCarty, Teresa L., and Ofelia Zepeda
1999   Amerindians. In *Handbook of Language and Ethnic Identity.* Joshua Fishman, ed. Pp. 197–210. New York: Oxford University Press.

McLaughlin, Daniel
1992   *When Literacy Empowers: Navajo Language in Print.* Albuquerque: University of New Mexico Press.

Meadows, William C.
1999   *Kiowa, Apache and Comanche Military Societies.* Austin: University of Texas Press.

Meek, Barbra A.
2006   And the Injun goes "How!" Representations of American Indian English in white public space. *Language in Society* 35:93–128.
2007   Respecting the language of elders: Ideological shift and linguistic discontinuity in a northern Athapascan community. *Journal of Linguistic Anthropology* 17:23–43.
2009   Language ideology and aboriginal language revitalization in the Yukon, Canada. In *Native American Language Ideologies: Beliefs, Practices, and Struggles in Indian Country.* Paul V. Kroskrity and Margaret C. Field, eds. Pp. 151–71. Tucson: University of Arizona Press.

Messing, Jacqueline
2007   Multiple ideologies and competing discourses: Language shift in Tlaxcala, Mexico. *Language in Society* 36:555–77.

Meza Cuero, Jon, Margaret Field, and Amy Miller
Forth- Rabbit & Frog. In *Inside Dazzling Mountains: Native American Oral*
coming *Literature of the Southwest.* David Kozak, ed. Lincoln: University of Nebraska Press.

Milroy, J., and L. Milroy
1985   *Authority in Language.* London: Routledge and Kegan Paul.

Milroy, Lesley
1980   *Language and Social Networks.* Oxford: Basil Blackwell.

Mitchell, Blackhorse
1968   The new direction. *Navajo Times,* Centennial issue, B8.
1969   Miracle Hill. In *The American Indian Speaks.* John R. Milton, ed.
         Pp. 110. Vermillion: University of South Dakota Press.
1972a   The four directions. In *The Whispering Wind.* Terry Allen, ed. P. 95.
         New York: Doubleday.
1972b   The path I must travel. In *The Whispering Wind.* Terry Allen, ed.
         P. 94. New York: Doubleday.
1972c   Talking to his drum. In *The Whispering Wind.* Terry Allen, ed. P. 96.
         New York: Doubleday.

Mithun, Marianne
1998   The significance of diversity in language endangerment and preser-
         vation. In *Endangered Languages: Current Issues and Future Pros-
         pects.* Lenore A. Grenoble and Lindsay J. Whaley, eds. Pp. 163–91.
         Cambridge: Cambridge University Press.
2004   The Value of linguistic diversity: Viewing other worlds through
         North American Indian languages. In *A Companion to Linguistic
         Anthropology.* Alessandro Duranti, ed. Pp. 121–40. Malden, Mass.:
         Blackwell.

Momaday, N. Scott
1970   The man made of words. Presentation at the First Convocation of
         American Indian Scholars, Dartmouth College, Hanover, N.H.
1997   *The Man Made of Words.* New York: St. Martin's Griffin.

Mooney, James
1979   *Calendar History of the Kiowa Indians.* Washington, D.C.: Smithso-
[1898]   nian Institution.

Moore, Robert E.
2006   Disappearing, Inc.: Glimpsing the sublime in the politics of access to
         endangered languages. *Language and Communication* 26:296–315.

Morgan, William
1949   *Coyote Tales.* Lawrence, Kans.: Bureau of Indian Affairs, Haskell
         Institute.

Mould, Tom
2005   The paradox of traditionalization: Negotiating the past in Choctaw prophetic discourse. *Journal of Folklore Research* 42(3): 255–94.

Neely, Amber A., and Gus Palmer, Jr.
2009   Which way is the Kiowa way? Orthography choices, ideologies, and language renewal. In *Native American Language Ideologies: Language Beliefs, Practices, and Struggles in Indian Country.* Paul V. Kroskrity and Margaret Field, eds. Pp. 271–97. Tucson: University of Arizona Press.

Nettle, Daniel, and Suzanne Romaine
2000   *Vanishing Voices: The Extinction of the World's Languages.* Oxford: Oxford University Press.

Nevins, M. Eleanor
2004   Learning to listen: Confronting two meanings of language loss in the contemporary White Mountain Apache speech community. *Journal of Linguistic Anthropology* 14:269–88.

Nevins, M. Eleanor, Paul Ethelbah, and Genevieve Ethelbah
Forth-   "Ndah Ch'iidn": A Journey between worlds. In *Inside Dazzling Moun-
coming   tains: Native American Oral Literature of the Southwest.* David Kotak, ed. Lincoln: University of Nebraska Press.

Nevins, M. Eleanor, Thomas J. Nevins, Paul Ethelbah, and Genevieve Ethelbah
2004   "He became an eagle": A contemporary Western Apache oral narrative. With Thomas J. Nevins, Paul Ethelbah, and Genevieve Ethelbah. In *Voices from the Four Directions: Contemporary Translations of Native American Oral Literature.* Brian Swann, ed. Pp. 283–302. Lincoln: University of Nebraska Press.

Nevins, Thomas J.
2005   *World made of prayer: Alterity and the dialectics of encounter in the invention of contemporary Western Apache culture.* Ph.D. Thesis, Anthropology Department, University of Virginia.

Nevins, Thomas J., and M. Eleanor Nevins
2009   "We have always had the Bible": Christianity and the composition of White Mountain Apache heritage. *Heritage Management* 2:11–33.

Norris, Mary Jane, and Karen MacCon
2003   Aboriginal language transmission and maintenance in families: Results of an intergenerational and gender-based analysis for Canada

          1996. In *Aboriginal Conditions: Research as a Foundation for
          Public Policy*. Jerry P. White, Paul S. Maxim, and Dan Beavon eds.
          Pp. 164–96. Vancouver: University of British Columbia Press.

Nuckolls, Janis
1992   Sound symbolic involvement. *Journal of Linguistic Anthropology*.
          2(1): 51–80.
2000   Spoken in the spirit of gesture: Translating sound symbolism in a
          Pastaza Quechua narrative. In *Translating Native Latin American
          Verbal Art*. Kay Sammons and Joel Sherzer, eds. Pp. 233–51. Wash-
          ington, D.C.: Smithsonian Institution Press.
2006   The neglected poetics of ideophony. In *Language, Culture, and the
          Individual*. Catherine O'Neil, Mary Scoggin, and Kevin Tuite, eds.,
          Pp. 39–50. Muenchen, Germany: Lincom. Europa.

Ochs, Elinor, and Lisa Capps
2001   *Living Narrative: Creating Lives in Everyday Storytelling*. Cam-
          bridge, Mass.: Harvard University Press.

O'Neill, Sean
2002   Northwest California ethnolinguistics: A study in drift. In *Proceed-
          ings of the 50th Anniversary Celebration of the Survey of California
          and Other Indian Languages*. Lisa Conathan and Teresa McFarland,
          eds. Pp. 64–88. Berkeley: Department of Linguistics, University of
          California.
2006   Mythic and poetic dimensions of speech in northwestern California:
          From cultural vocabulary to linguistic relativity. *Anthropological Lin-
          guistics* 48(4): 305–34.
2008   *Cultural Contact and Linguistic Relativity among the Indians of
          Northwestern California*. Norman: University of Oklahoma Press.

Ong, Walter
1982   *Orality and Literacy*. London: Routledge.

Opler, Morris
1996 [1941] *An Apache Life-way*. Lincoln: University of Nebraska Press.

Owen, Roger
1965   The patrilocal band: A linguistically and culturally hybrid social unit.
          American Anthropologist 67:675–90.

Palmer, Andie Diane
2005   *Maps of Experience: The Anchoring of Land to Story in Secwepemc
          Discourse*. Toronto: University of Toronto Press.

Palmer, Gus, Jr.
2003   *Telling Stories the Kiowa Way.* Tucson: University of Arizona Press.

Parker, Robert Dale
2003   *The Invention of Native American Literature.* Ithaca, N.Y.: Cornell University Press.

Parkhill, Thomas C.
1997   *Weaving Ourselves into the Land: Charles Godfrey Leland, "Indians," and the Study of Native American Religions.* Albany: State University of New York Press.

Parry, Adam (ed.)
1971   *The Making of Homeric Verse: The Collected Papers of Milman Parry.* Oxford: Clarendon Press.

Parry, Milman
1928   *L'Epithete traditionaelle dans Homere.* Paris: Societie Editrice Les Belles Lettres.

Parsons, Elsie Clews
1926   *Tewa Tales.* New York: American Folklore Society.

Pecos, Regis, and Rebecca Blum-Martinez
2001   The Key to Cultural Survival: Language Planning and Revitalization in the Pueblo de Cochiti. In *The Green Book of Language Revitalization in Practice.* L. Hinton and K. Hale, eds. Pp. 75–82. San Diego: Academic Press.

Perley, Bernard C.
2003   Language, culture, and landscape: Protecting aboriginal "deep time" for tomorrow. Electronic Document. http://projects.gsd.harvard.edu/heritage/program.htm.
2007   Tempus profundus: Warning from the village of the dammed. Presentation at the symposium From Magna Carta to the Sky Trust: The Historical Arc of the Commons, University of Wisconsin–Milwaukee.
2011   *Defying Maliseet Language Death: Emergent Vitalities of Language, Culture, and Identify in Eastern Canada.* Lincoln: University of Nebraska Press.

Peterson, Leighton C.
2006   Technology, ideology and emergent communicative practices among the Navajo. Ph.D. dissertation, University of Texas, Austin.

Philips, Susan U.
1983   *The Invisible Culture: Communication in Classroom and Community on the Warm Springs Indian Reservation.* New York: Longman.

Powers, Stephen
1877   *Tribes of California.* Contributions to North American Ethnology 3. Washington: U.S. Geographical and Geological Survey of the Rocky Mountain Region. Reprinted by University of California Press, 1976.

Prince, John Dyneley
1921   *Passamaquoddy Texts.* Publications of the American Ethnological Society 10. New York: G. E. Stechert.

Radin, Paul
1956   *The Trickster: A Study in American Indian Mythology.* New York: Pantheon.

Reichard, Gladys
1944   *Prayer: The Compulsive Word.* American Ethnological Society Monograph 7. Seattle: University of Washington Press.
1950   *Navaho Religion: A Study of Symbolism.* New York: Bollingen Foundation.

Reynolds, Jennifer F.
2009   Shaming the shift generation: Intersecting ideologies of family and linguistic revitalization in Guatemala. In *Native American Language Ideologies: Beliefs, Practices, and Struggles in Indian Country.* Paul V. Kroskrity and Margaret C. Field, eds. Pp. 213–37. Tucson: University of Arizona Press.

Rice, Keren
2004   Language contact, phonemic inventories, and the Athapaskan language family. *Linguistic Typology* 8:321–43.

Richland, Justin B.
2008   *Arguing with Tradition: The Language of Law in a Hopi Tribal Court.* Chicago: University of Chicago Press.
2009   Hopi sovereignty as epistemological limit. *Wicazo Sa Review* 24: 89–112.

Ridington, Robin, and Jillian Ridington
2006   *When You Sing It Now, Just Like New.* Lincoln: University of Nebraska Press.

Rothenberg, Jerome
1983   *Symposium of the Whole: A Range of Discourse toward an Ethnopo-etics.* Berkeley: University of California Press.

Royal Commission on Aboriginal Peoples
1996   *People to People: Nation to Nation.* Highlights from the Report of the Royal Commission on Aboriginal Peoples. Gatineau, Quebec: Minister of Supply and Services.

Samuels, David
2001   Indeterminacy and history in Britton Goode's Western Apache place-names. *American Ethnologist* 28(2): 277–302.
2004   *Putting a Song on Top of It.* Tucson: University of Arizona Press.
2006   Bible translation and medicine man talk: Missionaries, indexicality, and the "language expert" on the San Carlos Apache Reservation. *Language in Society* 35(4): 529–57.

Sapir, Edward
1921   *Language: An Introduction to the Study of Speech.* New York: Harcourt Brace.
1929   The status of linguistics as a science. *Language* 5:207–14. Reprinted in *The Selected Writings of Edward Sapir in Language, Culture, and Personality.* David Mandelbaum, ed. Pp. 160–66. Berkeley: University of California Press, 1949.
1930   Texts of the Kaibab Paiutes and Uintah Utes. Proceedings of the American Academy of Arts and Sciences 65:297–535.
1936   Hupa tattooing. In *Essays in Anthropology Presented to A. L. Kroeber.* Robert Lowie, ed. Pp. 273–77. Berkeley: University of California Press.
2001   *The Collected Works of Edward Sapir,* Vol. 14: *Northwest California Linguistics.* Ed. Victor Golla and Sean O'Neill. Berlin: Mouton de Gruyter.

Sapir, Edward, and Harry Hoijer
1942   *Navaho Texts.* Iowa City: University of Iowa.

Sarris, Greg
1993   *Keeping Slug Woman Alive.* Berkeley: University of California Press.

Saville-Troike, Muriel
2003   *The Ethnography of Communication.* New York: Oxford University Press.

Schaengold, Charlotte
2003   The Emergence of bilingual Navajo: English and Navajo languages in contact regardless of everyone's best intentions. In *When Languages Collide*. Brian Joseph, Johanna DeStefano, Neil Jacobs, and Ilse Lehiste, eds. Pp. 235–54. Columbus: Ohio State University Press.

Schieffelin, Bambi, Kathryn Woolard, and Paul V. Kroskrity (eds.)
1998   *Language Ideologies: Practice and Theory*. New York: Oxford University Press.

Schmidt, Annette
1990   *The Loss of Australia's Aboriginal Language Heritage*. Institute Report Series. Canberra: Aboriginal Studies Press.

Sekaquaptewa, Emory, and Dorothy Washburn
2004   They go along singing: Reconstructing the Hopi past from ritual metaphors in song and image. *American Antiquity* 69(3): 457–86.

Shaul, David Leedom
2002   *Hopi Traditional Literature*. Albuquerque: University of New Mexico Press.

Sherzer, Joel
1990   *Verbal Art in San Blas: Kuna Culture through Its Discourse*. New York: Cambridge University Press.

Shipek, Florence
1982   Kumeyaay socio-political structure. *Journal of California and Great Basin Anthropology* 4(2): 296–303.

Silko, Leslie Marmon
1977   *Ceremony*. New York: Penguin.
1981   Language and literature from a Pueblo Indian perspective. In *English Literature: Opening Up the Canon*. Leslie. A. Fiedler and Houston A. Baker, eds. Pp. 54–72. Baltimore: Johns Hopkins University.

Silverstein, Michael
1993   Metapragmatic discourse and metapragmatic function. In *Reflexive Language: Reported Speech and Metapragmatics*. J. Lucy, ed. Pp. 33–58. Cambridge: Cambridge University Press.
1996   Monoglot "Standard" in America: Standardization and metaphors of linguistic hegemony. In *The Matrix of Language*. Donald Brenneis and Ronald Macaulay, eds. Pp. 284–306. Boulder, Colo.: Westview.

1998a   Contemporary transformations of local linguistic communities. *Annual Review of Anthropology* 27:401–26.

1998b   The uses and utility of ideology: A commentary. In *Language Ideologies, Practice and Theory.* B. B. Shieffelin, K. A. Woolard, and P. V. Kroskrity, eds. Pp. 123–45. New York: Oxford University Press.

2000   Whorfianism and the linguistic imagination of nationality. In *Regimes of Language.* Paul V. Kroskrity, ed. Pp. 85–137. Santa Fe, N.Mex.: School of American Research.

2003a   From glottoprospecting to antiquarian curating: Dilemmas of reflexivity in the linguistics of local language communities. Presentation at the invited SLA-SSILA Joint Session on Endangered Languages, American Anthropological Association Annual Meeting, Chicago.

2003b   Indexical order and the dialectics of sociolinguistic life. *Language and Communication* 23:193–229.

2003c   The whens and wheres—as well as hows—of ethnolinguistic recognition. *Public Culture* 15(3): 531–57.

2005   Axes of evals: Token versus type interdiscursivity. *Journal of Linguistic Anthropology* 15(1): 6–22.

2006   Ethics and ethnicities: Naming names in the archive of culture. Department of Anthropology, University of California, San Diego, February 13.

Silverstein, Michael, and Greg Urban
1996   The natural history of discourse. In *Natural Histories of Discourse.* Michael Silverstein and Greg Urban, eds. Pp. 1–17. Chicago: University of Chicago Press.

Smith, Ian, and Steve Johnson
1986   Sociolinguistic patterns in an unstratified society: The patrilects of Kugu Nganhcara. *Journal of the Atlantic Provinces Linguistic Association* 8:29–43.

Smith, Kalim
2004   Language ideology and hegemony in the Kumeyaay nation: Returning the linguistic gaze. M.A. thesis, University California, San Diego.

Smith, David M.
2002   The flesh and the word: Stories and other gifts of the animals in Chipewyan cosmology. *Anthropology and Humanism* 27(1): 60–79.

2003   A gift of words, a gift of truth: A Chipewyan story of a hard winter. *Anthropology and Humanism* 28(2): 168–97.

Spicer, Edward
1962   *Cycles of Conquest.* Tucson: University of Arizona Press.
1975   *Indian Identity versus Assimilation.* Occasional Paper of the Weather-
           head Foundation. New York: Weatherhead Foundation.

Spier, Leslie
1923   Southern Diegueno customs. *University of California Publications in
           American Archaeology and Ethnology* 20:297–358.

Spitulnik, Deborah
1998   Mediating unity and diversity: The production of language ideolo-
           gies in Zambian broadcasting. In *Language Ideologies: Practice and
           Theory.* B. B. Schieffelin, K. A. Woolard, and P. V. Kroskrity, eds.
           Pp. 163–88. New York: Oxford University Press.

Spolsky, Bernard
2002   Prospects for the survival of the Navajo language: A reconsideration.
           Anthropology and Education Quarterly 33(2): 139–62.

Sturm, Circe
2002   *Blood Politics: Race, Culture and Identity in the Cherokee Nation of
           Oklahoma.* Berkeley: University of California Press.

Sutton, Peter
1978   Wik: Aboriginal society, territory and language at Cape Keerweer,
           Cape York Peninsula, Australia. Ph.D. dissertation. Department of
           Sociology and Anthropology, University of Queensland.

Tannen, Deborah
1993   *Framing in Discourse.* New York: Oxford University Press.

Tapahonso, Luci
1987   *A Breeze Swept Through.* Albuquerque, N.Mex.: West End Press.

Tedlock, Dennis
1972   *Finding the Center: Narrative Poetry of the Zuni Indians.* New York:
           Dial Press.
1983   *The Spoken Word and the Work of Interpretation.* Philadelphia: Uni-
           versity of Pennsylvania Press.

Toelken, Barre, and Tacheeni Scott
1981   Poetic retranslation and the "pretty languages" of Yellowman. In
           *Traditional Literatures of the American Indian: Texts and Interpreta-
           tions.* Karl Kroeber, ed. Pp. 65–116. Lincoln: University of Nebraska
           Press.

1997   Poetic retranslation and the "pretty languages" of Yellowman. In *Traditional Literatures of the American Indian*, 2nd ed. Karl Kroeber, ed. Pp. 88–119. Lincoln: University of Nebraska Press.

Tohe, Laura
1999   *No Parole Today.* Albuquerque, N.Mex.: West End Press.
2002   In Dinétah. In *Sister Nations.* Heid Erdrich and Laura Tohe, eds. Pp. 100–104. St. Paul: Minnesota Historical Society Press.
2005   *Tséyi': Deep in the Rock.* Tucson: University of Arizona Press.

Tsosie, Rebecca
2002   Symposium on cultural sovereignty: Native rights in the twenty-first century—Introduction. *Arizona State Law Journal* 34:1–14.

UNESCO
n.d.   *Interactive Atlas of the World's Languages in Danger.* www.unesco .org/culture/ich/index.php?pg=00206.

Uyechi, Linda
1990   Navajo fourth person: The ji-/ha- alternation. *Journal of Navajo Education* 7(3): 3–12.

Vizenor, Gerald
1999   *Manifest Manners: Narratives on Postindian Survivance.* Lincoln: University of Nebraska Press.
2008   *Survivance: Narratives of Native Presence.* Lincoln: University of Nebraska Press.

Waterman, T. T.
1910   The religious practices of the Diegueño Indians. *University of California Publications in American Archaeology and Ethnology* 8(6): 271–358.
1920   *Yurok Geography.* University of California Publications in American Archeology and Ethnology 16(5): 177–315. Berkeley: University of California Press.

Waterman, T. T., and A. L. Kroeber
1934   *Yurok Marriages.* University of California Publications in American Archaeology and Ethnology 35:1–14. Berkeley: University of California Press.

Watkins, Laurel J.
1984   *A Grammar of Kiowa.* Lincoln: University of Nebraska Press.

Watkins, Laurel J., and Daniel Harbour
2010   The linguistic genius of Parker McKenzie's Kiowa alphabet. *Interna-
            tional Journal of American Linguistics* 76:309–33.

Webster, Anthony K.
2004   Coyote poems: Navajo poetry, intertextuality, and language choice.
            American Indian Culture and Research Journal 28(4): 69–91.
2006a   'Ałk'idą́ą́' Mą'ii Jooldlosh, Jiní: Poetic devices in Navajo oral and
            written poetry. *Anthropological Linguistics* 48(3): 233–65.
2006b   The mouse that sucked: On "translating" a Navajo poem. *Studies in
            American Indian Literature* 18(1): 37–49.
2008a   "Plaza'góó and before he can respond . . .": Language ideology, bilin-
            gual Navajo, and Navajo poetry. *Pragmatics* 18(3): 511–41.
2008b   "To all the former cats and stomps of the Navajo nation": Perfor-
            mance, the individual, and cultural poetic traditions. *Language in So-
            ciety* 37(1): 61–89.
2009a   *Explorations in Navajo Poetry and Poetics.* Albuquerque: University
            of New Mexico Press.
2009b   The poetics and politics of Navajo ideophony in contemporary Na-
            vajo poetry. *Language and Communication* 29:133–51.
2010   On intimate grammars, with examples from Navajo English, Navlish,
            and Navajo. *Journal of Anthropological Research* 66:187–208.

Whitehurst, Lindsay
2007   More local chapters using Navajo names. *Daily Times* (Farmington,
            N.Mex.), May 22.

Whiteley, Peter
1988   *Deliberate Acts: Changing Hopi Culture through the Oraibi Split.*
            Tucson: University of Arizona Press.
2003   Do "language rights" serve indigenous interests? Some Hopi and
            other queries. *American Anthropologist* 105:712–22.

Whorf, Benjamin Lee
1956   *Language, Thought, and Reality: Selected Writings of Benjamin Lee
            Whorf.* Ed. John B. Carroll. Cambridge, Mass.: MIT Press.

Williams, Raymond
1977   *Marxism and Literature.* Oxford: Oxford University Press.

Wilson, Alan, and Gene Dennison
1970   *Laughter: The Navajo Way.* Gallup: University of New Mexico, Gal-
            lup Branch.

Wilson, Waziyatawin Angela
2005   Defying colonization through language survival. In *For Indigenous Eyes Only: A Decolonization Handbook*. Santa Fe, N.Mex.: School of American Research Press.

Witherspoon, Gary
1977   *Language and Art in the Navajo Universe*. Ann Arbor: University of Michigan Press.

Woolard, Kathryn
1998   Language ideology as a field of inquiry. In *Language Ideologies: Practice and Theory*. Bambi Schiefflin, Kathryn Woolard, and Paul Kroskrity, eds. Pp. 51–67. New York: Oxford University Press.

Woolard, Kathryn A., and Bambi Schieffelin
1994   Language ideology. *Annual Review of Anthropology* 23: 55–82.

Yava, Albert
1978   *Big Falling Snow*. New York: Crown.

Young, Robert
1989   Lexical elaboration in Navajo. In *General and Amerindian Ethno-linguistics*. Mary Ritchie and Henry Hoenigswald, eds. Pp. 303–20. Berlin: Mouton de Gruyter.

Young, Robert, and William Morgan
1987   *The Navajo Language*. Albuquerque: University of New Mexico Press.

Zepeda, Ofelia, and Jane H. Hill
1991   The condition of Native American languages in the United States. In *Endangered Languages*. R. H. Robins and M. Uhlenbeck, eds. Pp. 135–55. New York: Berg.

Zigon, Jarret
2008   *Morality: An Anthropological Perspective*. New York: Berg.

CONTRIBUTORS

PAUL V. KROSKRITY is Professor of Anthropology and Applied Linguistics and Chair of the Interdepartmental Program in American Indian Studies at UCLA. He received his B.A. from Columbia College, Columbia University, and earned his Ph.D. in anthropology from Indiana University in 1977. He has worked extensively with the Arizona Tewa and Western Mono communities since 1973 and 1980, respectively, and engaged in a variety of linguistic, sociolinguistic, language renewal, and language ideological studies. This research resulted in numerous articles and books on these topics including *Language, History, and Identity: Ethnolinguistic Studies of the Arizona Tewa* (1993) and *Regimes of Language: Ideologies, Polities, and Identities* (2000), the coauthored interactive multimedia CD-ROM *Taitaduhaan: Western Mono Ways of Speaking* (2002), and the coedited books *Language Ideologies: Practice and Theory* (1998) and *Native American Language Ideologies: Beliefs, Practices, and Struggles in Indian Country* (2009). His current projects include the completion of an Arizona Tewa dictionary and books on the verbal art and oral traditions of each the communities in which he has worked.

PAMELA A. BUNTE (1948–2011) was Professor Emerita of Anthropology and Linguistics at California State University, Long Beach, where she was chair of the Department of Anthropology from 1989 to 1995. She received an M.A. in French in 1974 and her Ph.D. in anthropology in 1979 from Indiana University. Her dissertation research was with the Kaibab Paiutes, and she later began working with the San Juan Paiute community in 1980 on a dictionary. Her research interests included verbal art, language socialization, intercultural communication, language maintenance and revitalization,

262   CONTRIBUTORS

and language ideology. She worked with the San Juan Paiute tribe on their successful federal recognition case, and this research produced the book *From the Sands to the Mountain: Change and Persistence in Southern Paiute Community* (1987). She continued to work with the San Juan Paiute Tribe on land claims and other applied projects. She had recently completed a five-year project working on federal recognition of the Little Shell Chippewas of Montana.

MARGARET C. FIELD is Associate Professor and Chair of American Indian Studies at San Diego State University. She received her Ph.D. in linguistics from the University of California, Santa Barbara. Her research interests include American Indian languages, language socialization, language ideology, and multimedia applications to language maintenance. Her current research focuses on the relationship between language ideologies and the development of lexical dialects in the Kumeyaay community of Baja California.

AMBER A. NEELY received an M.A. degree in anthropology and linguistics from the University of Amsterdam, Netherlands. She is currently a Ph.D. candidate at the University of Oklahoma, where her dissertation research focuses on language ideology, pragmatics, and language change among Kiowa speakers in Oklahoma.

M. ELEANOR NEVINS is Assistant Professor of Anthropology at the University of Nevada Reno. She earned a Ph.D. in anthropology from the University of Virginia. Her research addresses the interplay of language varieties, discourse genres, and language ideologies among residents of the Fort Apache Reservation in Arizona. In her published work she has addressed language ideology in relation to language maintenance programs, the relevance of discourse genres to appropriations of mass media, and contrasting uses of the Christian Bible by Apache evangelicals and traditionalists. Her work has appeared in the *Journal of Linguistic Anthropology, Language in Society, Language and Communication, Heritage Management*, and in edited volumes. She is currently working on a book that addresses the inevitably complex social dynamics of language endangerment and maintenance in indigenous communities.

THOMAS J. NEVINS is Adjunct Assistant Professor of Anthropology at the University of Nevada Reno. He earned a Ph.D. in anthropology from the University of Virginia. His research explores dialectics of alterity and identity in the invention of sociality. In collaboration with M. Eleanor Nevins, he has conducted three years of research on the Fort Apache Reservation with people who identify themselves as White Mountain Apache. During this time he worked with tribal educational offices on language and culture promotion efforts, grant writing, and NAGPRA documentation. His academic work has appeared in the *Language and Communication,* and *Heritage Management,* as well as in edited volumes. In addition to his work on the Fort Apache reservation, he recent research examines the role of new media in the construction of scientific authority and resistance identities in discourses of climate change.

SEAN O'NEILL is Associate Professor of Anthropology at the University of Oklahoma. His research broadly focuses on the role of language in human social life, including its place in identity politics, storytelling, and song, as well as its influence on thought processes. In more general terms, his work also focuses on the role of sound in anthropological thought, including the place of music, alongside poetry and oral narrative, in creating meaning and negotiating social identity. His books include *Cultural Contact and Linguistic Relativity among the Indians of Northwestern California* (2008) and *The Collected Works of Edward Sapir,* Volume 14: *Northwest California Linguistics* (2001), which he coedited with Victor Golla. In his work with the Apache Tribe of Oklahoma, he is currently studying the use of traditional songs in the context of language revitalization, with support from the National Endowment for the Humanities.

GUS PALMER, JR. is Associate Professor in the Department of Anthropology and the Native American Studies Program at the University of Oklahoma. He is a linguistic anthropologist whose main area of concentration is the Kiowa language, and he is presently working on a Kiowa dictionary with other Kiowa speakers in Oklahoma. A fluent speaker of Kiowa, Palmer teaches and has been teaching Kiowa since 1992. He spent several summers working with the Pawnee Nation language revitalization and preservation program, producing curriculum and updating original South Band and Skiri digital sound recordings for use by tribal members. Palmer has authored *Telling Stories the Kiowa Way* (2003) and published poems and fiction in several anthologies and literary magazines.

BERNARD C. PERLEY is Professor of Anthropology at the University of Wisconsin–Milwaukee, where he teaches linguistic anthropology and American Indian studies. He received his Ph.D. from Harvard University.

His research interests include language endangerment, language politics, repatriation, and American Indian sovereignty and self-determination. He returned to the his heritage community to examine the many factors contributing to the endangerment of the Maliseet language at Tobique First Nation in New Brunswick, Canada. While acknowledging the historical contexts of aboriginal language endangerment, he is actively promoting Maliseet language maintenance and revitalization through the incorporation of language, oral tradition, and landscape as everyday practices of aboriginal self-determination.

ANTHONY K. WEBSTER is Associate Professor of Anthropology at Southern Illinois University at Carbondale. He earned his Ph.D. in anthropology from the University of Texas at Austin. He specializes in linguistic anthropology. His research focuses on Navajo ethnopoetics, especially as it has emerged in contemporary written poetry that can and is performed orally. He has published articles on issues concerning Navajo poetics, the felt attachments to linguistic forms, and the role of iconicity in Navajo language and identity in *Anthropological Linguistics, International Journal of American Linguistics, Journal of American Folklore, Journal of Anthropological Research, Journal of Linguistic Anthropology,* and *Language in Society.* He is the author of *Explorations in Navajo Poetry and Poetics* (2009).

INDEX

Page number references to illustrations are in italic type.

Acculturation, 96, 192. *See also* Assimilation

"Across-the-Ocean Widower," 64–65

Agency, 89, 113, 143–44, 150, 157

Apache, San Carlos, 141

Apache, Western, 42

Apache, White Mountain, 15, 129–50

Archive of Indigenous Languages of Latin America, 124

Arizona Tewa, 4, 17, 76, 151–83; generational differences 174; language socialization, 159–60; linguistic curse, 157; youth, 171, 174

Assimilation, 196

Athapaskan, 149, 219

Australian (Aboriginal), 117, 119

Authenticity, 95–97, 100, 120, 144–45

Authorization, 54, 131, 142, 172, 182

Baja Kumiai, 117–18. *See also* Kumiai

Bakhtin, Mikhail M., 17, 30–31, 83–84, 92, 164, 172, 204, 223

Barth, Fredrik, 71, 76–77, 86, 95

Basso, Keith, 5, 42, 134, 139–40, 144, 149, 211

Bauman, Richard, 9, 13, 15, 43, 54, 115, 152, 173, 176, 191

Belin, Esther, 210, 221–22

BIA (Bureau of Indian Affairs), 45, 207–208

Boarding schools, 10, 71, 79, 92

Bourdieu, Pierre, 95, 152

Bright, William, 80

California Indians, Central, 8. *See also* Mono (Monache)

California Indians, Northwestern, 60–89; Gold Rush, influenced by, 75. *See also* Hupa, Yurok

Canada, 19n2, 184–86, 196, 203n5

Cheyenne, 98

Chippewa, 187

Choctaw, 106

Clan names, 210–11

Claw, Eugene, 208

Cochiti Pueblo, 114

Code mixing, 5, 32, 42, 219. *See also* Hybridity

Code switching, 5, 99, 158, 182, 208

Collaborative research, 146, 150

Comanche, 98

Communicative competence, 37

Compartmentalization, 77, 79, 87, 158

Contextualization, 25, 123, 145, 149, 167, 182n6, 192, 203. *See also* Recontextualization

Coyote, as myth character, 7, 49–50, 60, 78–79, 138, 170, 211; as negative role

Coyote (*cont.*)
  model, 57, 123, 161, 164, 167; as trick-
  ster, 48, 52–53, 66, 221; Coyote nar-
  rative framing devices, 214–15; Karuk
  stories, 85n7
Crow (people), 98
Cruikshank, Julie, 149
Cuero, Jon Meza, 120, 125
Cultural broker, 140
Cultural reproduction, 129–30
Cushing, Frank Hamilton, 8

Dauenhauer, Nora Marks, 11
Dena'ina, 219
Derrida, Jacques, 87n17
Diacritica of ethnicity, 76
Diegueño, 115–16
Diné College, 208–10, 221
Discourse markers, 99
Discrimination. *See* Narrative
  discriminations
Discursive consciousness, 156, 179
Discursive discrimination. *See* Narrative
  discriminations
Diyin, 133, 135, 138, 141, 145, 148
Documentation, 146, 153
Dorian, Nancy, 91, 96, 153, 182

Education. *See* Schools
Elder purism, 15, 139
Elders, 16, 44, 48, 80, 101, 114, 137, 150,
  223
Embodied communication, 168–69, 171
Emerson, Gloria, 207, 217–18
Endangerment. *See* Language
  endangerment
Erasure, 3–4, 17, 87, 90, 95, 147, 182n10,
  189
Ethnicity. *See* Identity
Ethnography of communication, 9, 39
Ethnolinguistic boundaries, 67, 73, 80, 83
Ethnopoetics, 9, 20, 23, 145, 214
Evans, Nicholas, 117, 119
Evidential particles, 99, 152, 156, 165,
  175, 181, 214–15

Footing, 39–40
Force, 10; moral force, 179
Formulaic opening, 39, 41, 213
Franklin, Robert, 4
Frog, 115, 123

Genre, 131; criterial attributes of (Tewa);
  163–64, 175; indigenous, 180–81; leg-
  end genre (Paiute), 47; myth (Paiute)
  57; oral genres, 218; signaling devices
  (Navajo), 213, 222; traditional storytell-
  ing, 145–46, 159, 196–97
Generic regimentation, 17, 152
Goddard, Pliny Earle, 80, 88
Goffman, Erving, 13, 39, 180
Golla, Victor, 80, 117
Gonzales, Alecia, 14–15, 90–91, 94–97,
  100–103, 107, 114n7
Gossip, 16, 136
Gramsci, Antonio, 19
"Grandpa Rabbit," 107
Graphic novel, 18, 198–99, *200–201*, 202
Gumperz, John J., 9, 123

Hale, Ken, 125
Hare, 7
Healing, Dewey, 160, 168
Hegemony, 8, 10, 19, 48, 58, 142, 173,
  179–80, 187
Heritage language, 11–12, 174; classes,
  35; curriculum materials, 131; regula-
  tion of, 181
Heteroglossia, 92, 223
Hill, Jane H., 73–74, 86
Hill, Kay, 193–94
Hinton, Leanne, 48, 80
Hoijer, Harry, 85, 211
Hopi, 45, 155–57, 160, 175, 180n1, 181n4
Hupa, 14, 60
Hybridity, 174, 197–98
Hymes, Dell H., 3, 9, 37, 39

Iconization, 32, 60, 71–72, 158
Identity, 227n1; discursive production of,
  115, 158; ethnic, 4, 14–15, 72, 76, 83,

Tricksters, 7, 19, 66, 105, 221. *See also* Coyote

Universal ownership, 4

Variationism, 119, 125
Village identity, 71

Wabanaki Confederacy, 162
Water Ouzel, 63

Whorf, Benjamin Lee, 83
Williams, Raymond, 206
Wiyot, 14, 60
Writing, 32–33, 208

Yellowman, 7
Yokuts, 8, 117
Yurok, 14, 60

Zigon, Jared, 151

CPSIA information can be obtained
at www.ICGtesting.com
Printed in the USA
FSOW01n1634190815
10067FS